What Women Know

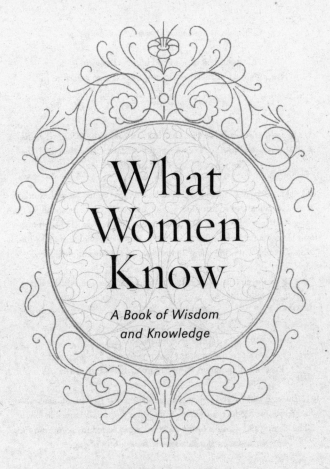

What Women Know

A Book of Wisdom and Knowledge

Michelle Jackson
and Dr Juliet Bressan

HACHETTE
BOOKS
IRELAND

First published in 2010 by Hachette Books Ireland
First published in paperback in 2011 by Hachette Books Ireland

1

ISBN 978 14447 2545 2

Typeset in Adobe Garamond
Cover, text design and typesetting by Anú Design, Tara
Printed and bound in Great Britain by Clays Ltd, St Ives plc

Hachette Books Ireland policy is to use papers that are natural, renewable
and recyclable products and made from wood grown in sustainable forests.
The logging and manufacturing processes are expected to conform to the
environmental regulations of the country of origin.

Hachette Books Ireland
8 Castlecourt Centre
Castleknock
Dublin 15
Ireland

www.hachette.ie

A division of Hachette UK Ltd,
338 Euston Road, London NW1 3BH, England

*Dedicated with gratitude
and love to all the women
we have had the joy of knowing*

Contents

Acknowledgements

Many wonderful women and men have been involved in the production of this book. Thank you to the Hachette team especially to our editor and publisher, Ciara Doorley and Breda Purdue, and to Peter, Ruth and Margaret Daly for your superb insight, enthusiasm and support.

What Women Know started out as a simple conversation between us and transformed into an incredibly inspiring and supportive community of women online. Without all of the fantastic women who contributed so honestly and generously this book would not have been written. Thank you so much to everyone who has joined our Facebook page and debated and posted over the last few months – this is really your book as much as it is ours.

We are especially grateful to all our artist and poet and writer friends who contributed enormously to the writing and editing of this book, and in particular to all the residents and staff of the Tyrone Guthrie Centre at Annaghmakerrig, Ireland.

Many thanks to Jackie Howard of Philanthropy Ireland and the Women's Fund for inspiration and ideas.

Our very grateful appreciation to the wonderful female role models whose wisdom has helped shape, and is still shaping, our lives.

Juliet and Michelle

Thanks to my dear friends who have been with me through school and college and work and life. Special thanks to my angels, Angela and Joy, who have helped me so much to find my path in life.

Gratitude always to my mother Pauline, daughter Nicole, grandmother Peggy and godmother Helen.

To my father Jim, husband Brian and son Mark who are duly qualified to now write 'what men know', thank you for being there.

Michelle Jackson

To my mother Jacqueline, daughters Molly and Jessica, niece Calypso, sister Rosa, auntie Luciana and godmother Marie Therese, my agent Sallyanne Sweeney, and to all my dear friends who have contributed to this book and to my life in every possible way. And to Peter, who knows women.

Juliet Bressan

Introduction

Every woman has a story that will inspire others. Every woman has a piece of advice that will solve a problem for a million other women. You've probably got a pearl of wisdom that you'd just love to share with all the women in the world because you know what a difference it would make. Helping other women to learn from your experience – if only they knew what you know now!

This is what this book is for. It's a collection of women's wisdom, a fountain of knowledge, a book that answers some of the big questions that women ask themselves on their journey through life.

Women have important power, deep levels of knowledge and vital wisdom and we need to share this knowledge with the world. The trouble is that we're so busy working, creating, nurturing, leading, healing and empowering others that we often forget to sit down and listen to ourselves!

Women are problem solvers. We listen. We learn. And we figure out what to do. Most of what we learn as women is through storytelling. All world religions and mythologies rely on stories to tell us what we need to know about life, humanity, morality, death, philosophy and ways of being. We learn about how to solve life's dilemmas from reading novels, watching movies, plays, following soap operas, reading news articles, and listening to human interest stories on daytime TV, because seeing what happens in stories is a powerful way of figuring out what works in life – and what doesn't.

Every day, we use other women's knowledge and advice – our mothers, sisters, daughters, girlfriends – to help solve our problems and to answer life's big questions. We reach out to each other when we need help. We meet in groups – around water coolers, in book clubs, restaurants, beauty salons, board rooms, operating theatres, staff rooms – and we lean on one another as a source of wisdom and support. We need the solidarity of other women to address much deeper questions, such as illness, widowhood, bereavement and death.

Imagine having all the women in the world to lean on when you need advice! Imagine the wisdom you could tap into if you could 'water cooler chat' with women from all over the world … imagine the fun you'd have if you could count on having your girlfriends with you at all times to solve your problems with you!

We wanted to find a way of getting at what is inside women's heads, and then collecting our shared experiences into a book … a book written by women for women.

Almost a thousand women from every corner of the world gave us their voices. We asked them questions about their daily lives, about what they believe, about what they want for their children, about how they spend their money, about how they work. We asked them about love, about friendship, about ambition and about power. About how they feel about their bodies, their beauty, their health and their fears. We asked them to tell us what they know. What came out of those hundreds of interviews is an amazing treasure of women's wisdom, inspiration and strength.

Women's wisdom is a quiet thing. The main institutions of wisdom are governed by men and are articulated by men: women's wisdom is sometimes ignored by the institutions of society.

But women are the main group bringing up the next generation. We are the educators, the healers and the managers of everyday finance, economies and social enterprise. In the past, the great gift of life and nurturing that we have has been used against us. Women's childbearing has been seen as a sign of weakness and has excluded us from participating in decision making during the time we spend nurturing. But we want to celebrate what it means to be a woman. It is time to take back the power and be the wonderful feminine creature that we are, inside and out.

What Women Know started off as an idea for a book only, but the most exciting thing that's come about as a result of all our interviews is the online community that has grown out of our search for ideas – and the group is growing! It just goes to show how important community development is and how wonderfully creative women are in their own homes, villages and offices, all over the world.

Collating this book has been an amazing journey of discovery for both of us. When we first started out to collect these stories, we had no idea how big this journey would become. We never imagined the breadth of our discovery. We were astonished and deeply moved by the honesty, the courage and the emotional strength evident in the contributions we received. And we were deeply touched by the depth and the power of so many of these contributions.

We wanted to create a book of wisdom that would inspire and empower other women. What we have found is that we have been truly inspired and empowered ourselves. As a result of reading these stories, both of us have grown – emotionally, spiritually and professionally. As a doctor, Juliet has been enlightened by the experiences women have shared with her of childbirth, miscarriage, happiness and health. She knows now that sharing ideas with hundreds of women has enhanced her own ability to practise medicine. As a mother and educator, Michelle has found a deep solace in the advice and wisdom that so many women have shared about children, sibling rivalry and teenage stress. She knows that the insight and knowledge she has gained from the stories in this book will be with her always as she continues to educate the next generation. Both of us have been inspired and deeply moved by women's stories about their traumatic experiences – divorce, abortion, widowhood, bereavement and violence. We have cried over some of the contributions. And thanks to the wit and wisdom of so many of the amazing women in this book, we have laughed at many, many more!

Some of the women who have contributed are friends of ours, some are relations, but the vast majority are complete strangers, women who found us through our web pages and who volunteered to share their wisdom with us. We feel so privileged to have been able to talk to all of these women and are so grateful to them for sharing their most important experiences with us.

We hope that you will love this book and that you will gain the same power that we have gained from it and from sharing the wisdom within it. We also hope that you'll want to use this book to gather your own wisdom, to pass your wisdom on to your daughters, your sisters and your friends. That's why we've included pages for you to write your own stories; to contribute to this living, learning book in whatever way you can. To celebrate your own wisdom with the wisdom of other women everywhere.

This book is our gift to you – *What Women Know*. For you to cherish and carry with you always.

Treasure it.

Michelle and Juliet

P.S. Visit us on www.whatwomenknow.ie or on our Facebook page What Women Know.

Friendship

*F*riendship isn't easily defined. It's about a range of relationships, some deep, some very loose, some distant and some close. Workplace friends, neighbours, lifelong school friends, yoga buddies, Facebook friends ... we need them all, to share our happiness, our sorrows, to share our burdens and celebrate our joys, to laugh, to cry and to make every little step on life's journey an easier one.

Friendship is incredibly important to women. We are naturally relationship-oriented, but our friends are more to us than just people we know. We use friendship as a source of wisdom. We nurture friendship to guard us in sickness and old age. Friendships are not always a source of joy, and we need to be powerful in our friendships as well as being empowered by them.

Toxic friendships can be a source of great misery, so it's vitally important that we recognise toxicity in all our relationships and make the changes we need to make to remove it from our lives. At the same time, the most important thing our friends do for us is to make us laugh, fill us with joy and bring us love, and it is our greatest privilege to give that love back in return.

What does friendship really mean?

It is really hard to be a good friend all the time, so we thought about a few of the most important things we value from friendship:

1. Feeling comfortable with each other.
2. Valuing each other's opinion and discretion.
3. Trusting each other to tell you the truth.
4. Always wanting the best for each other.
5. Knowing she'll always be pleased for you when things go well.
6. Knowing she'll always help you when things go badly.
7. Knowing that she'll forgive you when you don't live up to expectations or forget something that is important to her.

A FRIEND IS NOT A FRIEND when they tell you something that 'as a friend I think you should know' and then tells you in a way that takes away your confidence, respect and loyalty. A real friend will say the tough stuff that sometimes needs to be said in a way that shows you that they love you, care about you and only want the best for you – and then they give you wine and chocolate.

Lesley, 51, musician, County Dublin

❧

IF I WERE TO TALK to my teenage self I'd say, 'Friends are people who accept you as you are and you have got to be your own best friend.'

Carrie, 32, nurse, Nenagh, County Tipperary

❧

I THINK WE ONLY LEARN from making mistakes. The greatest gift we have is friendship, because no matter what bad things happen to us, it's our friends who are there for us. Being there for others is important too and it makes us who we are.

Cora, 39, grandmother, Athlone, County Westmeath

❧

MY FRIEND is very difficult to please. Every time I met her, she'd try to put me down. When something good happened for me, she'd always point out the flaw in it. She always boasted about her own achievements and if I got a pink sofa, then she'd have to have two pink sofas … It began to really bug me, and so I started backing away from her and avoided seeing her for a long, long time.

Then something very bad happened in my life and I was in a huge crisis. All of a sudden, my friend was there. She ran round doing errands for me, took care of my kids, cleaned my house, sat up late night after night talking my problems through – and if it wasn't for her, I don't know how I'd have coped. She was like an angel sent to rescue me!

What I realise now is that she is a foul-weather friend. When things are going well for you, she's full of negativity and spite. But when the chips are down, there's no better friend than she can be. I'll treasure her friendship always, and I'm much more tolerant now when she's being negative because I know how wonderfully kind she can be when you really need her! The interesting thing is that she's never needed anything in return – she's one of the toughest, strongest women I know, and she'll always sort herself out when her own chips are down. She has a lot of problems of her own, just like anybody, but she would rather die than ask anyone else for help!

Sonya, 48, doctor, County Dublin

❧

THEY SAY THAT FRIENDS are better than relatives because you can choose your friends but you're lumbered with your relatives. I never had any close relatives other than my parents and, as a child, was always very envious of schoolmates who had brothers and sisters to play with, so having friends was my major preoccupation.

I used to be amazed that they would disagree or quarrel with their siblings and disobey or argue with their parents, as it never occurred to me that this could be an option. But the necessity of acquiring friends at an early age has ballooned into a circle of lifelong acquisition of new friends all over the world, and it is a constant pleasure to hear from my former schoolmates, fellow students, my fellow young-married mothers of my children's friends, students I have taught and my professional colleagues, old and new neighbours in the three countries we have lived in.

We used to count how many 'best friends' we had when I was a child, and my grandchildren still do – I must tell you that the list of wonderful friends who have enhanced my life is enormous and, hopefully, is still not full.

Bernie, 64, Sydney, Australia

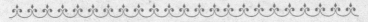

My favourite affirmation is this: When you judge someone, you don't define them, you define yourself …

Vicki, screenwriter, Australia

Guilt-free Pleasures

When our kids were very small, my neighbours, who were also mums on maternity leave or working parttime, used to meet up on a Friday afternoon in one or other's kitchen or garden and open a bottle of chilled white wine. We would sip and enjoy each other's company for hours before our husbands got home or the kids got too hungry. Rituals like this are worth the effort and make the best use of quality time with friends. Our little ones are now off kicking balls or doing activities, but we have those memories from when our children were so small that we were housebound. I now realise that it was a precious time.

Do try this at home:

Write individual letters to all your friends at Christmas. Everybody loves a few personal words much more than an email or a text.

Keep your address book up to date so you don't lose friends. It's one of the most valuable documents in your life.

Whenever you get a beautiful or special card, use it as a bookmark. Every time you open up your book you'll think about the friend or loved one who gave it to you and feel happy just to find it there.

Phone somebody today that you once had a deep friendship with, whom you hardly ever get to see. You'll have buckets to laugh about and it will make you smile for days.

For Mary H., Ann, Peggy and Eileen

MY BELOVED GRANNY died when I was fourteen. A few months later, my mother, who had long suffered with manic depression, killed herself. The two events were not unrelated. It took me many years to get over my shock and grief at losing these two very important women from my life at such a young and pivotal age.

No doubt because of this, I have always sought out the company and advice of older women, looking for nurturing, guidance and ways to live my life. I have met a number of them who were, and still are, very important to me. One was a friend's mother who provided unconditional love and warmth, another was a sister-in-law who helped me through many trials and tribulations about men, life, employment. She was always free to talk and give advice and encouragement. Another is an aunt by marriage whom I adopted, despite having health and other problems of her own. She was always there for me. Yet another was a neighbour for over forty years, again someone whom I could open up to, share my fears, sorrows, questions of how to be, how to live my life and come away feeling understood and affirmed.

From them I have learned that although you can have tragic losses in your life, if you reach out to people, by and large, they will respond positively. I want to thank those women, some of whom are now deceased, for the unstinting love, support and nourishment they generously offered me and for showing me that life is for living and growing.

Jean, poet, County Laois

᠀

I DON'T DO TISSUE-SERVICE for my friends any more. That's not what friends are for. My friends are for celebrating with, for having fun with. The Samaritans are professionals and they are very good at their job. That's who I tell my friends to call when they need a shoulder to cry on. I've been bereaved and I can't thank the Samaritans enough for being there for me in the middle of the night. I called them because I didn't know who else to call. You know when you're so full of grief that you think you're just going to die from it. But it works.

Beth, 50, make-up artist, County Dublin

᠀

SHOULD YOU BE FRIENDS with business clients? I used to always think not – but now I've decided that you can mix business with friendship as long as you are scrupulously honest with your friend/client. If a client wants to be your friend but they also are always looking for favours, then talk to them about what you expect from the friendship – your business needs to make money too! But if your friendship can't survive an honest working relationship, then you know what? It's not a real friendship.

Sheila, 40, consultant, County Dublin

*I trust the honesty I share
with my true friends.*

Toxic friends

True friendship is never jealous and it's never dishonest. It's never something you're ashamed of, and it's never one-sided. Our lives are too precious to be wasted by untrue friends. We talked to hundreds of women about what sorts of things cause toxicity in a friendship, and we found that the following is true: being a good listener doesn't mean that all you ever get to do is listen; being open-minded doesn't mean that you have to accept everything you hear; and being generous doesn't mean that you ever have to give your dignity away.

The worst thing about toxic friends is the time you waste on them, being hurt by them, when you could be spending time with nurturing friends or even being blissfully happy on your own. But when you've finally realised that someone is a toxic friend and you decide to ease them out of your life, there's such a great sense of freedom at that moment.

Like everything in life, a friendship can deepen, then move apart and then become vitally important again as the circumstances of our lives change. Every now and then, we need to loosen some unpleasant ties and reel some more important ones right in.

Friendships go up and down like the ocean's waves, and we shouldn't feel afraid to let unhelpful friendships wane to make room for more meaningful friends. Don't ever be afraid to streamline your *friends as your life changes. If you've stopped seeing as much of a friend because your priorities are different now, don't feel guilty or ashamed. Chances are she hasn't really noticed – or if she has, she's equally grown apart from you. If she's really feeling sore about it, then perhaps this is the very evidence you need to remind yourself why you've had to let her go. As long as we're honest with each other, we will always have the friends we need.* 🌿

A FRIEND IS NOT A FRIEND when she becomes the Queen Bee and I become the Wanna Bee!

Wolf, 42, Alabama, USA

A FRIEND IS NOT A FRIEND when you feel like crap after talking to them – toxic.

Keelin, 38, occupational psychologist, County Dublin

I HAD A BEST FRIEND for twenty-five years. I always thought she would be there for me. To me, a friend is always there, through the good times and the bad, the happy and the sad. Well, I was very wrong because when I told her that she had been very unsupportive to me when all I wanted was for her to 'be a friend', to call in just to say hi every now and then as she passed the door twice a day. Instead, she chose the men in her life as her best friends. They weren't married and they were always available for drinks at the drop of a hat. They were always there to see her fall off the bar stool drunk. They were there to have to put her in a taxi drunk and send her home. I was only there for her when her parents were sick. She had an affair with a married man and when it split up, I was there. She was my bridesmaid and my best friend and companion. But when I told her how I felt and that I was concerned about her drinking habits and who she palled with, she was not happy. It got to a stage where she couldn't, and wouldn't, stay in the bar if the lads were not out and I was.

So after my fortieth birthday, which she didn't get involved in celebrating with me, didn't join in the fun and dancing and, instead, proceeded to slag me and my husband off in public the next time we went to the bar with her, I decided I'd had enough and when she called me days later, I told her how upset I was and concerned about her behaviour on that night. She was not in contact for a year. We then met briefly when a problem arose at home and I asked her to be part of my life and be a friend. I invited her to my house again and she opted to stay in the pub with the lads! Two years have gone by. I miss her and the friendship that we once had.

The sad thing is a lot of others feel the same about her behaviour but won't say anything. Unfortunately I did. I am an honest person and think that you should be able to tell your friends their faults as well as nice traits. I have lost my best friend. So, before you say what you feel – think! I don't feel what I did was wrong. I thought we were stronger than that and could be adults and deal with the situation. So now not only are we not friends but a whole group of people have split up!

Isabella, 42, mother of two, County Dublin

MAYA ANGELOU WROTE that she had learned that people will forget what you said, people will forget what you did, but people will never forget how you made them feel. This is what I believe myself.

June, 38, journalist, County Dublin

❧

I'M ALWAYS WARY OF PEOPLE who instantly want to become friends and who are jumping to invite me places as soon as we've met – I work in television so I know a lot of celebrities and I'm very conscious of people wanting to be around me because they feel a bit of the 'fame' might rub off them. I've made a lot of friends over the years who seemed to be very interested in me but then I eventually discovered that they were only interested in how I could help them with their careers. The one thing you discover very quickly about the film industry is that people are very shallow and your new 'best' friend who spent every minute of the day with you on a nine-month job has moved on very quickly at the end of the series and you never hear from her again.

Jess, 29, script editor, Birmingham, England

❧

IF YOU'RE THE ONE doing all the running … then it's time to run!

Paula, fashion journalist, London, England

❧

WHEN YOUR YOUNGEST reaches a certain age, you are ready to get your life back in order. This means different things for different women. I had a very close friend who didn't like the way I changed after our children got to school-going age. She wanted me to stay in the zone of babies and nappies but I was ready to move on with my career and return to work – she hadn't worked since the day she got married and went on to have another baby. She resented me for my career and I couldn't understand why. Now that I am away from her and the toxic situation that developed, I see that she wanted us to remain the way that we were. The support of other women when you have kids at the baby stage is good. However, dependence is very unhealthy and will eventually lead to a toxic situation.

Ann, 43, teacher, County Wexford

Do try this at home:

Avoid gossip.

No matter how tempting it is to indulge, the facts on gossip are that it's simply not good for you! You can be much more powerful by being pleasant towards people you don't like. You can avoid having to offer an adverse opinion by saying, 'I don't know them very well.'

A DEAR FRIEND told me recently that when she was young, an older woman said to her, 'You can't change people around you, but you can change yourself.' At the time, my friend found this advice incredibly helpful. In some ways, though, it can be frustrating to hear this message. We want to ask, 'Why can't he/she change his/her annoying behaviour to make life easier for me? After all, I'm perfect, so why can't he/she be?' But think of it this way. I have the potential to change how I react to that behaviour. My reactions and emotions are within my control. Yes, there's work involved, but the pay-offs are worth it.

Jacinta, writer and GP, Melbourne, Australia

❧

COMPETITION is supposed to be good for us, to get us to work harder, be more productive, make someone or even a nation proud of us. It has its downside though as it can destroy friendships. I think women have a special sensitivity in recognising that competition is seldom between absolute equals, and that winning is not the end point, but achieving your potential is what it's all about. That's why real friends don't try to compete with each other.

Lynsey, 47, bank manager, Birmingham

Guilt-free Pleasures
Having a day off from work but not telling family or friends. That way the day really is all yours.

Jennifer, 47, outreach/case worker, Coolock, County Dublin

'I LOVE YOU BABY – the season's over.' It's a friendly way of saying, 'You're dumped.' What you find out at forty-five to fifty is that you need to dump those who are sucking the life out of you. Family and friends!

Beth, 50, make-up artist, County Dublin

秀

REMEMBER you only have to live with one person ... the one you see in the mirror each day, so that is the person to take care of.

Kasey, 55, personal assistant, Los Angeles, USA

秀

EVERY YEAR, I start a new diary and transcribe my lists of friends' phone numbers. I always come across friends who never phone or who don't stay in touch, people who are too busy for me or who haven't really ever been there for important events I've invited them to. Then you have to ask yourself, do I need to transcribe this phone number into the new book? Sometimes, it's good to let a few friends go. People change all the time. If you lose touch with friends, you don't need to feel guilty. Streamlining your friends is a natural process of letting go of the past and embracing all the new friends you're going to meet in the future. If you open your heart and invite new friends, you will always make new friends. I've made some friends in the past year, two years, who are dearer to me than people I've known all my life – family included! We should never be afraid to let stale relationships decline – and if a true friend is too busy to keep in touch, they will make an effort to reignite the friendship when their life has room for it. The most important thing is to look forward to meeting new people because you will make new friends wherever you go.

Ruby, 39, hedge fund manager, London, England

๛

IT CAN BE HARD to decide when to break away from a friend. But there are a few signs that always mean you should walk away. I mean, if you are constantly cancelling plans with someone just as often as you make them, then that means that you aren't really looking forward to being with that person. Sometimes, you start a friendship going because you think it's going to be good for you to have a friend like so-and-so, but the reality is that unless you fundamentally like the other person, you aren't going to benefit from that friendship!

Niamh, 32, PE teacher, County Galway

๛

I RECKON that if you find you are having the same conversation every time you meet, then you don't really have enough in common to keep up a friendship. I used to think that my friend Saran was such a great friend because we'd been friends since high school, but then I started to notice that the only thing we have to talk about is other people that we knew thirty years ago! I don't call her as often now, and it's OK because the friendship was getting boring.

Audrey, 46, Chicago, USA

The test of a real friendship is a shared holiday.

Magda, 34, nursing administrator, New Zealand

శ్రీ

I'VE LEARNED that sometimes you do have to 'catch yourself on a bit!' – and thank somebody somewhere for your lucky stars. I, for one, sometimes have been guilty of taking the good stuff for granted and advertising the imperfections of life by moaning to people close to me – but not shouting about the good stuff. It's worth the effort trying to create a happy atmosphere as a habit – it's amazing the negative habits we can fall into without even realising.

Jacinta, 35, development and outreach officer, Northern Ireland

I can let go of negative friendships and surround myself with people whom I love, who nourish me and bring me joy.

Can men and women ever really be friends?

We think so! Male friends can give us a different perspective, a male insight into our husbands and lovers. They can tell us when we look hot and they can fall in love with our female friends! But more importantly, sexual interest is only a very small part of the relationships between men and women anyway. How many times a day are you so distracted by your sexual feelings for your husband that you can't concentrate on your friendship? Having a close male friend is a great privilege and we cherish all of ours.

It's important to get beyond the boundaries of sexual interest and to see our male friends as individuals who need the same qualities from a friendship as female friends do. One of the things we love most about our friendships with men is the fact that our men friends don't have the same need to compete with our women friends. They are more likely to admire them! 🖋❤

I'VE LEARNED recently that a crisis brings out qualities in people that are not always what you expected. You will certainly find out who your real friends are (and it's not always the obvious candidates!) and you will always find huge support and strength from unexpected quarters. That is what makes just about anything cope-able with. Oh, and a last word from Mum, always wear good knickers, because you never know …

Laura, 40, journalist, County Dublin

꙰

WHAT I LOVE about men is when they make that giant leap and manage to get out of 'solution mode' and realise that you don't want them to solve your problem, just to listen, really listen.

Ciara, 40, software engineer, County Dublin

꙰

PRIOR TO THE 1950s my all-girls' convent school opened its doors to a minority group – boys. They joined the junior school in the room known as Bethlehem and were usually delivered by older sisters or mothers.

The boys are still remembered by their female companions due, no doubt, to the fact that they were a minority group and their behaviour in class and in the playground was often memorable. We are always impressed to see how well they have performed in their chosen careers. Some have left their marks on the community whilst the majority of female pupils of that time have hidden their talents under bushels.

It might surprise 'the boys' to know that at reunions or when past pupils gather together, they are often remembered. Some of the lessons were altered for the boys – when the girls practised the intricate stitches of needlework, they made model houses and plasticine animals for a farmyard – we watched with envy as we sewed on.

Our school days in Bethlehem were enhanced by the presence of the boys.

Today, so many years later, there remains a strong bond – their names are never forgotten. Did the school leave its mark on them? Are their memories of childhood richer for having known us?

Mary, secretary, Australia

꙳

I THINK IT'S POSSIBLE for men and women to be friends when you're younger, but as you get older, it does get more difficult. How many new male friends have you made in your thirties and older? I can't count the number of male friends I've lost when they eventually meet a girl and settle down with them. And I wouldn't like my partner to come home to tell me he'd met a fantastic new female friend!

Lynne, 31, accountant, County Galway

꙳

WITH MALE FRIENDS, there seems to be less competition on a personal level. I have always had male friends and you get what it says on the tin.

Deede, 27, nursery nurse, Manchester, England

WHEN I MOVED to Italy from the States, I had a lovely gay best friend called Mario, and I introduced him to a guy who had always had a crush on me, Alessandro. They hit it off immediately, and I was intrigued. Then I started to develop feelings for Alessandro that were probably inspired by jealousy. I knew that he was straight, and I had always assumed that he'd always have a crush on me, and now here he was flirting with Mario, my gay friend, and I'd introduced them!

I guess I kind of panicked, because then I decided that Alessandro and me should get married. We had this crazy, romantic, spur-of-the-moment wedding, but Mario was devastated and we stopped being friends. We have never really spoken since then, and Alessandro and Mario had a huge fight the night before our wedding and it kind of spoiled a lot of it. When Alessandro and I split up after two years of a bad marriage, he confessed to me that he had slept with Mario and he had enjoyed it, although he wasn't gay. Now it was my turn to be devastated. You can't always mix friendship with love and you can't make any man love you the way you want them – you have to take them as they come.

Sylvia, 29, graduate scholar, Rome, Italy

MY BEST FRIEND since I was four and a half also became my 'fall back', like in *When Harry Met Sally*. We vowed that if we were still single by thirty, we'd have our own 'open marriage' so we weren't alone. However, he came out just when I needed him most!

That's why there was never the spark and why our friendship lasted all this time – I just never realised. My parents always used to think it was weird that I'd meet up with him when I had 'another' boyfriend in tow – I think they might have thought I was a bit

Scarlett! We even tried snogging once and ended up in fits of laughter because we didn't like it – clearly I had 'something' missing. I know what it was now!

Violet, 39, art technician, Upper Maelstrom, England

🐝

I WISH SOMEONE had awakened me to the fact that as a teenage girl, most boys who are 'just friends' with you are either gay (perfect) or (more likely and not so perfect) hanging around in the hope that someday you'll succumb to their charms. I tried to pass this pearl of wisdom on to my own teenage daughter when she started hanging out 24/7 with her new best (male) friend. She thought I was being callous and old fashioned. The same daughter has recently started going out with a guy and guess what? Ex-best (male) friend no longer speaks to her. I rest my case!

Ger, novelist, County Dublin

🐝

IT IS CERTAINLY SAFER to have male friends who are gay vs. hetero-sexual. Hetero male friends can be platonic for years, then one night of boozing and loneliness and bam! You don't look at each other the same any more and it's really hard to go back. Sometimes it works out for folks, but mostly it's the horrible awkwardness that ensues, and a special friendship that's just not so special any more, having been tainted by the unmentionable. Yep. If you're going to have male friends, keep 'em gay. There are always exceptions, of course, but it works as a general rule.

Lesley, 45, law student, Canada

THE BENEFITS ARE when females are in their twenties and sometimes thirties and they do what I call 'games' when it comes to men and their friends. Men are pretty straightforward on what they want, so I was always attracted to their friendship over the drama of girls. This may not be a universal thing for women, but growing up in Los Angeles, I found that when one of my friends had a boyfriend or significant other, they pretty much gave up on friendship and devoted their entire life to their new person, not having time for friends. Guys I found were feeling suffocated by insecure women and always found time for their friends. I don't think men hold friendship in a higher esteem than women, I just think that friends are not a commitment to them, so they have the time.

Kimberly, 35, pre-school teacher, Indiana, USA

I HATE THE WAY my gay male friends think that just because I'm a woman I must be interested in their interior design and their obsession with *Sex and the City*! I don't give a hoot what my house looks like. And *Sex and the City* is an entertaining TV show – it's not a religion!

Alexandra, 43, violinist, County Dublin

I REALLY LOVED my friend Charles and looked forward to seeing him because we have so much in common – and my husband was only just a tiny bit jealous! But then I started to realise that Charles had feelings for me. I didn't want to stop being friends with Charles

– but now I'm too scared to contact him any more in case I hurt him. I just wanted to be platonic friends but I feel he spoiled it, and yet now I feel I'm punishing him for being attracted to me. I think this is why women tend to only have male friends who are gay, but it's a real shame.

Nancy, 37, interior architect, Devon, England

꙰

WHEN I CAME TO LIVE in Switzerland I made friends with two guys. We shared birthdays within two weeks of each other and all liked partying, so started a common project called the Aquarian Party. The two guys were enthusiastic DJs and I also liked the idea of being one. We rented rooms and sent flyers all over our neighbourhood to get everyone to come and dance. Although we've had loads of criticism about how we should run our parties, we have continued the tradition for fourteen years. They have become a local institution and one of the guys married an Aquarian girl, so there are now four of us! Although we don't have much contact throughout the year, I treasure my relationship with these people and the respect and reliability between us stands.

Nicole, 45, shoe designer, Switzerland

꙰

I DON'T FIND it difficult to be friends with a guy as long as I am not attracted to him! My male friends are just like my female friends!

Emma, 50, pharmacist, Wales

So can men and women be friends or does sex always get in the way?
The jury's out on this one. At some point in a friendship with a man,
one of the friends will inevitably ask themselves, 'Would I?'

We all do it. But it's just a question, we ponder it, consider it …
and then we move past it … and we're friends again.

Michelle and Juliet

Passion can be fleeting,
but friendship lasts.

Making new friends –
friends you just connect with

It's good to open your heart to new friendships. Friendships ebb and flow, but new people come into our lives all the time. Sometimes the deepest friendships can be with people we've only just met. Have you ever met someone that you just instantly connect with? We have! Sometimes it's tempting to believe that you've got to cling to your old friends forever or stay deeply loyal to childhood friends, but these relationships can hold us back as well as nurture us. Being open to new friendships all the time empowers us to value true friendship and to value ourselves. New friends bring new opportunities to grow in different directions, to explore new experiences of life. If you open your heart to new friendships all the time, you'll never fear loneliness and you'll gain an adventure of spirit that will carry you far through life. New friends come into our lives when we most need them to, and they always join us for a reason.

Juliet and Michelle met at a writers' course three years ago. Juliet was late, because she was having cold feet about whether or not to show up at all. Michelle had been introducing herself just before Juliet arrived and was trying to think of how to answer the question the tutor had just asked: 'What are you hoping to get out of this course?' Her answer had been, although Juliet didn't know it at the time, 'I just know I'm here for a purpose. I don't know what that purpose is yet, but I'll find out.'

At the end of the ten-week course, we had an informal drink together and we got to talk to each other for the first time properly. We discovered that we'd each had two husbands, have two children, and were each embarking with trepidation and excitement on our second career as a writer after a previous life – in Michelle's case as a teacher, in Juliet's as a GP. We are also the same age.

A week later, we were both approached by the same publishing house and began our new journey together as writers of women's books. We now know what the purpose to Michelle's being there that night was – and to Juliet's too. We were supposed to meet so that we could write this book, with all of you! ✍

How is it that, moments after meeting my neighbour, I felt as though we had so much history that our friendship spanned time itself? I know her and I want to know her. I want to know everything. I want to know what she's lived and how it came to be that despite the challenges and hardships she is *True* with a capital T. She traversed the divide, and it is these challenges, coupled with the very way she faced them, that transformed her into the whole person she is today.

My neighbour is grounded in a knowledge that only she knows, not unlike *Mona Lisa*, and it is this knowledge that makes her grounded, solid, yet a breath of fresh air. She enjoys her life tremendously, she has fun. She treasures what she has while exploring new avenues for her art – ultimately as a communion with the divine. Her courage, her sense of humour, her honesty, her healthy sense of irony and her open heart are but some of her extraordinary qualities. I've seen her landscape her magnificent garden, showcase her artwork at one of our city's premier events, teach at her renowned school, cook with gusto (with gorgeous results) and manage her artists' co-op. What sets her apart is the way she cares for her family, the way she kindles her relationship with each one knowing each moment is precious. She has looked after friends in need: she cooked for me and my family for weeks after the birth of our second child five months ago. My neighbour kept us alive, I tell you. We may have a third just to experience her cooking again. She is dear to me. I want to be there for her, to share with her whatever she needs, and to explore with her a world filled with possibilities.

Tania, 36, Toronto, Canada

MY NEIGHBOUR, Tania, and I have a special bond. She sends me beautiful cards to mark and encourage each significant event in my life.

I am close by to support her and to encourage her. We plan to have late night tea together after her children are in bed. We share our life stories.

This is such a happy, nurturing relationship!

Elizabeth, 55, artist, Toronto, Canada

WHEN I WAS SEVEN, I met a four-year-old girl who had the new Cola Chewits – I just knew we'd be friends! And we have been for twenty-five years! We've only ever had two arguments – one about marzipan and the other about Christmas decorations! I'm planning my wedding at the minute and she's going to be my beautiful bridesmaid!

Catherine, 32, student, Northern Ireland

SOMETIMES YOU MEET someone new that you like, at a dinner party or on holidays. I used to always be too shy to call this person afterwards, and I was quite lonely after moving to London. But then I was invited to a dinner party by a guy at work. There was a nice woman there, Ursula, and she and I sort of clicked at the table, we were laughing our heads off. She was the one who called me afterwards and suggested we go to a movie. And we've been best friends ever since!

If you meet someone you like, you should follow it up immediately and not expect that the other person will want to phone you. If you meet a new person and you think you'd like to become friends, just get their number and then phone them soon. Don't wait too long after the first meeting ... because they'll forget about you! The worst thing is to let a potentially great friendship go because of laziness or shyness. If there's a genuine friendship there, the other person will be thrilled you called.

Georgina, 32, sales rep, Kingston, London

❧

I MET MY BF at college studying French when we had to share a book. We were always being told off for giggling and Madame Jacqueline always used to say, 'Susanne et Linda you two are such naughty girls!' but secretly we were her favourites I think! Twenty-odd years later, we have remained solid friends and I even sang at her wedding in Rome. Our kids are friends too and she has moved house now so we manage to see each other a lot.

Susan, singer, County Dublin

❧

I BONDED WITH my best friend when I was twenty-seven, pregnant and using an online forum for mums-to-be. She announced she was expecting her third baby (her second being only four months old) and I thought she was off her trolley. I sent her some maternity trousers I didn't need (which once I met her I realised would have been completely ridiculous ... she is short and petite, I'm not) and she sent back a blue baby blanket for the son I was yet to have and a big bar of Galaxy for me. We have supported each other through post-natal depression. Those babies are now six and five respectively and she is my little girl's godmother.

Oh and she makes me laugh till I almost choke. Perfect.

As you get older, I think it gets harder to make true friends – the bonds you forge in your formative years (for me, in secondary school) will always stay but if you are lucky you will meet someone who understands the new you that adulthood has made you. My 'new' friends – especially my 'mammy' friends – are priceless.

Grace, 29, manager, Derry, Northern Ireland

Every person I meet is a potential new friend.

Nurturing friends – friendships for life

We know that children do better when we praise them, that managers who encourage their staff have happier workplaces with more productivity. You can't ever assume your friend knows how much you love her, but you can be sure that sharing affection is never a waste of time. It's wonderful to tell your friend that you are proud of her, that you think she's beautiful, that you love to spend time with her, and remind her that she's funny, clever, charming, kind, patient, talented, creative – all the things that make her dear to you. It's important not to just be a foul-weather friend, only there for the bad times, a rock, a shoulder to cry on – you've got to be there when your friend is succeeding too. Friendship is a celebration that lasts a lifetime if we want it to. ✍❦

A GOOD FRIEND of mine once said that your soulmate doesn't necessarily have to be your partner, and she was right. Myself and my best friend completely understand each other. She's been living in America for the past seven years but, if anything, our friendship has gotten stronger and we're closer than we ever were. That's the sign of a true friendship. When she and her husband move back to Ireland, we're going to make up for lost time on the cocktails!

Ciara, 31, editor, County Dublin

❧

GIVE AND TAKE is what life's about. Give with heart, accept with heart and if you have the balance right, you won't feel taken for granted.

Theresa, poet, West Cork

❧

YOUR OLD FRIENDS are comfortable like a great pair of old shoes you love, new friends are the exciting new pair you get to wear in by walking a lot of miles in them. I have done lots of miles in my old shoes and plan to buy many new pairs and do lots of miles in them. This is how I think of my friendships.

Caroline, 37, retail manager, County Donegal

❧

I TREASURE MY OLD FRIENDS – we have been through so much together. Recently seven of us who have known each other since we were kids all went to Portugal together for a weekend. We belly-laughed our way through the trip and when I came back home I felt refreshed and realised the value of our friendship. We have all had our ups and downs over the years but we are now at the stage where we can appreciate that there is no awkwardness or pretence between us. That is why it's important to nurture our old friends.

Wendy, 38, hypnotherapist, County Dublin

MY OLD FRIENDS are like a memory box. It's like we have 'history'. We've been there for the aftermath of a failed teenage relationship, the OMG I'm pregnant and delighted or OMG I'm pregnant my mum's gonna freak. The hold-me-I-need-a-hug moments, the sadness of infertility, the loss of parents and the joy of becoming new parents and all that new chapter brings. I have had my oldest and closest friend since we were sixteen – over twenty years. We've laughed and cried together and I love her to bits. We might not be in contact for weeks at a time but when we do, it's just magic. If you are lucky, you will meet someone who understands the new person that adulthood has made you.

Deborah, 37, computer technician, Northern Ireland

Guilt-free Pleasures
Spending time with your silliest childhood friend and laughing together at something that no one else understands.

TRUE FRIENDSHIP is being able to pick up a conversation where you left it off three months previously! Some of my 'old' friends have moved away, had families, etc., but I'm lucky that I can't say we've drifted apart. We may not talk as often as we used to but we're still linked and tuned in to each other. I think new friends are important too, although they will never know the real you in the way that your long-standing friends who saw you as a horrible teenager do!

Fionnuala, writer, Northern Ireland

꙰

I GOT A BEAUTIFUL Christmas card from a friend, it was a print of a painting of the bookshop in Skerries. I loved it that much I framed it and have it hanging in my hall with my other Dublin paintings.

Claire, 43, full-time mum, Holland

꙰

NEVER FORGET to thank someone for even the smallest present or courtesy.

Miriam, business coach, Newbury, England

꙰

MY SISTER IS AN INSPIRATION. We both look up to each other. We are best friends, not rivals. I believe insecurity comes from the way you have been treated by others, usually those in your workplace or, more so, those you once had a relationship with, loved and was hurt by through being undermined, devalued and criticised.

I never really compared myself with others, I didn't have to when I was made to feel so bad, but I have spent five years learning that I am a lovely, fantastic, beautiful, successful, independent woman … all the things my sister has always told me: all the things I think she is!

Maf, 38, Montessori teacher, Tain, Scotland

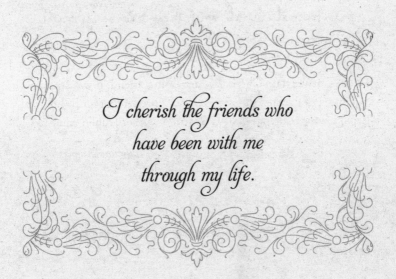

I cherish the friends who have been with me through my life.

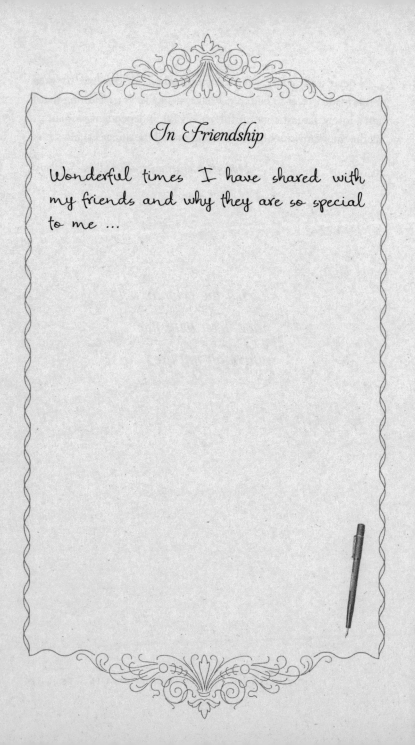

In Friendship

Wonderful times I have shared with my friends and why they are so special to me ...

Health

*I*t's important to realise your power as a woman to be the stronger, longer-living gender, the caretaker of humanity. Being a woman means that your health needs to be in tune with nature. It means listening to your body, nurturing your mind and being aware of what your body is telling you it needs.

Your body is unique in its shape, its strengths and its weaknesses. You inherit traits and characteristics in your genes, but your own unique interaction with the world has a special influence on the woman that you have become today and the woman you are going to become in the future. As women, we have an inner sense of how important it is to protect our bodies from illness as we grow through life.

Being a healthy woman means looking after your body and your mind. Women are more vulnerable to stress and depression and perhaps this is because of the responsibility we bear and the sensitivity we possess. So having a healthy mind means that we listen to what goes on in our heads, we seek advice, we share wisdom with other women and we learn to know our priorities, our values and we learn to trust our hearts. Choosing a healer or doctor is an empowering decision that we make with wisdom and intelligence. Growing older is a time to prioritise health and fitness, to look after our bodies and stay powerful as we enjoy maturity. Women who survive illness can teach us a lot about the value of self-care. Our gift of wisdom lives long with us into old age, and we cherish it!

Dealing with stress

Stress is the greatest cause of illness in modern society and, as the nurturers, women have to protect ourselves from succumbing to it. In turn, this will help those around us. There are many simple everyday ways of dealing with stress. Yoga and Pilates are popular amongst women because we need to be centred, balanced and calm to remain healthy. When stress becomes a bigger burden, we need to look at the root cause and examine ways of dealing with it in a powerful way. Most stresses are short lived. Those which are ongoing or deep in our lives need careful attention but should never be ignored. No problem is too deep to solve, too private to share, too shameful to reveal. The health care industry is full of strong women who are skilled and empowered to heal and advise – and our expertise is growing all the time. Together we have built up a vast knowledge base of stress-beating skills. If your life has become too stressful, you are going to have to reduce your workload or increase your fun. And very often, you need to do quite a lot of both!

MUCH ILL HEALTH is caused by stress and the environment we live in – I use a blue dot to help me to stop several times a day and take a deep breath before I move on to my next task. I put the dots on my watch – the steering wheel of the car – my mobile phone – it reminds me to take stock of how I am feeling inside and centre myself at stressful times.

Pauline, 66, counsellor and psychologist, County Dublin

※

WE HAVE TO KEEP in tune with the balance of our body and what it needs. Nothing does more damage or causes worse disease than stress. The more we are dominant or forceful in the old style of working, the more stress we will bring into our lives, so stop trying to behave the old way and try a new order that will not cause stress to you or your colleagues.

Irene, 53, choreographer, England

※

WHEN I FEEL STRESSED, I go for a walk outside in the rain, the sun, the snow or whatever, and I take in everything around me. When you stop to take stock of your surroundings, you realise the vastness of the world and the beauty of the simple things around us and you realise that you cannot control everything. This puts my role in the world and whatever was causing me stress into perspective.

Aoife, 32, teacher, County Dublin

※

I WOULD ADVISE women feeling stress to discuss and/or compare their situation with others (women if possible). It's amazing how many others are going/have been through similar situations. This is a great pressure valve and usually yields pretty sound advice. As the saying goes, 'A problem shared is a problem halved.'

Cesca, 45, eternal student, West Cork

❦

SEE IF YOU CAN pare down your life; declutter, organise, etc. and make absolutely sure you get your essential fatty acids; exercise; good food; and knock off the sugar and caffeine (those truly do make stress worse!).

And for heaven's sake, make one night a week a special night for you, to do whatever you want to do. Could be a special yoga class, shopping, movie, art class, whatever. It doesn't matter what it is, just do it for you.

Lesley, 45, law student, Canada

❦

Stress? Vitamin B complex works in about twenty minutes!

Ann, 54, writer, County Dublin

Do try this at home:

Stress is a major cause of heart disease and, it is now believed, cancer. If you suffer from stress, get help immediately – find the source or cause and deal with it. Then pamper and look after yourself – use methods to deal with it. Meditation and controlled breathing are very effective. If they don't work, try counselling – there is no shame attached. Let's face it, if your hair is in a mess, you go to a stylist, don't you?

Don't be afraid to say no (make up an excuse if you must). During times of extreme stress, drop your standards and put off anything that you can. Talk out your problems with friends. Make sure you have some personal time to do something for yourself. Have some early nights; even if you can't sleep, your body is still resting.

I acknowledge that when I feel stressed it is because I've been doing too much.

Nourish your body

Diet is for life. Many women have a tortured relationship with food, but the simple fact is that we need to eat foods that nourish our bodies. Every time you go to eat something, ask yourself, 'Will this food nourish me? Give me energy? Provide me with vitamins, fibre, protein, minerals? Will it hydrate me and give me the strength to fight disease?'

There are a few golden rules that we can live by when it comes to food.

Don't focus on weight or diet or think about it too much – if you're dieting, you are thinking about food all the time and this only makes you want more of it. Try to eat when you're hungry. Most of the time when you feel hungry, you are actually thirsty! It's the same feeling and a drink of water can stave off the craving for sweet food. If you eat, try to make it real food – and if you hate veg and fruit then make smoothies or juice to get live food into your system – that will get rid of any hunger craving too. And finally (this pains us to write), no matter how much we try to convince ourselves that the antioxidants in that glass of vino are actually good for us, nothing piles on the weight like alcohol! It's a bitter pill, but true.

Your body is an engine – what you put into it reflects how it will perform.

Lisa, 34, fitness instructor, County Kerry

⚜

IF YOU THINK ABOUT IT, the role of women has always been to feed our children – from the watering hole to the campfire, to the supermarket, we preoccupy ourselves with food. It's no wonder that it can become easy to confuse feeding with love, anorexia with rejection, dieting with self-control! Feeding children and babies should be just that – providing them with nourishment. And love.

Rhonda, 40, counsellor, Australia

⚜

MY FRIEND was very overweight. She was chronically unhealthy, living on doughnuts and fizzy drinks. Whenever we got together, she was always exhausted and grumbling about being tired, and she got every single cough and cold going. She was always putting her husband and her son first as well – whenever I suggested we go out, she always had to ask her husband first. Whenever I wanted to go clothes shopping with her, she only wanted to buy things for her son. She's a great wife and mom but I couldn't help feeling frustrated that she would never do anything nice for herself, and she was always apologising for the way she looked. She was always complaining that she felt unwell, but she never tried to change anything about her diet or the way she lived. Whenever I was with her, I always felt thin (which I'm not!) but I couldn't actually enjoy her company. I began to realise that the energy around her was very negative and that she was making me feel depressed. I felt she was slowing me down. So I started avoiding her at work because I felt I couldn't enjoy my job around her. I felt guilty about this but something had to change.

For about a year, I didn't see my friend, and then one day she rang me out of the blue. Her husband had recently become ill. She'd had to take time off work to nurse him, and she began to realise that if she didn't get healthier herself that she'd be no use to anyone. She'd started to lose weight, was taking care of her diet and was walking to work – and her energy was completely different. I felt comfortable being around her for the first time in years. I have my friend back.

Niamh, 37, receptionist, London, England

꙰

EVERY MOTHER WORRIES that her daughter will become anorexic – and when she starts to gain too much weight, we worry that she'll become depressed, diabetic and lonely! The fear and powerlessness we associate with food has got to be one of the most negative consequences of our ability to feed ourselves a surplus to our fundamental needs.

Linda, 32, psychiatric nurse, County Dublin

꙰

Take echinacea. Put a few drops in a small glass every morning during term time for your kids – we have made it a tradition in our house and say 'down the hatch' and knock it back like a shot before breakfast!

Michelle

SHOPPING AND COOKING FOOD should neither be a chore nor a creative art – it's a practical task that contributes to a family's health and well-being. Food is not a treat – it's something we nourish our bodies with. The treat is the energy, vitality and joy you experience when your body is in good health.

Jane, paediatrician, Liverpool, England

Do try this at home:

Become food aware.

Every day eat something green, something blue or red and a handful of seeds or nuts.

Choose brown rather than white food.

Eat fish more often than dairy or meat.

Drink plenty of fresh, clean water!

I GET FED UP with health scares. A bit of what you fancy does you good. It speaks volumes that people were healthier during the war when there were shortages. But people were encouraged to eat better than the poorer sections of society did before the war, and again now. There is an added dimension of fad diets causing dietary deficiencies.

Deede, 27, nursery nurse, Manchester, England

My husband says the only thing that I can make is a reservation.

Jacqueline, 41, fashion designer, New York, USA

❦

I meet a lot of patients who have gained weight but are at the same time suffering from malnutrition because they aren't eating enough vitamins and minerals in their food. The right foods will protect us from illness. Coloured fruits and vegetables prevent cancer. Omega 3 in fish protects your joints and your brain. Nuts and seeds contain the minerals and phytochemicals that nourish your breasts, bones and womb. The most important thing is to make sure you're getting the foods you actually need, so make sure that every day you eat something red (tomato, strawberry) or something blue (aubergine, blueberry, plum), something green (broccoli, peas, spinach) and a handful of seeds or nuts and some whole grains. Drink some water, eat five fruits. Red and blue foods contain powerful antioxidants (the blue and red pigment of the plant), which fight infection, cancer and ageing in cells. Then, eat fish three times a week, meat only once. Nourish your body!

Juliet

❦

I'M NOT SURE I know that much about health because I spent most of my life working with the unhealthy! However, I know the theory and spread the gospel of maintaining a healthy lifestyle based upon fresh air and exercise, moderation in all things, eating regularly and not confusing rest and relaxation with inactivity. My advice is to look at the lives of those who enjoy good health.

What does that mean?

Enjoyment is the key to good health. It's not much good if you ruin everyone's dinner party because you're living on a lettuce leaf to keep the weight down.

It's no fun either if you're jogging round the stadium in the pouring rain just because you're in training and can't afford to miss one day.

It's not enjoyable to drink too much alcohol and feel decidedly unhealthy the next day.

It may be enjoyable to smoke but it's not enjoyable to sit near a smoker in a closed space.

It's very enjoyable to have a good laugh and to cheer someone up, and you'll feel much healthier if you do this at least once a day.

And if you've had a row, it's very bad for your health if you go to bed without making it up or saying you're sorry!

April, 42, family practitioner, Florida, USA

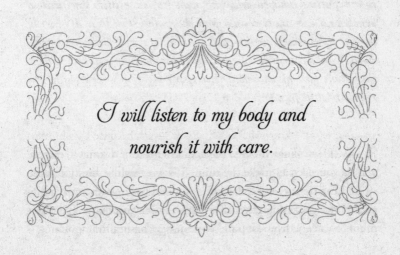

I will listen to my body and nourish it with care.

Exercise for health

Women differ enormously in the kind of exercise they like to do – and for many women, exercise is a chore, something that has to be done because we want to stay slim. But no woman can afford to be a couch potato for life because we need the protection that exercise gives to our bones, our breasts, our immune system and our minds.

Exercise, fun and friendships can be neglected if we don't prioritise them. The body heals more slowly after middle age, so you need to make sure you prioritise your health every day. Sometimes, that means putting yourself and your own free time first. You need to pencil your exercise time into your diary and stick to it. It's easy to let that time go to something else, so think of it as a vital investment. Even if you don't care about your body fitness, your mind is the most important part of your body. Exercising vigorously makes sure you keep a healthy mind!

RECOVERING FROM ILLNESS or childbirth makes it difficult to exercise and so you need to make the time. It is worthwhile spending time to find the right exercise that suits you and fits in with your family and working life. Children always love to play outdoors with their mum. Soccer, catch, skipping, swimming, chasing, trampolining –

what child doesn't want their mum to join in?

Marion, 36, post-natal physiotherapist, County Galway

჻

I DON'T LIKE EXERCISING – I hate sweating – but instead of dreading going for a walk or a run, I focus on how good I feel after the exercise and slowly I began to crave that feeling, so when I don't exercise, I feel uncomfortable and sluggish. Now I look forward to stretching my legs and getting the heart rate going!

Lorna, 29, beautician, County Offaly

჻

A LOT OF WOMEN spend a huge amount of time feeling guilty about not taking enough exercise. But it's not just about vanity. You need to take vigorous exercise to protect your bones against osteoporosis in later life. It's just a thing you've gotta do – like flossing! Vacuuming is vigorous and if you garden also you will be using more muscles than you imagined.

Delli, 58, family lawyer, San Francisco, USA

჻

HULA HOOPING, well, hoop dance to be exact. Brilliant fun as well as good exercise.

Audrey, 32, London, England

WALKING THE DOG on the beach, dancing around the kitchen with my kids and lots of – you've guessed it.

Susan, 42, full-time mum, County Dublin

Do try this at home:

Use your body – all of it. And give your heart a good workout.

WALKING AROUND THE SHOPS is surprisingly underrated. Even a once-a-week, one-hour jaunt will keep the (waist) pounds off. And then if you're like me, you're a seasoned shopper. So, you'll see what you want in the very first shop and then just to be sure you'll see what else is about … when suitably satisifed with your reconnaissance … head back to said first shop after say … four hours of investigative price comparisons/stock taking … and buy the 'must have' item. Satisified that yes, indeed, it is the best in town. Calorie burning and shopping addiction complete. Mission accomplished.

Mary Ann, jewellery designer, County Donegal

I exercise because I want to have fun.

Healthy breasts

Our relationship with our breasts is such a love–hate thing. When you're young, your breasts are all about looking sexy. All we worry about is their shape, their perkiness, their size … it's all about the way they look for other people! Having your breasts cut and trimmed into a different shape is one of the most traumatic operations you can have – but for many women, their breasts are so important that it's something worth spending a fortune on.

One in every five women gets breast cancer eventually. But we also need to empower ourselves to prevent disease.

Every woman is aware nowadays that she must check her own breasts. We need to find out what young women can do to avoid having to find a lump in the first place. And what middle-aged and older women should be doing to reduce their risk of breast cancer and to prevent recurrence of cancer if they have already been diagnosed. ✍

The World Cancer Research Fund has found that there are some important links between diet and lifestyle factors and cancer, including breast cancer. Keeping slim turned out to be one of the most important things a woman or man can do to lower the risk of cancer. Because the hormones that can influence breast cells (oestrogens) and the development of breast *cancer are made in fat tissue, excess body fat can increase a woman's chance of developing breast cancer after menopause.*

The other biggie is alcohol – this has been found to be associated with an increased risk of breast cancer. There aren't many health scares that can keep me away from a nice bottle of wine, but this is definitely one of them. One of the best things that's happened for women in the West is that we are free to socialise, hang out in bars, share wine with our friends and have as much fun as we want to, whenever we want – and women love to party. We've got a lot to celebrate! But we need to be careful about the amount of alcohol we drink, just like any other toxin we put into our bodies.

Juliet

※

WE STARTED TO NOTICE several years ago that women who came from cultures where there was less alcohol had fewer breast cancers. When we looked back through their histories, we realised that Western women were drinking an awful lot. Now we know that oestrogen can cause hormone-receptor-positive breast cancer to grow and alcohol can increase the amount of oestrogen in a woman's body. This increase in oestrogen may be part of the reason for the link between alcohol and breast cancer risk. Drink lightly, ladies! Avoid alcohol as often as possible for healthy breasts!

Sharon, 53, breast cancer histo-pathologist, USA

※

I remember the day after my son was born and I was taking to breast-feeding very well and enjoying the experience of being a mother and nurturing my baby. The breast-feeding nurse sauntered in with all sorts of horrible things like pumps which terrified me and warned me of how sore my nipples were going to get. But the piece of information that shook me was a flippant comment she made as she walked out the door – 'Oh and don't use any deodorants or antiperspirants when you are breast-feeding.' She was gone before I could ask why. Later that evening, I asked the staff nurse why she had said that.

'Well, deodorants usually contain aluminium and it will flow through the glands in your armpit and go into the baby's milk.'

I was a bit shocked and said, 'That means I am putting aluminium into my system even when I am not pregnant?' She nodded. Since then I only use natural deodorants that you can get in health food shops that don't contain aluminium.

Michelle

Do try this at home:

For healthy breasts:

Always maintain a healthy weight – keep your body mass index less than 25 for life.

Avoid meat and dairy foods – low animal-fat diets protect breasts.

Eat plants, seeds, nuts and soya – phyto-oestrogens from plants protect breasts.

Red, blue and purple fruit and vegetables fight cancer cells – so make sure to eat more than five a day.

Exercise and sport protect your breasts – so do something physically active for at least an hour a day.

Seven hours a week of vigorous exercise from middle age prevents breast cancer risk.

Eat healthy. Spray fewer chemicals. And break a sweat!

Watch your drinking – we now know from the Million Woman Study that alcohol is associated with cancer of the breast.

HORMONE REPLACEMENT therapy (HRT) definitely increases our risk of breast cancer. I think everyone who works in health care knows that. But most doctors won't tell you that nature is full of foods that replace oestrogen in our diet and don't affect our breasts. Evening primrose oil protects breasts from lumpiness and tenderness at period time, and relieves menopausal symptoms too!

Andrea, 50, radiographer, Australia

❧

BREAST CANCER SURGEONS say that soya is more breast-friendly than dairy. This is because soya foods contain phyto-oestrogens, or plant-based oestrogens, which are thought to block the body's response to the cancer-causing natural oestrogens that every woman has.

I grew up in Korea and we rarely heard of women with breast cancer. Then I moved to the US, and breast cancer was all that women talked about! Asian women have low rates of breast cancer compared to Western women. But eating soya (tofu, miso, soy milk, etc.) can definitely help with symptoms of menopause for women who don't want to take oestrogen. And soya in the diet definitely reduces the risk of osteoporosis after middle age.

Soon, 60, food scientist, Kansas, USA

ALWAYS MASSAGE your breasts with massage oil because you'll find it much easier to feel any abnormal lumps and you'll keep them much perkier and younger looking.

Emer, 38, plastic surgeon, London

Love your breasts.

Choosing the right healer

When we talked to women about their choice of healer, most women seem to favour women doctors, nurses and complementary healers. The interesting thing is that research into practitioner preference among patients shows, in general, that most men prefer women doctors too. Women have a gift of empathy, we are relationship people, we tend to read body language with sensitivity and so we make natural healers.

Self-help for women has always been a necessary alternative to professional care. And this isn't a new thing. As far back as the middle ages, women have made an effort to instruct one another to help themselves with female problems, rather than consult with a male physician! In 1500 a woman's health manuscript was written and was reprinted in 1981 under the title Medieval Woman's Guide to Health. Today, we can all benefit from the huge variety of consultation style, of approach and of theory that is available in modern holistic healing.

The most important thing is to find the healer or practitioner that you like and trust. The therapeutic alliance you develop with your healer is the source of much of the benefit in your health. Trust *your practitioner, but be honest and strong in your health-seeking relationship. And, most importantly, trust your own body to tell you how it feels, what has gone wrong and what kinds of treatments are working best.* 🌿

It is common in Western society to feel your heart race after you pass the age of fifty and, for some, it can happen in their thirties. My mother went through numerous tests and investigations to deal with this when it happened to her at sixty. None of the medication worked or helped her ailment until an alternative therapist told her about magnesium citrate – it's a supplement that can be bought over the counter and really does work. Look into the alternatives and try to find the cause of the problem rather than a quick-fix tablet that will ultimately lead to further health problems.

Michelle

🐦

I WILL GO TO THE DOCTOR and I am also open to seeking alternative medicines and methods of preventative medicine. But, I think after women have families, we do put ourselves on the back burner.

Julia, 39, Oxford, England

🐦

I THINK A WOMAN will go to a doctor when there's something wrong more often than a man does. Maybe this explains why we outlive the men! Conventional medicine always works for me, but I do think holistic healing has its place. Our health service is terrible in this country but, despite that, I've always been well looked after by GPs and hospitals, especially during my pregnancies. They never took any chances with me – if anything, I thought they were too fussy altogether.

Veronica, 34, florist, County Waterford

※

MASSAGE IS WONDERFUL for anything stress-related, great for mental well-being as well as ironing out the knots, but then not advisable in pregnancy or for someone with a cancer diagnosis. I find it beneficial, but a friend says she feels bruised after deep-tissue massage, so it depends on the person too.

My medicine cabinet has Paracetamol as a mainstay, but also echinacea and citricidal (taken for all kinds of ailments from sore throats to sinusitis) and also arnica (for bruising/shock). I believe in keeping the antibiotics for when you absolutely need them – I think they have been vastly over-prescribed.

Theresa, 41, administrator for mental health services, West Cork

※

HOLDING A HAND (skin-to-skin contact) can do wonders. Apparently, it has been proved that just having a hand to hold can lower trauma anxiety and increase pain toleration. This can be seen when brain activity is measured in a MMR scanner.

Any mother knows that just a wee touch to her child can stop the child's tears in an instant. I have always said, 'Never underestimate the power of a hug.'

Now, I am not saying that a touch or a hug can heal all, but I am saying that it can make a huge difference to the 'patient'.

I believe that modern medicine is truly amazing (yet still has a way to go), but I also believe that we have lost sight of some of the natural ways.

Many of our medicines are derived from natural ways: galantamine, for example, which is used to treat early to moderate dementia, is derived from the snowdrop! The rainforest in Australia has plants that are poisonous which live alongside a plant which has the antidote. The Aboriginal people know this. And when I think about it, where there are nettles, there can also be found dock leaves! I think we ought to embrace modern medicine and all it can do for us, but we would be very short-sighted to turn our backs on what we call alternative healing methods, medicine that has been around for thousands of years.

Getting back to the humble hug as my example: if it helps the patient in any way, then surely it is 'good medicine'.

Maf, 38, Montessori teacher, Tain, Scotland

૭૪

I HAVE HAD AMAZING RESULTS with reflexology. Finding a practitioner who can tell you your problems before you have to tell them is key. The young man that 'did me' was Romanian and totally amazing. He also did the most fabulous massage too. If only I could have him on the NHS.

Caroline, 43, Hampshire, England

I find reflexology fantastic. It's amazing what you can be told about your physical and mental well-being. Would still revert to traditional medicine though where necessary, but it's nice to try the non-drug route first.

Susan, 38, manager sharehold services, County Dublin

⁂

My GP is a life-saver. She made me visit her every day when I was at my worst with hyperemesis [severe morning sickness] and she just listened while I cried and cried and cried. I don't know what I would have done if I had not had someone so sympathetic to listen to. The other great life-saving healer in my life is a lady who I went to for Angel Reiki at the same time … I walked out of her treatment room assured everything would be okay.

Claire, 34, writer and journalist, Derry, Northern Ireland

⁂

Women feel pain differently to men. This has been proven in scientific research. I think it's important that medicine acknowledges this, and that there are enough female practitioners in nursing, medicine and physiotherapy so that we can learn from the patients. Childbirth is changing, but the advances in anaesthesia in midwifery are all thanks to the fact that more women are working in medicine and the midwives are more powerful now!

Margaret, 46, radiographer, County Kilkenny

ARE WE GOING from one health scare to another? Pretty much! We would be living in bubbles if we took on all the warnings, but, sure, even that would be unhealthy. If knowledge is power, I'm afraid I don't want all the power. Sometimes ignorance is bliss – not always, I know, but we don't have the time or the energy to stress and worry about everything! That's unhealthy too!

Rebecca, 32, teacher, Bolton, England

I will work with my healer to protect my health.

Working through illness

Being a woman means that your health matters. If you're working outside the home, your colleagues rely on you, but most importantly you rely on your income, so don't take good health for granted. And if you work inside the home as a full-time carer, full-time mum or home-maker, you'll find that taking a sick day is pretty much impossible because you're always at work. Take the time to listen to your body and make sure you are prioritising good health at every age.

Middle age is a time of significant health change for women. This is the stage when we gain weight, when many of us develop serious diseases of the womb, breasts, bones and gall-bladder. Yet, quite often, we are working in full-time jobs or caring for children, husbands and elderly relatives … it can be tough and it's no wonder that our health can't take the pressure. Being a powerful woman means you put your health before your career, even if this means staying out of work because you are ill. Taking care of your health when you are ill is a sign of wisdom, not a weakness, and our colleagues will thank us when we are fit and healthy for the job we have to do. ✿

WHENEVER THERE'S A COLD going around my office, it's always the women who struggle in to work whereas the guys are very happy to take time off. I think that women need to be more assertive when we're ill and not feel ashamed of staying at home. Why bring something into work to give to everyone else? Nobody thanks you for coming into work ill!

Mary, 49, administrator, County Kildare

WE NEED AN EQUITABLE and fully funded health service to remove financial and all other stress. Properly funded so the staff – the majority of whom are women – get paid a proper wage. Fully funded public primary health care which approaches health from a community response approach, feeding back into how our communities are managed.

Less pollution, proper housing, public transport that's regular, no stealth taxes, crèche facilities where they are needed (and affordable too). A woman's right to choose to have an abortion in Ireland instead of sending women off into the silence of going to Holland or the UK. These are some of the things I know about health, my health and health in my community. My community has two chippers, two pubs, four off licences, a bookie, two pharmacies, a gourmet deli butchers, a post office, one ATM machine, no benches, no community spaces, no green areas. No wonder our health is in rag order!

Paula, photojournalist, film-maker and social activist, County Dublin

TRY NOT TO WORRY or think about it (like me!). I knew I had college to go to this semester and for a few weeks I suffered badly with panic attacks and my stomach was also in a state – every time I started to feel unwell or panicky, I automatically went home (although it was probably just the panic attacks that scared me – I'm slowly but surely handling them better). I'm not a great patient and worry like hell, so stay calm is my advice because worrying only makes you feel worse.

Geraldine, 19, student, County Galway

🐝

I HAVE FIBROMYALGIA and work part time. My advice would always be to keep working, as being at home when you are ill gives you too much time to think which, in turn, makes you worse. I was told in 2006 that I would never go back to work but I took this as a challenge and although I am not able to work full-time and need help to achieve this, I know I am much better fighting to carry on working as I would go batty if I stopped.

Debz, 52, independent mental health advocate, Manchester, England

🐝

FROM BITTER EXPERIENCE, if you have a course of antibiotics – or more, one after another – take some probiotics afterwards to put the good bugs back into your gut. I don't mean these piddling drinks – get some strong suckers from the pharmacists. Look after your gut.

Avis, 55, writer, England

I DID A LARGE STUDY on women's health and one of the outcomes was that women 'listen to their bodies' and seek health information from friends and colleagues, as well as family and medical practitioners, so work/community is very important for women's health, as it provides a backdrop network of word-of-mouth health information. That might be part of the reason why we are so keen to go to work when we are ill, because we find similar souls there who will listen and care. My advice would be to trust your instincts and look after your body – you only get one set of internal organs!

Also, I think some women have no choice but to go into work when they are ill. Two women I work with tell me they feel guilty if they are off sick, as they need their jobs to survive and worry that they will be sacked. When I was a single parent with young children I was literally 'one pay packet away from poverty' and paid by the hour, so if I wanted to eat/pay the electric bill, I had to work. Even though I'm not in that situation now, the urge to work no matter how ill I am has remained.

Jacqueline, 48, chief executive, Manchester, England

❧

BEST WAY TO DEAL with illness is prevention, Vitamin C, various herbs, garlic, plenty of veggies topped off with exercise and variety!

Louisa, 29, marketing executive, West Cork

❧

IF YOU'RE WORKING through illness, then you should listen to your body, slow down when you have to and take care of yourself. Don't ever listen to people who believe you will never get better. Find a coping mechanism that works for you and work through your illness. Keep a positive state of mind even after you've had a bad day … just get back up again.

Valerie, author, County Kildare

❧

Being sick means bed. Men or women. I really, really hate when people come to work sick. They spread germs and put the whole office at risk. Don't be a martyr – stay in bed and read the ditty about a bucket of water.

Victoria, 45, scriptwriter, Tasmania, Australia

I will trust my body to tell me when it's ill.

Sleep

Sleep is probably a woman's greatest luxury – and there's no substitute to the health benefits a long sleep brings. The average woman needs 8.3 hours a night – but many of us are lucky to get half of that!

Sleep happens so that the body can heal itself. When our mind switches off, our body and muscles relax deeply and our brain waves change completely. We need this period of 'stand-by' for the brain and muscles to completely rest so that we can heal and repair.

First thing in the morning is when we are at our most creative, the time when we are boosted with creative energy for the day, the time when our mood hormones are fully switched on for all the vital tasks we need to do during the day. It's so important to get enough sleep, so take the time to prioritise sleep as a necessary health and beauty boost in your life. Power naps of twenty minutes in the middle of the day can recharge your batteries when you feel exhausted, and even that short snatch of sleep is sometimes enough to take on a new task with energy … but there's no substitute for night-time sleep, so do whatever it takes to make this a target in your life.

Serotonin balances your emotions and your mind. If you aren't sleeping properly, wakening up during the night, have trouble getting to sleep or can't stay awake during the day, these are all signs of physical or emotional ill health. It's no wonder that the first symptom of emotional illness is always difficulty with sleep. It's important to have a full cycle of sleep every night so that your body and mind are in tune with one another. During sleep, your brain secretes human growth hormone, which repairs your body too. Sunshine is the only thing that stimulates the production of melatonin in the brain. Your brain needs enough melatonin to stimulate the sleep centre at night. If you aren't getting enough sunshine during the day, it will quickly disturb your brain's ability to fall asleep. That's why people who live in dark places in winter get so depressed, and why suicide rates are higher in northern countries. We think it's a lot of the reason for the increased life expectancy in the Mediterranean countries too.

If you suffer from real sleep problems, seek help. Problems with sleeping can be the first symptom of depression and anxiety: don't leave it too late to attend to this. And finally, there's nothing like a great holiday to boost sleep. Never underestimate the healing power of a week off. 🌿❤

I CAN NEVER GET USED TO night-working! I've been doing it for years, and the first few hours are always OK, you feel great, everything's nice and quiet but then – it happens every night – at about five in the morning, you get into this weird space where you feel totally depressed and you think you're probably going to have to punch someone! Then that passes and you look forward to going home at dawn … I wouldn't do it except that I love driving home at seven in the morning just in time to have breakfast with my kids. Then the day just flies by and I'm back on the next night shift again. I'll get used to it some day!

Sarah, 36, night nurse, Birmingham, England

It's easy to get into a habit of staying up late to watch TV when you've got nothing to do the next day. When I didn't have a job, I just used to stay up till all hours and I found it very difficult to sleep. I used to get sick a lot when I worked as a teacher because I didn't like the work – but now I'm running my own business, I'm working harder than ever. I sleep like a baby and I'm much healthier too. I'd advise anyone who's having difficulty sleeping to examine their routine. Make sure you enjoy the work you're doing. Get up in the morning, get busy, get out during the day, get to bed early, and if none of that helps then get help!

Sam, 36, PR consultant, Edinburgh, Scotland

Do try this at home:

Eat your largest meal in the middle of the day.

Eat bananas and drink camomile tea in the evening instead of tea or coffee.

Exercise early in the day.

Quit cigarettes! They definitely keep you awake.

Invest in the most beautiful, comfortable mattress you can afford.

Keep your bedroom spotlessly clean and dust free – dirt in the room creates bad energy that interferes with sleep.

Make your bedroom a haven of tranquillity. Use the bed only for sleep, reading and sex.

Remove the TV, computer and mobile phone. They give off microwaves and disturb sleep.

PHYSICAL EXERCISE definitely helps sleep. The body needs to feel fatigue in order to send a 'fatigue' message to the fatigue centre in the brain to stimulate sleep … I always advise people to work out in the mornings so that they'll sleep well that night.

Cheryl, 27, personal trainer, UK

We were married for ten years and our bedroom still had the rose duvet that we had been given as a wedding present. Then one day, over the Christmas holidays, I went into Arnotts and went mad in the sales – I bought a feather and down duvet and some cosy flannel sheets and exotic shiny duvet cover – it set the mood beautifully. Now all we have to do is get the kids to go to sleep earlier!

Helen, chef, 37, County Wicklow

I am grateful for the healing power of sleep.

Mindfulness

Women suffer from anxiety and depression twice as much as men. Doctors who study depression in women find that much of the gender difference is because of women's more vulnerable social status. Many women are economically dependent on men. And poverty, unemployment and stress may affect women more deeply if we have dependent children or parents. But it is important to remember that emotional illness is as treatable as any other illness. When depressive feelings interfere with sleep, appetite and will to live, it is vitally important to seek help.

Women are much less likely than men to become violent when emotionally unwell. If you feel suicidal, this is rare and dangerous and you must consult your doctor or a trusted friend. Suicidal thoughts are always abnormal and a sign that you are most certainly ill.

If you are prone to episodes of low mood, make sure to seek happiness in your life. Examine your sources of unhappiness and try to eliminate them. Painful relationships, toxic friendships, miserable work, dysfunctional families, unhappy memories and physical illness can all cause deep, permanent sadness. Physical and mental exhaustion burns out your brain by using up all your happiness hormones to deal with stress. Antidepressants replace the happiness hormones at a neurological level, but changing the causes of unhappiness in your *life is essential to prevent depression from recurring again. Seek out the sources of happiness in your life and nurture them.* ✍❤

I'VE SUFFERED FROM DEPRESSION on and off during my life but I find that exercise is the only thing that really works. I play golf every day now, I swim in my local hotel pool in the winter and I'm absolutely mad about gardening. I used to get very ill with depression and I was in and out of hospital for years. I don't think I'd be alive today if I hadn't decided to make sure I get a good dose of exercise every day.

Nora, 65, retired teacher, County Limerick

※

WHEN MY HUSBAND DIED, I was very depressed and I couldn't get out of bed for weeks. I couldn't believe that this thing had happened to me, and I kept asking myself what I'd done to deserve this pain. I didn't want to take antidepressants because I didn't believe that there was anything wrong with my brain. I was convinced that life is just full of pain for everyone. I'm very against taking medicines and I felt that antidepressants were just a way of turning you into a zombie. My doctor eventually persuaded me to take medicines but I didn't stay on them for long. I think they were good because they gave me the energy to get out of the bed and start to make the changes that I needed to make in my life. But what I really needed to do was to change a lot of the way I was thinking, all the work I was taking on, and to stop taking a lot of toxic relationships seriously.

Rose, 45, community activist, County Dublin

Do try this at home:

Be grateful! Studies of happiness in communities have found that practising gratitude makes a big difference to your mood. Keeping a gratitude diary has been proved to make life happier for whole populations of people. Psychologists and counsellors are now using a gratitude diary as a technique for treating long-standing depression.

MY FRIEND RECEIVED a corneal transplant recently and wrote this to me: 'I am deeply grateful that an individual and his or her family, who will always remain anonymous to me, generously chose, at the time of death, to donate his or her cornea. I often think, Who was he/she? What did he/she see? It's hard to put it into words but I will say a prayer for him/her every day for the rest of my life.' With the donor forever unknown and unable to say thank you to the family, I was led to reflect on what inspires the generosity and love we get from each other.

Miriam, administrative officer, Melbourne, Australia

Do try this at home:

Focusing on the here and now is the key to mindfulness. The past is over: don't dwell on it. The future is unknown. But *here and now* is all that we can experience in our minds. Try to be aware of the moment. Forget strong emotions, beliefs, memories, regrets. Forget fears, anxieties and worries. Concentrate on the here and now and what is happening in the moment. Breathe deep. Learn to meditate and be in touch with yourself.

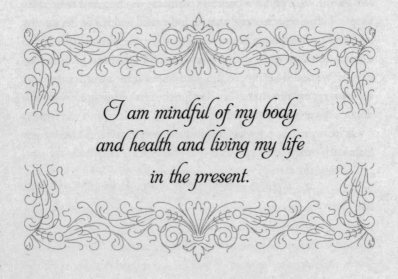

*I am mindful of my body
and health and living my life
in the present.*

Ageing
magnificently

For women, growing old is more than just the physical aspect – it's also about the emotional journey. But ageing is inevitable, and therefore the important thing is to grow old powerfully. When we talked to women about their ideas of ageing, the fear of illness and the fear of death, the one strong message that came out was that no woman would swap her aches and pains and wrinkles for the insecurity, anxiety and self-loathing of their youth, no matter how small a waist she could get!

Everybody dies – but not everybody gets to grow old. If you are afraid of ageing, think about the millions of truly wonderful women throughout the world who never got to age. We have all lost someone who died before they grew old, and we all know someone who has outlived all expectations. Think about the magnificent older women you know and how honoured you are to have been in their company. Relish the thought that one day, with luck, you will be an old, wise, fascinating woman, who other women adore and respect, and who is, after decades of living history, living gracefully, at great peace with the world.

Ageing magnificently means listening to your body: it's telling you what to eat. If you're having indigestion problems, gaining too much weight, having bowel problems – these are all signs that you aren't feeding your body what it needs. Taking the time to eat carefully means that you won't risk increasing the toxin levels in your body over time. The earth provides us with the nutrients we need to live to a very great age – the fruits of nature are all there to be enjoyed.

Being stressed and worn out is not the way to honour your gift of life! We only have one life and it's important to spend it wisely, joyfully and meaningfully. Make sure you examine your job, your family, your friendships and check that all are fulfilling you, providing you with the nurturing you need to live long and happy, healthy and wise. Use your time in youth wisely to prepare your journey into old age so that you have built up investments in love, in friendship and in health. ✿

MY GRANDMOTHER SAID to my brother and me, 'The best Christmas present is good health.' I have good health already – so I would like an iPod instead!

Dina, 13, schoolgirl, Australia

❧

WHY DO WOMEN LIVE LONGER than men? I'm with the superior evolutionary power! No, seriously, we are just used to having to get on with things when sick and when under pressure, and when we need to go to the doctors we go, it is not seen as a moment of weakness. Our systems are built to withstand horrendous things like periods and the dreaded childbirth (and the memories of the pain never fades) so we can deal with living a few extra years.

Ria, 35, manager, Derry, Northern Ireland

ॐ

NEVER FEEL LIKE you're past it. I turned sixty this year and feel like I've never looked better. My daughter is a beauty therapist and keeps me looking young with lots of facials! Always make an effort – you'll feel like a million dollars.

Marie, 60 retired teacher, Belfast, Northern Ireland

ॐ

I THINK WOMEN OUTLIVING men is an evolutionary advantage aimed at maximising the human population so that there are more females to protect the younger, more vulnerable members of the group – plain and simple.

Deede, 27, nursery nurse, Manchester, England

ॐ

The vagina sustains life, too bad, boys!

Wolf, 42, Alabama, USA

I'M IN MY SEVENTIES now and this is what I know about staying healthy and enjoying life: don't eat a meal while watching TV or listening to loud music. If you're going to give up smoking or chocolates or drinking, don't tell anybody until you've been off them for a week.

If you skip off work early, everybody will see you leaving: if you stay late, nobody will notice. Always take your full holiday entitlement. You'll feel refreshed, everybody will have missed you and you'll have something new to talk about at morning tea. Always have something to look forward to – a holiday, losing weight, spring flowers in the garden, a new baby, your partner coming home.

Never have a new hairstyle or colour just before going out on a first date – you might not be recognised …

Say 'I love you' to your family every time you say goodbye on the phone, and give them a hug every time you meet. You never know the day it will be your last opportunity. Learn a skill – knitting, crocheting, folk singing, dancing, playing an instrument, painting, sketching, miming – and then teach your children.

If you move to a new area, why not offer to walk a dog for a neighbour – you'll soon make friends after you've been round the park a few times.

Join a community choir – there is nothing quite like the joy of making music together. It's impossible to be angry or impatient when you're singing in harmony.

Noelle, 74, Wellington, New Zealand

෪

THERE'S ONE REALLY GOOD THING about ageing that I can think about, and that's the lack of inhibition which makes us confident enough to admit our inadequacies. Surely we can all remember the terror of waiting to be asked a question in class, the humiliation of mispronouncing a word to hoots of laughter, the day we came into work wearing casuals having forgotten that there was a formal lunch, the day you had to sing solo and couldn't get a sound out, the agony of waiting to be asked to dance, the fear of blushing beet-root-red with embarrassment or burping loudly in public. My heart goes out to the young women who believe that they have low self-esteem and that it matters. Heaven knows people who have high self-esteem are generally insufferable show-offs!

I would advise the low self-esteemed women to age rapidly and lessen their inhibitions. Don't be afraid to put your hand up at a meeting to ask, 'Does everyone understand that point except me?' – odds are you'll see half the room smile in agreement. Dress for comfort in styles that you love – you can wear 'car to bar'– stiletto heels only from car to bar without agony. Smile sweetly and ask the underage occupant of a seat for the elderly or incapacitated on public transport – repeatedly and loudly, if he's listening to his iPod, to move; stay in on a Saturday night whenever you feel like it, with a good book or the TV – it's much better than dreading not having been asked out on a date!

Gemma, 72, retired vet, Brighton, England

Sometimes, I hate having to slow down, hate aches and pains, hate grey hair and toothache and wearing glasses and not being able to hear properly … but not for long, because I absolutely love wisdom, confidence, peace and all the pleasure you get from your own company in old age – and really that's all I care about when I come to think of it. If something hurts, I just take painkillers and have a glass of wine and put my feet up for the night … the great thing about being older is that you don't worry as much, you don't worry about anything really. You're just grateful for every day, people are nice to you and you look forward to things all the time. It's magic, actually. I thoroughly recommend it!

Sinead, 75, retired teacher, County Dublin

Do try this at home:

Ageing magnificently means preparing your body for life.

Weight-bearing exercise from youth – walking, cycling, running, tennis, going to the gym, dancing, skiing – all protect your bones from hip fractures and prevent a humped back in old age.

Give your heart a good workout, feel the buzz, get a natural endorphin high … and protect your breasts and bones.

Make your holidays action-centred and feel like a million dollars when you return. Cycling with your family. Scuba diving with your lover. Hill-walking with your friends … enjoy the wonder of nature, stretch your bones, let your heart beat with joy!

I KEEP VERY ACTIVE – that's the trick. I've got two artificial knees but it's not going to stop me playing golf. Now that I'm retired, I've got lots of time to play, it's brilliant.

Bennie, 73, County Clare

❧

I WAS OVER FIFTY before I learned that my body is smarter than I am, knows much better what is – and isn't – good for me, and responds more authentically and quickly than ever I could. However, I was several years older before I really began to listen to what it tells me.

And I don't seem to be alone. Because more and more women are telling their stories, I am learning that many of our bodies have ways of telling us when to extend a hand, when to notice that something isn't right for us, when to step away from a situation, when to set a boundary.

Just as there are various ways that we each have positive physical reactions when we've met someone's needs without condition or been of service when it's really needed, I'm beginning to understand that we can each have our own physical reaction to people and situations that have the potential of being toxic for us.

My body's signal begins with a slight queasiness, which often gets worse before I consciously recognise it. Lately, I've got better at responding to the sensation early enough to do something about whatever is causing it before I'm too far into a situation to get out easily and before I've done myself or anyone else any real damage, for which I'm increasingly grateful.

But that hasn't always been the case. I was fifteen when I first began dating my former husband. A bit sooner than the appropriate length of time designated by our culture for such a thing, he kissed me. At the time, I was surprised that he had moved so 'fast' and thought that the sick feeling in the pit of my stomach was due to his breaking the 'rules'. That queasiness, however, was strong enough for me to 'drop' him. Over the next six years, that scenario played out over and over again, until in the seventh year, the queasiness disappeared, I fell in love and I married him.

Over the next thirty years, I ignored, denied, ate something, quit eating, and kept really busy in order to fight the sporadic bouts of nausea, which after five years were most often directly related to trouble in my marriage. Looking back on that part of my life now, I can see that if I had been willing to put all those occurrences together rather than package them up individually and shelve them away where I wouldn't have to deal with them, I would have learned to listen to my body way before my fiftieth year.

I now see the queasiness as my body telling me that I was about to be knocked away from my centre onto uneven, unstable ground where I wouldn't be able to keep my balance, that my instability and vulnerability would bring on nausea as the toxicity of the situation got worse and worse.

For a close relative of mine, her body's early warning system is a lump forming in her throat; for one friend, it's a headache caused by a muscle tightening in her left shoulder; for another, a cold sore on her lip. Of course, there are physiological explanations for all our reactions and ways of treating them medically and psychologically. What I know is that it is important for me to trust that my body will tell me when I need to pay attention, to recognise the message quickly, and to work with my body to overcome, eliminate or avoid whatever is causing the reaction.

I am incredibly grateful to be working in an environment that often gives me an opportunity to practise what I've learned and hopefully to continue to get better and better at walking the walk.

Sue, director, County Cork

*Age
magnificently*

Staying well - happiness for life

Women have always been the more willing gender when it comes to trying something different in our pursuit of good health. And we are constantly seeking out new ways to improve the way we deal with stress. Women realise that a calm mind in tune with a relaxed body is one of the best ways to counteract our stressful society. Disease is taken from the term dis-ease, implying that ill health can happen when you are not at ease with yourself. Many forward-thinking doctors are looking to patients' mental and emotional states to help diagnose and find a cure for physical ailments. Homeopathy, for example, works on the principle of treating the cause of the symptoms and not the ailment.

Taking time to go to a health-related class is one of the most important parts of women's social lives. That's because women are always prepared to look outside of themselves and not worry about appearing foolish. It's why we ask for help when we're sick – we seek advice and we share knowledge.

Illness is what happens when our bodies are out of balance, and taking the time out to pay attention to your body is what's really important. Finding the health-seeking activity that suits you is a *powerful way of protecting your future health. When you go to yoga, Pilates or Reiki you're having a fun evening out as well as investing in your future self. Finding the time for health-activity isn't always possible, but we need to listen to our bodies and make health-seeking a priority as often as possible.*

Medical research has shown that gratitude, friendship and love will protect us against illness. Seeking joy wherever possible, seeking laughter, seeking strong friendships and nurturing the people we love will all mean that we benefit from longer, healthier lives. We need to balance everything in our lives in order to stay alive!

Knowing what makes you happy isn't as easy as it sounds! But it's worthwhile taking a bit of time to figure it out. This means spending time alone with your thoughts. It means finding a place where you can think about yourself. Every woman needs what Virginia Woolf called 'a room of one's own'. Spend time getting to know yourself – you deserve a healthy mind and a healthy body for life.

HAVE YOU EVER NOTICED someone say 'he is a pain in the neck – she is a pain in the neck'? The chances are that at some stage that person is going to end up with a pain in the neck themselves. My friend Angela told me such a story one day about a woman she knew who referred to situations and people that annoyed her as always being 'a pain in the ass'. She was sad to say that very same woman was diagnosed with colon cancer. If you moan and complain after others, the only one you will ultimately end up hurting is yourself.

Teresa, teacher, 44, County Meath

Do try this at home:

When you go to visit someone who's ill, make sure you are there to entertain them rather than comfort them: the best visitors tell jokes or talk about something interesting or amusing that has happened to them. And don't stay too long!

Nature protects us from dis-ease. Seek out remedies in nature to stay well!

Vitamin D prevents colds and chest infections and boosts the immune system. Lots of people nowadays suffer from vitamin D deficiency because they don't get enough sunshine – we work in offices all day and use sunblock all year round. But you need to get into the sun for your body to manufacture vitamin D, we don't get it from food alone. Get plenty of sunshine and daylight in the wintertime and take cod liver oil!

Cranberry juice prevents and treats simple cystitis and can prevent urinary tract infection – drink it every day and you'll have a healthier love life!

Vitamin A cures acne. Dermatologists actually use this in high doses in Roaccutane, an anti-acne treatment which is very toxic. Carrots contain natural, non-toxic vitamin A in safe doses. If you've got acne, you should drink carrot juice every day and you'll see your skin improve very quickly! If you hate the taste of it, mix it with apple or orange juice too.

Here's a thought – laughter is a reflex. That means it's a human behaviour that's essential to our survival. Here's another thought – animals don't laugh, only humans do. So does laughter have a purpose? Studies have found that laughter protects against infection, depression, insomnia, and promotes love and fertility …

I ACTUALLY ENJOY helping people who have problems and count myself a good listener – but I often found that people were dumping stress on me. Being a doctor means that you spend your day listening to other people's sorrows – and helping people can be very rewarding but you have to make sure you don't end up absorbing too much misery. I used to come home exhausted and drive everybody mad with my moaning sometimes … So I decided that outside of my working life, I'm going to go out of my way to try to seek out people who make me laugh. Turns out, you can be a good listener without absorbing misery – and you need to make sure that you neutralise other people's sorrow with someone else's laughter every time.

Sinead, 36, GP, County Tipperary

I BELONG TO A WOMAN'S Walking Group and a Woman's Book Club. The walking group has been together for ten years and we walk at 7 a.m., three times a week. The book club has been together for twenty-one years. I have been a member for nine. All the members are married with children! We are all in the forties and fifties age group.

We have supported each other in woman's health issues; children's and adolescent illnesses; career advice and help with employment; suggestions for sources for the care of the elderly; support after the death of a parent; international exchanges; home repair and maintenance; family and solo travel; and many more things!

In our groups, we have a visual artist/educator, health care communications specialist, businesswoman, musician/ educator, lawyer, accountant, literature scholar and community volunteer and educator.

I cherish these women and the nurturing relationships!

Anonymous, mom and dancer, Canada

❧

MEDITATION, living in the moment, realising it's pointless worrying about things that are out of your control, some sense of spirituality – all of these lead to a happy, healthier you!

Jeanne, 47, unemployed, County Dublin

❧

IF I COULD SIT DOWN and talk to my teenage self, I would tell her this: Keep your figure, don't eat junk. Don't go back with a man because he cries for you! Don't be so serious, enjoy life, and fate will take care of the rest. Don't worry, there's plenty of time to get married in your thirties, you've not even lived half your life at that stage. Save some for a rainy day. Love yourself and life will love you back!

Caroline, 37, retail manager, County Donegal

Do try this at home:

Did you know that children laugh on average four hundred times a day and that adults only laugh about fifteen – what about the other three hundred and eighty five that we should be having? Please try to do something about this – the world needs your help!

THE ESSENTIALS for happiness are good health for yourself and family … and don't ever worry about money because that will always be there … enjoy every day as much as you can …

Angela, 39, single mum, County Longford

LIFE IS TOO SHORT to live a mediocre life. Play and live full out – you only get one chance.

Caitriona, 34, mumpreneur, County Laois

BE GRATEFUL. Love yourself as much as you can regardless of size or shape, you are the best you are today. Really live your day, for we are never guaranteed tomorrow, this life is not a dress rehearsal, it's the real thing. Enjoy it.

Linda, make-up/hair designer, County Dublin

THE MOST IMPORTANT LESSON life has taught me is that that the only thing that I will never live without is oxygen … but happiness is the thing that we work to get … I guess the most important thing for happiness is health. Seeing that the people you care about are in good health and happy, this makes you happy, and when you find people who love you for yourself and love them back … you always smile.

Hanein, 21, medical student, Libya

❧

GOD TAKES SOMETHING away from you to give you something better … and karma is real.

Yasmine, 18, beauty therapist, County Dublin

❧

THE MOST ESSENTIAL ingredient for happiness is peace of mind. Definitely. Health and love pretty good also!

Oonagh, food scientist, Northern Ireland

❧

Seek out friends who make you laugh. When you're feeling sad, don't always run to the friend who is a great listener, who soaks up your misery, who wallows in your misery with you. Instead, make sure that the people who make your heart sing out with joy are always in your life. Nurture these friendships. Surround yourself with people who make you laugh.

Make sure you have people in your life who are happy for you as well as those who will console you – and make sure that the consoling friends are also those who will make an effort to make you laugh again.

Juliet and Michelle

꙳

BE GRATEFUL FOR YOUR HEALTHY BODY!
I had a period last week – I really enjoyed it.

Perimenopausal woman, 43

꙳

NEVER TAKE ANYTHING or anyone for granted, count your blessings, live each day to the full, laugh until your sides are sore, smile! Try not to judge, think before you speak, love with all your heart.

Marie Louise, 37, teacher, Derry, Northern Ireland

꙳

YOU DO NOT HAVE TO CHANGE yourself for someone. And don't ever let something fall from your eyes, don't look behind and look forward.

Koka Bofa, 24, student, North Africa

꙳

Guilt-free pleasures for a healthy, happy life: breakfast in bed.

Oh God, I adore a Saturday morning lie-in. And none of that on-the-hoof rubbish I shove down my throat during the week. Proper free-range scrambled eggs on seeded toasted bread with a few strips of smoked salmon on top if I'm feeling really decadent. This is no ordinary breakfast, oh no … this is a Saturday morning lie-in breakfast … Mmm.

Debs, 39, non-teaching assistant, Bedford, England

※

Sometimes people are asked about the best or happiest moment of their life, a landmark event, or what was their best achievement. It may be self-indulgent, but I'm more interested in what makes a person's heart sing – little things, places, works of art, beauty, memories. Of course these can change with time but, for now, this is what makes my heart sing:

1. Rainbows.
2. Coming home on the train.
3. Listening to my iPod, all alone in the bath.
4. Flying above the clouds.
5. Having a meal out with my best friends.
6. Going to a brilliant gig of a band I really love.
7. Talking to family or friends on the phone, anytime!

Marion, 49, Blackrock, Dublin

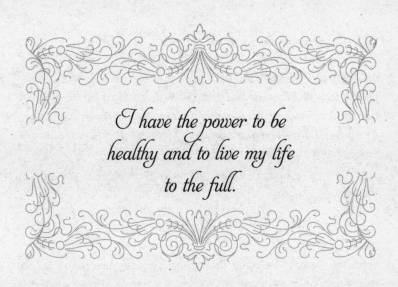

*I have the power to be
healthy and to live my life
to the full.*

In Health

Make a magic wish.

If I could have a magic wish, what
I want is ...

Beauty

*I*s beauty important to every woman? Certainly the beauty industry thinks so. As women, we spend more on beauty products than on medicine, literature, entertainment, sports, education and, in some cases, food. Beauty treatments are more than just a way of looking better for others – we use the beauty parlour as a social group, a chance to be alone, a room where we can be ourselves, an escape from the city streets, a place to celebrate occasions with friends. For many women, the beauty rituals we enjoy regularly are a way of rewarding ourselves for having worked so hard and having succeeded in life.

Why is physical beauty so important to women? Is it vanity, or is our desire for beauty a primal instinct? It's tempting to believe a lot of old-fashioned ideas about women needing to attract men, the urge of reproduction, the survival of the fittest – but human females are the only animals who tend to adorn themselves more than males! Look at male birds, fish and other primates – it's always the male of the species who needs to be the most attractive.

Women love to look beautiful – because we can. We are sensitive to aesthetic values in every part of life – in music, art, poetry, literature. Looking beautiful, giving ourselves a beautiful self-image, is just another part of wanting to make our world a better place. When we look in the mirror, everything we choose to add to what we see, from our clothes to our jewellery and make-up, is like a palate from which we paint a beautiful self-portrait to present to the world, every day.

Inner beauty,
outer strength

When we talk about inner beauty, what do we really mean? Most women are beautiful, but even the most stunning, prize-winning beauties amongst us rarely feel that we are pretty enough. Our tendency to be self-critical is a huge waste of our power and our ability to enjoy our bodies and our minds.

Caring about what you look like is an important part of being confident and strong. If we really believe in inner beauty, then why not show this on the outside as well? The beauty inside of us is brave. It is wise. It is powerful, sexual, emotional, spiritual, philosophical and deep. The image we have of ourselves in our physical appearance is an important reflection of this inner beauty.

Looking into the mirror should empower us. We should see the person in the reflection. See her intelligence, her wisdom, her kindness, her wit. We should see her softness, her courage and her heart. Painting and adorning this image is a part of the aesthetic pleasure that women find in every creative part of life. Strong women are proud to show their faces to the world! ✑❤

WHAT I KNOW about women celebrating their identity is that it's easier to be who you are the older you get. The need for pretence disappears and being comfortable in your own skin replaces it.

Lesley, 45, law student, Canada

🐝

A FRIEND OF MINE wouldn't be classically pretty. She's such a gorgeous person, however, always laughing, upbeat, generous and unselfconscious and this makes her a stunner. Guys fall in love with her all the time and girls want to be friends with her. Looks will fade, but she'll have that inner sparkle forever.

Jessica, 28, shop worker, County Limerick

🐝

TO ME, nothing is more beautiful than a clever person.

Kasey, 55, personal assistant, California, USA

🐝

AVERAGE INTELLIGENCE over smug cleverness any day, and beautiful is what's inside a person surely? Classic example: my friend's five-year-old once told me that I was beautiful, while we were browsing through pics of airbrushed celebs in a mag. I asked him what made someone beautiful and he replied 'people who smile' – out of the mouths of babes!

Theresa, poet, West Cork

WHEN I LOOK in the mirror, what I love about what I see is my lips. Always wear red lipstick. It's just me, makes me feel good. If I had to have a tattoo it would be of Betty Boop in black and white but with bright red lips.

Deborah, 37, computer technician, Derry, Northern Ireland

❧

I THINK it is important to be clever. Beauty fades with time, but if you're clever, you can try to hold on to it for a bit longer.

Valerie, author, County Kildare

❧

WHEN I LOOK in the mirror, what I love about what I see is my shoulders. I have great shoulders, girls, and I like to work them to my advantage. Ha!

Susan, singer, County Dublin

❧

WE ARE BOMBARDED day in day out by unrealistic standards being set by media. Depending on the publication and the age group involved, the ideal woman is size 6, confident, beautiful, in control of her life and, of course, successful in her chosen career and has a flat tummy three days after giving birth. Whether we are insecure or not depends on how much we allow this constant drip-drip to affect our self-esteem.

Carrie, 32, nurse, Nenagh, County Tipperary

ALL BABIES are beautiful to their parents. You have always been beautiful and you always will.

Meg, 50, retired dancer, Glasgow

⁂

IF SOMEONE GIVES YOU a compliment, you should listen to it and relish it! You only imply that their judgement is a bit iffy if you respond to every compliment with 'What? This old thing?' or 'I got it cheap in a sale at Bargain Basements' or even 'I don't really like this colour.'

I'm not sure if this is news to any of us, but one of the best bits of advice (which I have diligently tried to follow for twenty years) is always to smile and say, 'Thank you, I love it too!' when someone says you look nice in what you're wearing.

Orla, 48, accountant, County Kildare

Do try this at home:

Smiling will always make you more beautiful. Enjoy your friends. Make time for people. Be generous and open your heart. Show the world your inner beauty and live a life of joy!

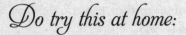

Do try this at home:

This meditation is very good for your body, mind and soul. Lie or sit in a quiet place. Begin at your toes and say, 'I love my toes. I appreciate my toes. I love my toes.'

Move to your feet and say, 'I love my feet. I appreciate my feet. I love my feet.' Moving up the body, go into a much detail as you have time for, acknowledging your ankles, calves, thighs or just your legs.

Be sure to include all the major organs in your body, especially your womb, ovaries, intestines, spleen, liver, gall-bladder, lungs, heart, thyroid, breasts, throat, neck, head, eyes, ears, nose, brain, arms, hands, fingers and five senses.

We spend so much time criticising our bodies and being told by the media that we should look a certain way that we are all conditioned not to love our bodies. This meditation has a calming effect. It gives us strength and peace. It affirms the true beauty of you.

If you really want to change a part of your body that you don't find attractive, tell it constantly that you love it. You will find yourself putting in place what you need to put this right. Solutions will appear!

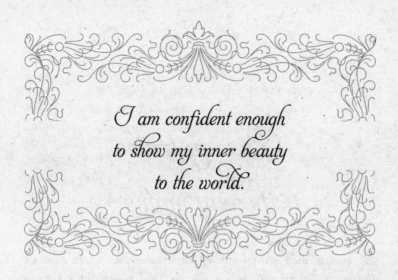

*I am confident enough
to show my inner beauty
to the world.*

Beauty truths, beauty myths

As women, we're always seeking the beauty secrets of the icons we adore. It's tempting to believe that we need to live up to extreme standards, but the truth is that red carpet goddesses have worked very hard to be on the front page of magazines. Real beauty is so much simpler to achieve in our daily lives, and most women don't have to have their photograph air brushed for the world to scrutinise. Finding what suits your lifestyle and brings out the best in your beauty is liberating and empowering.

If there's something that deeply bothers you about your appearance, think carefully about why this is so and what you hope to gain by changing it. Cosmetic surgery and dermatology are very sophisticated nowadays but are expensive options and can cause a lot of pain. Your face has more nerve endings and is more sensitive and expressive than any other part of your body, so think carefully before you seek to change it. And don't forget, it's important to remember that others rarely see us as we see ourselves. The most important thing is to be true to yourself and to feel empowered to change the things you don't like about yourself and love the things you can't change.

Sometimes our friends have the best beauty advice we need.

Simple remedies can change a lot about the way we look. We don't need to spend a fortune on the beauty regimes of the stars. The cleverest beauty wisdom can be the simplest. ❧

I THINK THAT the most important thing is to be clean and neat. Simple clothes: nothing awkward, uncomfortable, tight or scruffy-looking. Clean hair, good haircut, healthy skin, tidy nails and a warm smile to greet the day. Then I put my glasses on, look in the mirror and say, 'Fabulous!'

Chrissie, tax attorney, Ohio, USA

❧

WHY BLONDES have more fun … blondes can get an extra day out of a hair wash by brushing talc through it when it starts to get greasy!

Karen, 32, hairdresser, County Dublin

❧

PALE IS BEAUTIFUL TOO: not everyone should let themselves be pressured into thinking they need fake tan.

Marissa, 32, model, Italy

❧

IT'S A MYTH that not having a proper skin routine ages you – life bloody ages you, a bad attitude ages you. I have never been organised or methodical with my skin care as I was blessed with good skin in my teens and got into a lazy habit early on, but I truly believe that the right positive mental attitude is what keeps us all sane, feeling good about ourselves but most of all young, be it at heart or otherwise.

Ber, 39, mother and community worker, County Cork

🐝

THE ONLY THING that gets rid of eye bags is staying off the booze.

Sorcha, 38, nurse, Belfast, Northern Ireland

🐝

I THINK THE COSMETIC surgery industry plays on our innate fears of our own physical and mental view of ourselves and manipulates them so that we think we're not good enough … it makes us judge ourselves against some supposed societal views of the norm that are damaging emotionally, physically and mentally. Whilst there is always the case for plastic surgery for those who actually require it (burns victims, etc.), I don't believe that this cynical marketing used by cosmetic surgery firms should have a place outside of medical requirements.

It is a total myth that more expensive cosmetics will be better for you – and I should know, as I make my own! My other life is making handcrafted soap and body butters but I also make my own facial moisturiser, shampoo and cleansing oils – and my skin has never been better! I wash my face every day with the soap I make and cleanse every night with my cleansing oil and use my own moisturiser daily. Last week four people said, 'How the hell do you look younger today?' I was chuffed! I think treating your skin well and with care will not only make it feel good, but you'll feel good about yourself too and people will notice and comment and you'll feel great. There's a lot to be said about loving yourself enough to treat yourself well, but that does not have to mean expensive lotions and potions!

Celine, 42, cosmetics manufacturer, County Dublin

DAB TOOTHPASTE on a blemish before you go to sleep, it extracts germs and bacteria and lessens redness. Wash applicators thoroughly and often.

Diane, 32, secretary in Mid-Antrim Animal Sanctuary (musician/artist), Ballymena, Northern Ireland

THERE IS NO PERFECT SIZE for a pair of breasts – they all grow like watermelons when you are pregnant and droop to your belly button after you give birth or turn forty. So what! When you are lying beside your lover, he thinks they are the most wonderful breasts in the world, and if he doesn't – dump him and get another lover!

Martina, 46, editor, County Wicklow

WHEN I WAS GROWING UP, most girls had average-sized breasts. I was a little light in the cups but never, ever had a true problem with it. I grew up thinking, gee, I wish I'd been granted a little bit more, but that's it. Never felt unsexy. Never felt less than 100 per cent female. My idols didn't have giant breasts, so I guess I never really felt there was anything that wrong with my own.

Of course, I also didn't have such readily available plastic surgery, as they do today, nor was anyone touting it to me as the next best thing since sliced bread. Now, I see young women, some as young as eighteen, having implant surgery, liposuction, etc. It's shocking! I also see women running out for Botox injections. Does anyone know that a single gram of the botulism toxin can easily kill 1 million people? Yes, I know it's professionally handled in proper facilities but jeez! Injecting that stuff into yourself just so your lines aren't as pronounced. I often despair that women don't seem to understand the real and lasting effect of happily succumbing to the 'you're not good enough as you are' campaign, and running to plastic surgery because 'it's their right to choose'. Unless there is a genuine need (i.e. mastectomy, disfigurement, etc.), why are you not good enough as you are? In fact, why are you not absolutely brilliant?

On the surface, some choices may appear 'empowering' but actually end up robbing women, as a whole, of their true power; their belief in themselves, just as they are.

Sammy, law student, Canada

❧

THE COSMETIC INDUSTRY, I feel, targets low self-esteem/body image. I think more women buy into it than men because it goes back to the Dark Ages, thinking men are superior, the breadwinner, etc. and women have to work hard to stay young to keep a man. I live in Los Angeles and work for people in the entertainment industry. I can honestly say I know very few people through work that have not had Botox or something except myself! I know quite a few who are never satisfied and keep going back again and again.

Kasey, 55, personal assistant, California, USA

☙

EXFOLIATE YOUR BARE FEET by walking barefoot in the sand – they
will be super soft and smooth afterwards.

Nicola, 30, receptionist, County Dublin

☙

SHADE FROM THE SUN. Forget sunbathing your face. Never wear
base in hot weather. Total sun block on your body will block so much
sun, you'll lack vitamin D. Shade is the smart woman's beauty block.

Karen, 45, dermatology nurse practitioner, Arizona, USA

☙

YOU NEED TO GET as much sleep as you can. I love to get the house
to myself, make the bed with crisp, fresh sheets, have a cup of
chamomile tea or hot milk and honey, a lavender bath and get an
early night. I'd advise anyone who sleeps badly to invest in a new
mattress – a mattress costs about as much as you'd spend on one
weekend of beauty spa and facial treatments, and you'll get years more
value out of it. Then at least once a week take a day off, leave the alarm
clock off in the morning and sleep until you wake up naturally.

Annette, 53, business coach, Manchester, England

SMILE! There now! You've just become more beautiful!

Miranda, agricultural scientist, Spain

❧

SPEND YOUR EVENINGS doing something beautiful. Nobody needs to watch TV. A TV in the bedroom keeps you awake at night because it emits radiation into the room. I got rid of my TV and go to bed to read a beautiful novel or poetry instead. I like to bring flowers into the house. If you surround yourself with beautiful things, you'll feel more beautiful. Sleep is very important too. You should make your bedroom a sanctuary for beauty, peace and love.

Helen, 40, gardener, UK

❧

THE WONDERS OF VASELINE (and this little tip isn't X-rated!). Isn't it sometimes the case that our tired old hands give away our real age just when we thought we'd covered all the other bases? My advice is to put Vaseline on your hands at night and they will look and feel ten years younger in the morning. I once read an article in a magazine about a foot model who would always put Vaseline on her feet at night so that they would plump up and look younger in the morning and then I thought I'll try it on my hands and it works!

Marigold, TV producer, Jordan

❧

EVERY WOMAN should invest in a good bra. It is the secret to a good shape and figure. Most women are wearing a bra that is not the correct size for them. Sizes change hugely after having babies and every woman should get fitted at least once a year. If embarrassment is stopping you from asking the assistant in the department store to size you, just remember that she has a pair too.

Kate, 27, lingerie assistant, County Dublin

꙳

IF YOU CUT your fingernails very short, your manicure lasts three times longer! And it looks neat too.

Yasmine, 18, beauty therapist, County Dublin

꙳

Never overpluck your eyebrows!

Joyce, 24, hairdresser, County Sligo

꙳

Never, ever get a perm!

Katrina, 23, colourist, UK

꙳

NEVER PUT anything on your body that you wouldn't put in it – your skin is a living, growing organ.

Tina, 47, herbalist, County Dublin

Respect the Sun

We are blessed to have this wonderful star in our solar system that nourishes the earth, bathes us with heat and light, enables us to grow food. Humans have a unique relationship with the sun because we need its light to stimulate the production of vitamin D in our skin. Only the sun can stimulate our bodies to manufacture this vitamin – and we need vitamin D to protect our bones, for our immune system, to fight cancer and to balance our mood. Lack of vitamin D causes bone pain, arthritis, chest infections, asthma, skin infections, acne, hair loss and depression.

*Looking in the mirror
and loving what you see
is the key to feeling and looking
beautiful every day.*

Feeling fat and ugly – what's gone wrong?

As women, we are constantly aware of each other's bodies and of the bodies of women we admire in entertainment, in public life, in our own workplaces and social lives. Being a woman means that your body is unique to you. Be grateful for it. Nourish it. Be proud of your feminine shape! Enjoy the sexual feelings your body gives you. Relish the power of your intellectual mind, your creative imagination, your senses of listening, seeing, enjoying all the sounds, scents and sensations of the world in which we live. Your body is a living, breathing organism, equipped to carry your brain around – it's not just a set of boobs, a bottom and a tummy that will never be flat enough.

The woman that you are today is a different person from the child you were born, from the teenager you became, from the mature woman you will be. Life leaves its memories on your body and our skin, muscles and hair change as we move through the magnificent journey of being alive. We are shaped by our environment. Everything we interact with affects our bodies, from the food we are given as children, to air we breathe in the cities we inhabit, from the desk we write at, to the bed where we go to dream. The lifestyles we live can change the shape of our breasts, our bones and our minds.

Too many women spend their lives worrying about food and shape, yet at the same time, too many women are suffering from obesity, while others suffer from eating disorders and life-long malnutrition. We need to live the life that gives our bodies the most power to enjoy the world we live in. Food should never become a tyranny in our lives. Our food is our nutrition – it's fuel, for our brains, our hearts, our limbs, our glowing skin and silky hair. We need to love what we eat, as well as sharing what we eat with those whom we love. If we've eaten too much and we aren't living in the body that we need to enjoy our life properly, we can fix this. But we don't have to fix it all immediately! Weight loss and adjustment can take a little time – and we will get there eventually. The important thing is to be confident in your ability to do whatever it takes to enjoy the body you've been given.

If your body has become a burden to you – don't blame yourself. Seek help – from your friends, doctor or nutritionist to support changes you need to make, and to prioritise the foods you need to eat to nourish your body and your mind. Doctors and nutritionists are experts in their field and want you to feel healthy – lean on their knowledge base.

DIETS DON'T WORK. The secret to weight loss is to eat less and walk more!

Deirdre, 40, sailor, County Dublin

WHEN I WAS YOUNGER, I was always slim and never had to watch my weight. As I got older, I started to put on weight that was impossible to shift and I became very paranoid about the lumps and bumps and obsessed about them. Then I started a relationship with a guy who made me feel like a supermodel. We've broken up since, but it's just a shame that I need the approval of someone else to feel attractive. That's definitely something I need to work on.

Lauren, 34, designer, County Offaly

ॐ

I'VE SPENT MY WHOLE LIFE dieting. I know all the tricks. Vomiting, laxatives, diet pills, low carb, low fat, no matter what you do you can get fat again at the drop of a hat. Basically, I've given up weighing myself because it makes me too depressed. The worst thing is the low self-esteem. That's a lot worse than the clothes you have to wear! But I now realise that even though I feel like an elephant most of the time, other people don't always notice the rolls that I'm so conscious of. I make sure no matter how fat I feel to always wear lipstick, dark clothes, great jewellery and a great pair of shoes – and I remind myself I'll lose it again, one day. And I don't let it get me down any more or make me feel ashamed. I just tell myself that I've only gained too much weight again because I've been having too much fun!

Sandra, 43, personal assistant, Glasgow, Scotland

ॐ

IF YOU DON'T THINK you are overweight, you will give off the impression that you are slim. Notice how you want to eat less when you lose weight and feel better as the pounds fall off. The positive effect of getting fitter and slimmer creates a more positive attitude.

Karen, 26, fitness instructor, Australia

WOMEN PUT THEMSELVES under so much pressure to conform. It's not just about competition with other women, but men also look at TV and mags and judge. It's very sad really.

Lonisa, 29, marketing executive, County Cork

❧

MYSELF AND MY FRIEND were looking at the same photo taken of her walking along a country lane. I thought the photo was completely amazing – she looked slim and gorgeous. She couldn't stop obsessing about how big her thighs looked and she really hated the photo. I was completely amazed because they looked totally normal to me. We should really learn to listen to others and think, Yes, I do look good.

Ellie, 26, student, Southampton, England

❧

I'VE BATTLED with my weight since I was sixteen – basically, I've been on a diet of some kind for the past twenty years. Thankfully, I've never been obese, just marginally overweight. The media throws up these images of LA Lovelies and skeletal supermodels and women and makes you feel if you are not stick thin without lumps and bumps then you have failed in some way. There is a lot to be said for being happy in your own skin. We shouldn't feel pressured to conform to the skinny extremes. There should be a healthy happy medium with weight, somewhere between size zero and size thirty. I've just dropped a dress size and I'm over the moon. I think self-acceptance is the key, not social acceptance.

Marie, 39, technician, Northern Ireland

FOR THE PAST THIRTY YEARS, I have had a problem with binge eating. Sometimes, I just can't stop even when I feel full to the gills! My weight goes up and down all the time. I have clothes from size fourteen to size eighteen in my wardrobe and I am size sixteen right now!

Some people see themselves as fat even when they are not. I have always had the opposite problem. I look in the mirror and think I look quite slim and OK but other people point out that I am weighty! Or I see it in photographs. Weird. I convince myself I look OK and eat more. I am in my forties now and still haven't got a handle on the whole thing!

Claire, 44, administrator, County Dublin

๛

THE FUNNY THING IS that women are constantly criticising themselves – their bum, their tummies, their bingo-flap arms – but a guy will never even notice these things. You'll never hear a guy saying he didn't ask a girl out because her stomach wasn't flat. Men aren't that picky!

Lorraine, 54, dentist, County Cork

๛

IN UNDERDEVELOPED countries the curvy woman is seen as attractive, healthy and fertile ... our society is meant to be better developed, with better education and health care and we're the ones who aspire to thinness – because the 'ideal' is blasted at us on every corner, magazine, TV show, etc. Who loses in the body image argument though?

Theresa, poet, County Cork

We love looking at pictures of Nicole Kidman, Jennifer Aniston and all the other goddesses on the red carpet. We think they look beautiful and they are very thin ... And then we can't help thinking, God help them – they must be absolutely starving!

Michelle & Juliet

❧

When my mother developed anorexia related to her chemotherapy, she said we shouldn't even think of going on a diet because it was such a loss not to be able to enjoy a meal. I feel so sad for people who think that keeping slender is worth losing the joy of sharing a meal with friends.

Jackie, 72, doctor, Melbourne, Australia

❧

JUNK MIGHT TASTE GOOD but it isn't actually food – as in feeding your body. Sugar-based junk might give you a quick energy boost but it really is only temporary – you need to eat more live food and raw food to actually feed your body. A jelly or piece of chocolate is a dead food. Same goes for well-done meat – eat it rare, because when it's well done all the nutrients are cooked out of it. Never, ever over-cook your vegetables!

Anne, 50, home economics teacher

❧

FORGET TEA AND COFFEE, have warm water and lemon in your break at work. Your face and skin begin to glow with all the vitamin C in fresh lemon juice and the toxins flush out of your tired, puffy eyes. I never drink alcohol when I'm on TV the next day. If I need to shift a few pounds, quitting alcohol is the quickest way to do this!

Donna, 29, TV journalist, Manchester

✺

I'M LUCKY, I don't have the worrying-about-my-figure thing. To be frank, I couldn't care less. I try to stay healthy. I eat well, because I like grub, I drink a little and I get on with it. I make the best of what I have – sometimes making an extra effort, sometimes not! I'm not vain (at all) but a healthy dose of checking myself in a long mirror now and again doesn't hurt. I have been skinny. I have been fat. But at least I can do something about how I look if I want, other things maybe not so much. Saying all that, I empathise with anyone with body issues/eating disorders and don't wish to appear at all flippant about that.

Jacinta, 35, development and outreach officer, Northern Ireland

✺

WOMEN CONSTANTLY COMPARE themselves to others (I know I do) and we always want to be a better version of ourselves. It's like that saying about how when a man looks in a mirror, he notices all the good things about himself, but when a woman does, she sees all her flaws. I guess it's just by nature that women are like this.

When the media stop hounding us with images of what is 'perfect' and so on, then women may be less critical, but I know, personally, I always want that bit more, there is always something I will want to change. Listening to other people's opinions can often be damaging too – listen to yourself and just learn to be happy with who you are. That is really the only way we will learn to love ourselves.

Geraldine, 19, student, County Galway

❧

A LOT OF WOMEN I know tend to be unhappy with their bodies as they are, and when they look back at photos, they wonder what they were complaining about because they love their body the way it was! I'm guilty of doing that myself too. I think the media certainly doesn't help out body image because of the airbrushing and impossible images they try to pass off as 'normal'.

Rebecca, 32, teacher, Bolton, England

❧

IT STARTS IN CHILDHOOD and it's not just a modern-day thing. Even in the 1970s, when I was growing up, we had Sindy dolls and Barbie dolls. Granted, Sindy looked a little more normal, but Barbie was the popular one and still is. Then there were the comic books. I remember Bessie and Billy Bunter, characters that were ridiculed for being pudgy and needing glasses etc., mocked for not being perfect. Progressing on to the teen magazines was no different, with stories about ugly ducklings transforming into swans. Then it's the glossies and the celeb magazines and most print media, not to mention the many TV programmes. It's no wonder women feel inadequate about their bodies.

I spent most of my twenties and thirties dieting and trying to be what I am not. The great thing about getting older is that most of us realise that the only important thing is to be healthy in mind and body. Learn to accept the things about yourself that you cannot change and learn to love them.

Claire, 44, administrator, County Dublin

৯১

KEEP AWAY FROM THE MEDIA, watch less TV, look at fewer magazines and newspapers. Then there is nothing to compare yourself against. Yes, that is easy for me to say, I know. I live rurally, where most women rarely get the chance to dress up/wear make-up and life is too practical to worry too much about all those issues. I am aware that living in towns and cities it is harder to get away from all that, but it is possible.

Yes, it does start in childhood. How we feel about ourselves and others, what we let our children watch and read all influences them greatly. I brought my daughter up without television/magazines, etc. (again, yes, I know, easy for me to do because, either I or my partner was always at home to care for her – and, no, not an easy task if you are single and/or work full time). I also have been lucky enough not to have any body issues myself to pass on to her. Now that she is thirteen, she is healthy and fit and wonders what on earth all her friend's body issues are about. (And no, she isn't a little mouse, she's all purple hair and mad clothes, as you'd expect.)

What we need is a magazine with plenty of pics of un-airbrushed celebs, but also normal people airbrushed, just to show how it can work the other way and what a cheat it is. Lots of (un-glamour model) nudes to show what real bodies look like, and lots of tips on how to have a balanced, down-to-earth, healthy life. Fancy taking that on girls?

Mairi, 47, ceramicist, County Cork

Do try this at home:

Ancient monks only ate the amount of food that they could fit into their cupped hands … calorie counting made simple, for life.

Eat fruit: Vitamin C is the body's natural healer for skin, hair, nails and all connective tissues, and it protects the body against viruses and colds. And fibre is the body's natural laxative. Studies in diabetes now show that the most effective, long-term weight-loss diet is a high-fibre (low GI) diet. You never need a colonic if you eat loads of fibre, and you'll never be overweight. Nutritionists in France recommend eating ten pieces of fruit a day – twice as many as the UK/US guidelines! Fruit satisfies your sugar cravings, so you won't be hungry for junk.

Walk vigorously: Walk for at least an hour a day, or in two bursts of half an hour. Walk to work. Walk around your neighbourhood in the evening. Ditch the TV and join a gym. Get out of the office and walk around town at lunchtime. Play with your kids in the park. Run with the dog. Cycle to the supermarket. Hoover the stairs. Mow the lawn. Feel joy in your heart as you put it through a good workout! Break into a sweat.

IT HAS TAKEN ME thirty-eight years to realise that I am me! And I like me and the people who matter to me like me just as I am. Like many women, my weight and shape change from year to year, depending on the factors of my life that make me the me I am. I wouldn't mind flattening my tummy or lifting my boobs or shedding a stone or two, but it just takes one cuddle with my boys, who love my pillow tummy, my cosy boobs and the fact that the curvier me is a happier me, to realise that I am just fine!

I am very real, very alive and happy to be alive and to be the mummy to the two most fantastic wee boys out.

As women, we ought to lavish one another with positive comments about one another's bodies, so that we are no longer critical of others/insecure of ourselves. I have a friend who is from Russia (maybe women act differently towards one another there) and she is always complimenting me on how I look, how intelligent I am, how strong I am and what a fantastic mother and friend I am … I could go on but it kind of embarrasses me! She has taught me that approval from another woman means more than the approval from a man, at least it makes me feel stronger, I don't know why. In my opinion, men are far less critical and they see the positives in women rather than the negatives. (Well, some men do!)

I hope that there will be a change. I encourage my two boys, and the children I teach, the adults of tomorrow, to see the beauty of a person rather than an image of what society/the media think. So I hope for change. I believe it could happen but I know that, sadly, it may take generations to happen.

Marianne, 38, teacher, Scotland

I THINK A FAIR AMOUNT depends on the attitude of your parents when you were growing up. 'Irish mammies' typically did not give you many compliments (to your face), as they didn't want you to get too big-headed and act conceited. I remember when I was first living in the States and I mentioned to one woman that her daughter was lovely/pretty and her reply back was, 'Yes, isn't she?' My instant thoughts were, 'Jaysus, that kid is going to be so big-headed by the time she is in her teens.' Usually, when I got a compliment on how I was looking, I felt compelled to explain that the dress was on sale or borrowed, the hair was just done that day and I'd promise that the following morning, I'd be looking like I was pulled arseways through the bushes! Finally, one day, someone told me that when I am complimented, all I have to do is say thank you ... full stop! I've tried to practise this ever since, though sometimes I do forget.

Once when I was my heaviest, my husband and I were on vacation in Cancun and as we walked along the beach, he said to me, 'Do you realise how beautiful you are to me?' Funnily enough, it's been a good while since I've heard those words. I find these days that I'm hinting for compliments!

For me, it has always been the person inside. I try to treat others as I would like to be treated and have found out to my dismay and heartbreak that it's not always a two-way street.

God, I would love to be swept away for a few days and given a new look and total makeover and then maybe understand what the mystery is about expensive clothes, as right now, I could never justify spending money on them.

Ruth, 45, special needs assistant and author, County Clare

WHEN OTHER WOMEN allow us to be 'what we are', we will be free. There are none so harsh who judge than she who sits next to thee (with the same dress only two sizes smaller!).

Victoria, 45, scriptwriter, Tasmania, Australia

🐚

OH, THE ETERNAL impossible question about 'loving our bodies just the way we are'. Well, how simple and beautiful life would be if everyone could just accept that we women are all different, but equally beautiful. Instead, we (as women) allow ourselves to fall into the trap set by magazines and TV of their idea of what the 'perfect' woman should be, and no wonder we end up feeling disappointed in ourselves.

I have been a serial dieter (yo-yo!) for years, since my early twenties, and it has taken me twenty years (and Weight Watchers!) to realise that nobody has the perfect body (unless they are in the wax museum!), but that we should strive to be healthy and happy in ourselves and be content with what God has given us. The frightening thought for me is how far our disillusionment will drive not only us, but our beautiful children. Will they be contemplating tummy tucks/face lifts, etc., etc., while still in their teens? I hope not. We need to stop being so materialistic and get back to more basic stuff (OK, still shave under the arms and wash, but other than that …) and just accept ourselves and each other as beautiful inside and out.

Mary, 43, logistics controller, County Limerick

🐚

I FEEL IT ALSO GOES DEEPER ... my mother passed away four years ago with lung cancer, but she also had an eating disorder. She was fifty-two and she suffered badly with it all her life ... it is a disorder that affects women that mentally you see yourself as fat, even though you weigh like six or seven stone. It goes back years despite that in this day and age, I agree women feel they have to conform to media expectations.

Elaine, 34, single mum, Derry, Northern Ireland

How to lose weight and keep it off ...
1. When you're hungry, eat.
2. Eat what you want.
3. Eat consciously (put down the knife and fork between mouthfuls).
4. When you think you are full, stop.
5. Always leave some food on the plate.

Pauline, 66, counsellor and psychologist, County Dublin

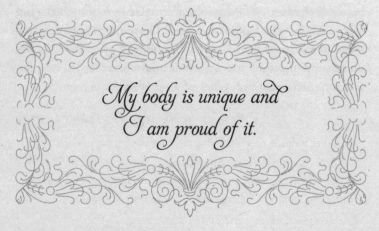

My body is unique and I am proud of it.

Fashion for now

Fashion is something we all have an opinion on as women. It's more than just a term we use for style that is prevalent at the present time. Fashion is a wonderful documentation of how we view ourselves socially and culturally as women. It is also a statement of its wearers.

To be truly stylish means having a sense of self and individuality. It is more than being one of the nameless, faceless crowd shouting praise at 'the emperor's new clothes'. So has the time come when we no longer feel the need to be labelled by brands or guided by the advertising industry?

Clever women realise that a few classic staples will hold their wardrobe together. It is good to feel nice about yourself and what you wear and how you look. Remember when you turn fifty, you will think of your thirty-year-old figure as a thing of grace, and wish you had worn that bikini that you were afraid to wear. When you turn sixty, you will be pulling turtleneck pullovers over the neck that you were too shy to expose when you were forty. There has never been a better time to enjoy wearing clothes than now and there is enough choice out there to look your very best, whatever you choose.

There is an ever-constant influx of cheap, attractive clothing flooding our stores – the origins of some of this clothing are completely untraceable and if we knew how our clothes were made, would we still choose to wear them? We have a responsibility as women to decide what is right or isn't right for us. Choose wisely and independently and remember fashion always repeats itself, so if you don't want to throw out something you love because it's no longer in fashion, keep it! ✍♥

I THINK FASHION will always evolve, but I think it's important to stick to your own style. Just because it's in fashion doesn't mean it will suit you. Labels will always be around, but the high street stocks such good clothes now anybody can look amazing on any type of budget.

Sophie, teacher, County Wicklow

※

WOMEN MAY BECOME a little less obsessed with labels and reuse their clothes more perhaps. Couldn't care less to be honest, not the shopping type! I do admire those that seem to have the 'eye' and have their own innate style. Each to their own.

Cesca, 45, eternal student, County Cork

※

I KNOW IT'S A CLICHÉ but you always feel more confident in something you feel comfortable in. There's nothing worse than going out in something you have to constantly fix all night or a pair of heels that hurt like crazy. And buy clothes that fit – ill-fitting clothes are the worst!

Sheila, 53, housewife, County Westmeath

I LOVE FASHION and brands but I think mirrors are more important. I mean we need to pick what is suitable for us and our bodies … make your own style! And then we'll be modern women in a beautifully unique way.

Aya, 22, medical student, Benghazi, Libya

※

I HAVE ALWAYS FELT very uncomfortable with the whole 'fashion' scene. I am the wrong height or shape for anything designer or trendy (and never had the budget for it either!) and have never had much confidence about the way I look. I would love to have a session with a stylist but worry that they would pick out all sorts of unsuitable or expensive stuff that I would feel obliged to buy … Yes, I am willing to try on different things but, help, how do I change the habits of a lifetime? I would love to look in the mirror just once in my life and feel I look fab …

Lesley, 51, musician, County Dublin

※

BUY CLASSIC – it will never go out of fashion.

Grainne, 40, nutritionist, County Cork

※

Do try this at home:

Too many women hang on to clothes that they don't even enjoy wearing. Give away anything in your wardrobe that you don't love. Give away anything that you don't feel beautiful in. Give away anything that doesn't make you glamorous, chic or elegant. Give away anything you don't look forward to wearing. Give away anything that makes you feel fat, boring, lumpy, ugly, frumpy, sad or that fades you into the background. Anything left? Put it all on the bed and try it all on. Then get rid of any of it that fits into the list above!

IF YOU ARE HANGING on to unflattering clothes, think of all the people who'll discover your hand-me-downs if you get rid of them. Think of all the joy you will bring vintage-shoppers who love rummaging for a bargain. Think of all the people in poverty crises who will benefit from your clothes, who will be able to keep warm, sleep cosily, wrap their children, have something smart to wear socially. Then, get something new, feel beautiful and don't spend a fortune. Your shape and tastes change over time so refresh your wardrobe and enjoy giving your clothes to other women who will love them.

Melinda, 34, Australia

I USED TO BUY A LOT of expensive classic clothes, I used to shop online and I couldn't pass a trendy boutique without an impulse buy. But now since the credit crunch I can't afford to splash out any more. So I only buy clothes with a specific use or occasion in mind. This really helps to keep my budget down. I don't want to wear old things and I hate looking poor, but I buy a coat now because I need something warm for winter, some boots because I need to keep my feet dry, everything in my wardrobe has a purpose and a job to do. Now I love all my clothes. I can't believe I wasted so much money in the past on impulse buys, on fashion trends and 'labels' – the best part is that I actually think I look better than I used to when I shopped all the time.

Doreen, 37, interior decorator, Warwick, England

BEFORE YOU GO SHOPPING for that 'special' outfit for an occasion where you have to look your best, get your hair blow dried and put on your make-up. An outfit will look different when you are looking and feeling your best.

Karen, 30, hairstylist, County Dublin

Wardrobe Essentials

What's in your wardrobe? We asked hundreds of women all around the world.

A KILLER PAIR OF HEELS, a little black dress that goes down well at any function, a well-cut coat and knee-length boots, which look good every year, and a lock on the doors to keep the daughters out!

Louise, 37, lady of leisure, County Donegal

✣

I HAVE A GIRAFFE-PRINT adult romper suit made of the softest fleece. As much as I enjoy getting dressed up and going out, I couldn't get by without my nights in. There's a wonderful feeling in spoiling yourself with comfort. Every woman deserves the softest, warmest comforts from time to time (without even remotely trying to be sexy – in fact, just the opposite).

Diane, 32, secretary in Mid-Antrim Animal Sanctuary
(musician/artist), Ballymena, Northern Ireland

✣

FOR WINTER, WEDGE HEELS, knee boots, opaque tights, selection of dresses that can be worn over trousers or on their own. For summer, white linens, dresses for layering, wedge shoes, deck shoes. God, I wear the same layered look all year. Seasons just change! I love it.

Venetta, 42, mother of four, County Dublin

✣

WITH THE RIGHT JEWELLERY and hairdo, you can look a million dollars dressed from Penneys or Oxfam! The light in the eyes outshines any amount of bling!

Caroline, public health doctor, County Galway

COMFORTABLE BUT CLASSY jeans that don't give you a muffin top that you can wear with heels; smart but casual top that can be dressed up or down with classic jewellery; black dress; trendy heels that go with jeans or dress; selection of costume jewellery but not tacky stuff!

Lynda, 38, mother of four, County Clare

❧

A GOOD, WELL-CUT, comfortable suit or two, matching shoes and handbag, always handy for weddings, funerals and interviews.

Fran, 39, County Carlow

❧

I DON'T KNOW if underwear would qualify as part of your wardrobe, but I think it's an essential item for every woman. Whether it is casual, formal or out for the night wear, it can make or break an outfit! It can also make you feel so comfortable, confident and, when you want, sexy!

Linda, 44, mum, County Dublin

❧

A GOOD PAIR OF BOOTS, ditto black heels. The obligatory little black dress. Well-fitting jeans/trousers, whichever you prefer and last-ly a winter coat that will not be a one-season wonder.

Caroline, 43, Hampshire, England

DON'T SAVE YOUR GOOD UNDERWEAR for a special occasion. So what if you spend all day, every day in jeans or a tracksuit running from supermarket to school, from play dates to piano lessons? Put on that lace red number underneath, it will make you feel sensual and confident and people will notice. You might hear comments like, 'Have you lost weight?' or 'Did you do something with your hair?' Or maybe it'll come with a lingering look, a cheeky smile. Whatever the reaction, it's your secret … or not, depending on who's giving that smile.

Siobhan, 43, health therapist, County Dublin

Handbags and shoes – and flip-flops at weddings

Shoes have an important emotive role in women's wardrobes. We associate shoes with power, sex, wealth … shoes are what we need to get places. High heels give you elegance, get you noticed, make you look slim – but low heels give you speed …

My friend Grainne bought a stack of flip-flops before her sister's wedding. She put them in a basket beside the dance floor. When the party got into full swing, the glamorous women guests were delighted to kick off their killer heels and swap them for flip-flops! She also provided a pile of pashminas that came in very hand as the night got cooler for the female guests who wanted to take a stroll outside.

Michelle

Two-inch black courts for business, some pretty flats/pumps for work, a pair of beautiful killer heels for night-time, a pair of knee-high boots for wearing with skirts in winter, sneakers you can walk home in, flip-flops for summer and some waterproof all-weather boots for snow and ice.

We'd like to add – a pair of comfy slippers/Uggs, for slobbing in front of the TV …

Juliet

What Women Know about travelling light

Here's a list of the only summer holiday clothes you'll ever need – and it fits into an overhead locker on a budget flight.

Two swimsuits.

Three sleeveless vests, wear one with a pair of jeans for travelling with a warm cardigan.

A very large pashmina that also works as a sarong, a pair of socks for the plane, a pair of sneakers.

A pair of jewelled or silver/gold flip-flops that go from poolside to bar, one crush-proof sundress and enough knickers to last three days (you can wash everything in the hotel using their shampoo … and this capsule will last a fortnight, honestly). *Bonnes vacances!*

What's in your handbag?

Handbags and purses have such an important place in women's lives. Our handbags are not just fashion accessories, status symbols or adornments – they are our working mobile offices, our children's mobile nursery, our home from home wherever we carry them.

I HATE BIG BAGS. In my bag right now: tissues, house keys, earphones for my mobile, headache pills, cleaning gel for hands, a couple of tampons and my purse. That's it. When I leave the house I throw in my phone and iPod.

Claire, 43, full-time mother, Holland

✆

Ha ha. A penis straw – bet no one else has one of those! (From my hen do last weekend, honest!)

Suzie, 30, administrator, Portsmouth, England

✆

TOO MUCH RUBBISH! Nappies, dummies, a sun hat, glasses, receipts, my purse (with very little dosh), my Weight Watchers folder, a pen or two and my son's swimming lessons pass.

Claire, 34, writer and journalist, Derry, Northern Ireland

TOTE HANDBAGS are a nightmare to find things in and small bags never hold enough. I prefer something in the middle. But the perfect handbag's like the Holy Grail, isn't it?

Jennifer, 28, personal assistant, County Dublin

🔖

IN MY BAG, the usual (mobile phone, wallet) and then lipstick, mints, address book, sun block and the memory stick with all my books on it, in case my house catches fire while I'm out and ten years of work is lost.

Suzanne, In Her Prime, author, County Tipperary

🔖

A PURSE, SEWING KIT, diary, pens, markers, highlighters, keys, many receipts, euro coins, sterling coins, lip balm, driving licence, perfume, hair clips and bobble, blood donor card, letters, bills, water, make-up, inhalers, aerochamber, urine sample bottles, mobile phones ... think that's all, just don't ask me what's in my purse!

Ria, 35, manager, Derry, Northern Ireland

I COULDN'T TELL YOU where my handbag is at the moment as I tend to fit everything I need into my pockets when I go out ... having a one-year-old complete with nappy bag, pram and various toys means that carrying a handbag is the least of my worries!

Brenda, 37, psychiatric nurse, Northern Ireland

꩜

MY HANDBAGS have evolved into tote bags lately. Is it because of the following I wonder ... lippy, perfume, hair bands (kids, am too old for ponytails!), nail file, passport covers, today's post not yet opened, as I know they are bills, gum, hand cream, two bangles, phone, fags, several lighters . . .

Ber, 39, mother and community worker, County Cork

꩜

The world and a little bit more ...

Dora, 53, mom of triplets, Brazil

꩜

My life ...

Laura, 40, journalist, County Dublin

It's not just a purse – it's a life-support system.

Melissa, 37, political journalist, Washington DC, USA

What Women Know about the portable life-support system!

Is it large enough to hold lipstick, touch-up make-up, hairbrush, mobile phone, wallet, notebook and pen and a laptop if you ever need one?

You can always buy a larger holdall that folds up into a tiny one to bring with you. Use your fold-up bag for the days when you need to shop, carry shoes, sandwiches.

Is it small enough to fit on the floor of your car in front of the passenger seat, in the basket of your bicycle, under your arm tucked safely on the train?

Has it got a long enough strap to be carried on your shoulder and keep your hands free?

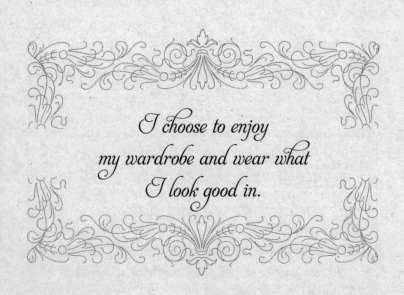

*I choose to enjoy
my wardrobe and wear what
I look good in.*

Beautiful at every age

We asked a woman we know who is in her mid-thirties to suggest a topic for this book that concerned her. This woman is beautiful – she has adorable children and a husband who loves her and provides very well for her, keeping her in a comfortable home with many luxuries most would only dream of. So when she told us that she was concerned about ageing, we were a bit taken aback. Surely with so much going for her, she would have the confidence to grow older gracefully and enjoy the wisdom that comes with it? Then it struck us, that if she was feeling this way, then other women must have strong feelings about ageing.

We asked a single woman who is slightly older and a psychologist by profession the same question and she was quick to tell us that she was interested in ageing, but for a very different reason to the first woman. She told us all about her grandmother and the knowledge and sense that she spoke and how she had helped her when she found herself confronted by different difficulties throughout her life. This older woman was grounded and earthed in ways that younger women are lacking. Her grandmother often had the answers to problems she encountered and a way of dealing with them that she lacked herself.

This knowledge gives us such an insight into our abilities and creativity as a species and as a sex. To fear getting older is to fear life itself and all the growing that comes with it – for with the demise of the outer shell comes a greater insight. As the layers of superficial importance of unblemished skin and flowing hair disappear under the greying temples, so, too, comes the wisdom to see that those who value you for your looks and youth are not worth the importance they may have been given by innocence.

Modern medicine has developed all sorts of techniques to disguise the effects of ageing, making lines and wrinkles a thing of the past. In many circles of urban women, having Botox or fillers is almost as ordinary as having your hair coloured or your legs waxed. Pretty soon, women who've left their faces to age naturally will look as socially unacceptable as women who don't shave under their arms or colour their grey hair.

Today, most women in cinema, TV and fashion photography are pretty much all touched up for photographs and most have had cosmetic work. Celebrity women are in the limelight and on camera all day long, where every little line and flaw is visible a hundred-fold. But for most women our tiny lines and gradual changes to our face are really only noticeable to us! Cosmetic work is very expensive. Injections into your skin are painful and can leave you with bruises and altered sensation. If cosmetic work is important to you, empowers you and gives you the confidence to do your job, then go for it. Whatever you choose, make sure that you are empowered by your decision to have any cosmetic work done. Make sure your expectations of the results aren't unrealistic, as most of the differences are really very tiny or barely noticeable afterwards. Have a thorough consultation with your physician before you spend, and make sure that you are really going to benefit from the results.

Do try this at home:

Take out a photo of yourself from ten years ago. See how beautiful you looked. But do you remember how you felt about your looks back then? How self-critical you were that day, despite the beauty you can see now, ten years on? Sometimes, what we dread most about the ageing process is the reminder of the passage of time, rather than the presence of tiny lines!

WHEN I TURNED THIRTY, I felt my biological clock go into over-drive and thought that I was roller-coasting headlong into middle age, but I was really only a few years away from being a kid! Realising that made it a lot easier to become forty.

Imogen, 47, designer, Norfolk, England

MY MOTHER ONCE TOLD ME that at twenty you care about what others think of you – at forty you don't care what others think of you and at sixty you realise that they haven't been thinking about you at all!

Leah, 48, potter, County Sligo

I WAS WATCHING a daytime American television programme around the time I turned forty and was feeling very sorry for myself; coincidentally, the topic of conversation was ageing. Then a clever old woman who was being interviewed said something that resounded in me: 'Age ain't nothing but a number!'

Fiona, 43, accountant, Athlone, County Westmeath

❧

YOU ARE ONLY as old as you feel! It may have been said many times, but it is true. No matter what your birth cert says, you are the age you feel inside right now. I often travel with a fascinating group of five women who vary in age from mid-forties to mid-sixties – we have the common interest of the arts and take regular cultural weekends around European cities for pleasure. The twenty-year gap in age dissipates whenever we sit down together, as we always have the common bond of being interested in each other and what we all have to say. Whenever the subject of age comes up, we always say the same thing – we all feel years younger than the age we actually are – most settling somewhere between sixteen and twenty-six. I think that being in good, positive company can make you feel younger, and breaking the boundaries of groups with similar age opens a whole new way of looking at the world.

Maria, 54, lecturer, County Dublin

❧

I've had collagen fillers: it hurt like hell! I cried and cried with the pain and then, afterwards, I was covered with bruises. I vowed I'd never go there again! But then, after that, when all those bruises had settled down, I couldn't help admiring my new chin, which absolutely no one else noticed, except my daughter, who asked me who had hit me. But it was an interesting experience because I found that the more I had something to look at in the mirror, the more concerned I became about my looks. I can see how women become 'addicted', and want more and more 'done' – it's so tempting to think, I'll have just a little bit more injected here, and then, wow, what a difference that would make! What I want now is to feel happy with my face the way it is, and I know it's going to change even more in the future. I notice a lot of women who've had collagen injections now, and Botox, and I respect their choice to spend a lot of money on their appearance. But I kind of feel sorry for them too because I know it really hurts.

Linda, dermatology nurse, County Dublin

What Women Know about ...
an instant, pain-free, non-surgical face lift

Breathe clean air! Traffic pollution, cigarette smoke and stale office air age your skin. An hour's walk in clean, fresh air drops ten years off your skin-age overnight.

Green tea lifts tired, ageing, dehydrated skin overnight as it contains antioxidants: it's a face lift in a teacup.

Lots of water to drink plumps skin naturally.

Vitamin C heals skin: eat oranges and find a moisturiser or toner that contains this magic anti-ageing ingredient.

Plastic surgeons use vitamin E creams to heal burns: find a skin-food cream that gives you this rejuvenating boost.

And finally … nothing looks prettier than a smile – at every age!

*I am at peace with my age.
Each age has its own special joys
and experiences. I am always
the perfect age for
where I am in life.*

In Beauty

Ten beautiful things about me ...

Work

Women make great workers. Our gift of empathy makes us focused as colleagues and means we excel in the caring professions. Our ability to multitask makes us invaluable in a rapidly changing world.

We both grew up in Ireland in the 1970s and 1980s, and both our mothers worked. But in Ireland in the 1970s, this was rare – there was a law in place that prevented married women from working in certain professions and the civil service. Both our mothers were role models who knew the importance of financial independence, personal development and self-esteem. Today, we both work within and outside the home – Juliet is a doctor and a writer, Michelle is a teacher and writer – and while both still want to ensure our personal relationships, family and children come first, both of us feel that our jobs are a very important part of who we are.

Having a job isn't just about having an independent income and the luxuries we love in life. The job we do is where part of our social life takes place. It can be a place where we find our sense of purpose and where we can get to make a difference to the world. Doing a job you love is a luxury that's rare but it's a prize that women should reach for. The biggest challenge many women face is balancing the excitement of a career with the desire to have children – and then finding time for both. Powerful and wealthy women can more easily do both, but for ordinary women, we need to keep fighting for a balanced opportunity to be happy in our job and happy with our families.

Successful women can be great role models, but we need to make sure that women still trapped beneath the glass ceiling are given a helping hand. Success is a celebration to be shared. Being creative is what being a woman is all about: thinking imaginatively all the time to make sure our skills and talents are not wasted and that our lives are as full as we could ever imagine them to be, whether we work inside or outside the home.

Being passionate about work

Work is the key to financial independence, but your work should be fulfilling in itself. It should be worth doing, and worth doing well. Be proud of the job you do, be it in your home, office, farm, factory or wherever you make a living. Celebrate your achievements. Look for role models and be a role model for women everywhere. All work is dignified and all work is worth doing well.

Finding the right career shouldn't be a chore – it should be an adventure. We have both changed careers several times during our lives. Michelle started off as a designer in fashion and went on to be an artist, lecturer, teacher and author. Juliet explored all the different branches of medicine and now uses her medical background in a creative way working with musicians, as a television presenter and as a novelist. What we both know is that there is no single career for anybody – people change all the time. The important thing is to be true to yourself and follow your heart and you will find the career that you will love at every stage of your life. ♡

'If you are what you should be, you should set the whole world on fire.'

St Catherine of Siena

꙳

WHAT ADVICE WOULD I GIVE other women? Never, ever, ever turn down an opportunity. If life opens a door for you, walk through it. If you don't like what you find there, you can always walk back out again, but if you walk past an open door, you may never get that opportunity again. Never let self-doubt or fear of change hold you back from a new experience – nothing ventured, nothing gained! And you'll be amazed what comes your way once you make yourself open to things. All of the best things that have happened to me in both my personal and professional life have come as a result of taking a chance. And that includes presenting *Ireland AM*. I had zero TV experience when I went for the job, so didn't think for a minute I would get it, but I did. If I hadn't given it a shot, I would have missed out on the best job I've ever had!

Sinead, TV presenter, County Dublin

꙳

A JOB IS NEVER WORK when you love what you do. I'm in marketing and there is never a dull day, the only thing that makes it drudgery is when you don't get paid on time! If I could give everything up and run a bar on a beach in a hot (politically stable) country, I would jump at it. Every day in shorts and zero stress, now that's a dream!

Alison, 34, owner of a marketing company, West County Cork

❧

I WAS A FIRST-YEAR UNDERGRADUATE in my first week at York University. I always felt slightly as if I'd blagged my way on to the course as I'd got into what was considered one of the best literature courses on the back of an interview and my own reading list of about eight books. I'd changed my career from medicine and decided that the world of literature was for me and, luckily, the world of literature seemed to want me.

So in walks our wonderfully eccentric professor with his mad white hair and blustery manner and, as an opener for his lecture, asked us who hadn't read *King Lear*. You could see that everyone looked aghast, it wasn't on the A-Level syllabus and we hadn't been told to prepare by reading it. 'Come on,' he said. 'Who hasn't read *King Lear*?' Gradually, a couple of hands went up sheepishly, then a few more ... I wasn't going to put my hand up! Then, to our surprise, he burst out, 'You are so lucky! Those of you who haven't read or seen *King Lear* are so lucky! You have such a treat in store, reading it for the first time, something I will never have again!'

Brilliant, the best advice I could ever be given and I've taken that with me ever since. Instead of being overwhelmed by that great canon of literature I haven't read, even after studying literature for three years, I welcome all unread books as being future treats that, at some point in my life, will one day delight me. How lucky I am to have that treat in store! And so that's how I approach all subject areas I don't feel I have specialist knowledge in, with delightful anticipation of what that subject will, in due course, reveal. And it has helped, as I have wiggled my way through an unusual career path, to never have fear of a learned body of knowledge.

Marigold, TV producer, Jordan

Do try this at home:

When thinking about starting a career or studying for it, find your passion and everything else will follow.

YOU NEED TO RETHINK your career every ten years – you've only got about seven decades in your life. No one tells you when to run.

Aine, 45, teacher, County Westmeath

YOU SHOULD HAVE SIX or seven careers during your life. After a decade in the same career, you've got to ask yourself the question – is there a point to it any more?

Jay, 41, musician, teacher, writer, scientist, sailor and mum, County Sligo

I AM DOING MY DREAM JOB, Montessori teacher. I enjoyed the travel business – I don't regret doing it and I don't miss it one bit. Going to work is a joy, it doesn't feel like going to work. If I'm in bad form, the kids have me in good form in no time.

Carol, 45, Montessori teacher, County Dublin

❧

IT'S A FUNNY, LIGHT-HEARTED place to be. A place where I thrive and I love. I love the banter, *craic*, people and stories. Hairdressing brings us lots of exciting dramas every day. Lots of fun and stories and fun people. Some famous, some not. Some just ordinary like myself. Being the elder lemon, I see a lot differently to my younger colleagues. My clients are more mature, like cooking, clothes, holidays and diamonds!

Some of the girls have lots of clients who like dogs and these stylists have dogs themselves. The clients are drawn to the stylists that like what they like.

We had a girl once that didn't like kids – funny thing was neither did her clientele. She would grow horns when kids came into the salon.

The young stylists attract the men too. They get great tips and have a good laugh.

We meet millionaires, movie stars, housewives and students. It's a fantastic career to have. You can work all over the world, can never be replaced by a robot or computer and will always have a laugh.

Twenty-seven years later, I never regret doing it – it's my passion!

Lisa, 42, hair professional and salon proprietor, County Dublin

*I am proud
of the job that I do and I will
never stop chasing my dreams.*

Glass ceilings

Climbing to the top can be very tough for women, in virtually every career, but we can't let our power of reproduction be thought of as a flaw in our skills any more. Having children should never be seen as a failing in a woman who works. With more and more powerful women running companies, being involved in politics and influencing society, we need to ensure that the power of reproduction is upheld as a triumph that should be supported wholeheartedly by all of us.

As Mary McAleese, the President of Ireland, said in a speech in May 2010, one of the main problems with the world economic crisis is that the political economy of the world has been testosterone-driven.

Women in positions of responsibility and power should support their women colleagues to smash through the glass ceiling that exists in many professions and companies. Workplaces with a workforce that is gender balanced are so much more pleasant, productive and less alienating than workplaces that are skewed with a dominance of either men or women. We firmly believe that all workplaces, institutions, government departments, boards of management – wherever society is organised – should have a mandatory gender balance to make the world a more pleasant, more productive and more peaceful place for all!

Critics of the 'glass ceiling', which prevents women from becoming

leaders of businesses or the professions in which they work, fail to
appreciate how few of us are willing to compromise our lives by trying
to break through that barrier — our common sense tells us that it can
be lonely up there. Being powerful can be hard work and you have to
fight for it for as long as it takes. Sometimes you'll lose and sometimes
you'll want to give up, but the important thing is never to give up with-
out having given it your best shot. Deal with criticism professionally,
not personally. Look for role models in others and see how they operate
to get where they are. Network with your rivals, be a good colleague
and seek support from people you can trust. And make sure to always
celebrate your achievements, every day! 🖋

IF YOU HAVE SELF-BELIEF, then there is no glass ceiling, the sky's
the limit. You just have to be driven and motivated enough to strive
for what you want in life.

Marie, 59, Derry, Northern Ireland

🖋

I KNOW A WOMAN who is hugely successful with her own business
and she makes an appointment in her diary every day to see her
children. The nanny brings them in for fifteen minutes every
day. You might think that's mad, but at least she sees them every
day, because most successful women who have got to the top of
their profession don't! How many men at the top of their game only
get to see their children at weekends and nobody thinks this is
strange!

Joan, 47, accountant, County Kerry

I'M LUCKY ENOUGH to work in publishing which is, by and large, a female-dominated industry, so there's really no such thing as a glass ceiling. All the women I know juggle their professional lives with their private lives and do so successfully. It shows that women can have it all – children and a high-powered and creative career.

Linda, 35, editor, London, England

❧

I WENT TO A PSYCHIC ONCE – as one does when a life crisis has to be faced! While I am fairly sceptical of these things, I was also desperate to hear something positive so rather than pay money to a psychologist to tell me why I was so unhappy, I decided to go to a psychic so she could tell me why I should be happy. Unexpectedly, the woman started talking about 'petty tyrants' ... I'd not heard this term before and was interested as she began to talk about these people who can make your life miserable and have such a strong influence over your life and decisions you make.

I started to recognise what she meant, as I'd left a job not long before because of an intolerable colleague. She told me I had a lot of them around me, partly due to the fickle nature of the business I work in. She explained to me that the reason they are called 'petty tyrants' is because they are petty people and the only way they can have this power is if you let them. They don't have power over you unless you give it to them. They are the little people, the miserable ones who have miserable lives themselves and enjoy making other people feel bad. They tell you gossip that may or may not be true. They tell you they heard rumours about you. They wonder if you should lose some weight because they are worried about you. Little things like this that can have a huge effect on your life. Her advice to me was invaluable and is to this day – recognise a petty tyrant and deal with them accordingly. Only you can allow them to influence your life so you have the power.

Vicki, screenwriter, Tasmania, Australia

THE GLASS CEILING is there for everyone – not just women who look for a work–life balance. Men typically don't feel the need to nurture and spend time with their families in the same way as women and this is why they can afford to give so much of themselves to their careers.

Kiara, solicitor, County Dublin

I SEE SO MANY WOMEN at work, still doing cheesecake to get ahead. Unless you work in a very specific type of business, stop wearing micro-minis and heels to work if you truly want to be taken seriously! The power of sex is only temporary. Lasting power comes through achievement, which is the result of diligence and hard work.

Sammy, law student, Canada

I THINK WOMEN BECOME more focused and are less prepared to put up with the male ego shit after having a child. This is why women choose not to work in that type of environment and why some companies do not employ strong women who have had children.

Caroline, 37, retail manager, County Donegal

☙

WORK HARD AND DON'T BUY into the patriarchal idealism of a 'man's world'. Understanding (not playing) the power dynamics of gendered aspects of the world can often, in my opinion, highlight the different and equally valid ways men and women perceive and operate power. And by supporting other women and not begrudging them when they do well – not all women do this, but it really is a joint effort.

Jacqueline, 48, chief executive, Manchester, England

☙

I GRADUATED IN MEDICINE in the 1980s and had a baby straight away. I found that no matter what job I went for, I wasn't taken seriously because I had a baby and then when I got pregnant with my second, I was pretty much fired. It was devastating. It absolutely knocked my self-esteem out of me and my marriage fell apart. I took a series of dead-end jobs and tried to keep a career on the road but it was impossible, as my (single) colleagues had no compunction about rostering me for night duty, which was a nightmare with two small kids! Around that time, I heard that the hospital matron used to do the same thing whenever one of the nurses got married – she'd put them on nights, just to teach them a lesson!

I decided that I'd spent enough time trying and putting my colleagues first and that my kids had suffered for it, so it was time to put my kids first. I did a series of part-time jobs, and developed a more portfolio career – and this actually paid off for me in the long run because, due to an episode of unemployment, I was able to completely rethink my career. I'm now very happy and fulfilled as I'm working outside of clinical medicine now. I run my own business from home, and the most astonishing thing is that many of my former medical colleagues now envy me! Also, I've learned not to let others put me down, not to take crap, not to put my colleagues' interests before myself or my kids, and I've learned that I am talented, diligent, reliable and that I'm very good at my job.

Breaking the glass ceiling isn't about punching your way to the top – it's about believing that you deserve to be treated well, to have your voice heard, and that if you put yourself and your own family needs first, career success will follow.

Elaine, 43, medico-legal consultant, England

☙

I WAS HIRED BY MY COMPANY because of my managerial and operational background. However, I am unable to pursue my position aggressively because I am the single mom of three children. I no longer have a husband/children's dad around. I have a partner, who is wonderful, but he does not replace me. That is the nature of it. I am still the responsible party when it comes to illness, schedules, school, so I am not free to work late, go on luncheons or business trips to secure business. I must work 8:30–4:30. No more, no less. I am not at liberty to focus on my work 120 per cent. I must be the mom first. So, the three men in management have taken a higher status than mine. They are wonderful to me and very understanding, but, my priorities are now as a mom. It is frustrating, as my stature and income could be triple what they are. But, it is what it is.

Kirsten, 39, office manager and director of communications, Illinois, USA

WHAT A WOMAN ASPIRES TO depends on where the woman lives and what the political or cultural system decrees the limits to what she can achieve are. Some aspire to the right to choose their own life partner, while others choose the right to equal work opportunities. The feminist era was clear cut – we burned our bras and got equal educational and job opportunities with men. Cue Germaine Greer and Nell McCafferty as role models.

Post-feminism put us on a more equal footing with men in social and cultural areas but in a retrograde step. Idealised 'celebrity' and a body image for women only attainable through starvation or cosmetic surgery. Cue Victoria Beckham, *Desperate Housewives*, etc.

So where to, now that economic collapse has forced us to rethink our priorities? Finding and holding on to a job, feeding and educating children, repaying huge mortgages – these are the current priorities. So maybe our new role model will come from the area of social justice – perhaps someone like Mary Robinson who has worked endlessly for a fairer sharing of wealth and resources. A woman who is not afraid of either the power brokers or her own innate feminine qualities of caring and empathy.

Mary, 50, author, County Cork

❧

THE WHOLE POINT of 'equal' seemed to be about having choice – but the choice many made was to become that which we all disliked about men in the first place – how warped and stupid is that?

Aisling, 41, Montessori teacher, County Cork

I ENTERED THE WORKFORCE after having children had given me a drive to succeed. It brought out a competitiveness I was unaware I had and a ruthlessness in order to provide for my family. It gave me courage to apply myself and to take risks I would never have taken.

The only problem I have ever faced is prejudice and insecurity from those in higher positions unable to see past their own preconceptions.

Debz, 52, independent mental health advocate, Manchester, England

The glass ceiling is very low and if I reach up I can easily smash it.

Juggling the work-life balance

Being confident to do all the jobs you have to do as a woman takes a lot of courage and a lot of preparation. If you know what it is you have to do and how you're going to do it, you can perform any task. Being able to perform everything takes organisation and determination. Surround yourself with supportive women who share your self-respect and have similar values and views as you. Keep close to you people who will always tell you the truth, but with love. And listen to your heart, every day.

For working women, time is the greatest luxury. We've never got enough of it.

When talking to women about their busy lives, the one strong message that came across is the importance of scheduling time to be alone, time away from responsibilities, time to listen to your own thoughts, to enjoy being yourself. If we could give one strong message to women everywhere it would be this: if possible, always make sure to schedule yourself a half-day off every week.

For many women, developing a career is the key to self-determination and independence. But our lives are much fuller than the hours of the working day. Being balanced means seeing our job as just one part in our journey though life, the source of income for the fun we are going to have, the comforts we enjoy and the future we plan with our partners, our children and ourselves.

Women bear children, but this has been twisted and turned against us on numerous occasions and many women experience some form of prejudice when they take time off to have a baby. For some women who are fortunate enough to stay at home and mind their families, the struggle will always remain between being a successful mother and having a career outside the home.

We need to take time to think about the balance we want for our busy lives. Having a plan for the amount of time we want to devote to work, the amount of time we want to spend with our children and making a firm decision that we are not going to suffer from guilt about either will empower us to be strong women with healthy, comfortable and fulfilled lives. There will always be times when children come first no matter what – and we should never feel guilty or ashamed of being a mom first and wanting to enjoy every moment of our children's lives. And there are times when children need to come second because a great career opportunity comes first – and we shouldn't be afraid to explain this to our kids and to reward their patience afterwards.

MAKE SURE THAT the person/people you live with are jugglers too!

Mairi, 47, ceramicist, County Cork

PUT ON YOUR OWN OXYGEN mask first! I read that in the book *Waiting for Birdie* by Catherine Newman and it stayed with me. You can be neither use nor ornament to anyone else if you allow yourself to burn out. So put your own essential needs first and remember you still exist as a person in your own right.

Claire, 34, author and journalist, Derry, Northern Ireland

❧

THE MORE MISTAKES you make, the better you become. There is only one person you must keep happy … and that's yourself, and your children if you have them.

Jaydee, 16, student, Leamington Spa, England

❧

WHEN I MOVED in to my new home in the woods (my little wooden house, an identikit for the three bears' house in *Goldilocks*), an old lady down the road with silver hair in a bun and glasses (the perfect grandmother from *Little Red Riding Hood*!) told me her biggest regret was spending so much time cleaning her home when her children were young. I often think of her … usually when I'm fighting with the hoover and the sun is beckoning from outside.

Caroline, public health doctor, County Galway

❧

I grew up in the West of Ireland in the 1970s. Women didn't work. Not married women, anyway. Until the early 1970s there was actually a ban on married women working in the public service. My mum was a doctor and she was extremely proud of her job – but all our neighbours were housewives. Quite often, other kids would say to me, 'It must be awful having your mother out at work all day,' and I would feel quite hard done by. Most of these women were clever women married to successful men, and they tended to have large families. We lived in the countryside just outside the town, and so the women in the neighbourhood were married to retailers, estate agents, headmasters. Our next-door neighbour was a gorgeous, leggy blonde who 'didn't have to work' because her husband was a bank manager. Her home was a show house. Ours was a giant mess. She was terribly glamorous, always sunbathing, always playing golf, tennis, baking wonderful treats for her kids. My mum would be racing in the door, frazzled after doing a theatre list all day, trying to cook chips for tea while smoking a fag and having a glass of sherry at the same time, while we whinged like mad because dinner was so late.

One day, our glamorous neighbour popped around to Mum for some advice about her health. As they chatted in the kitchen, our neighbour said to Mum, 'We should do this more often. Why don't you call around some time for a coffee?' I remember my mother's face — she looked so resentful when she said through smiling but gritted teeth, 'Well, I have a job. I don't get to call round to people's houses in the daytime for coffee.'

Our neighbour nodded and looked sad for a moment. I assumed that she was, like a lot of the other women, pitying my mum. Then our neighbour said, 'I really envy you, you know? I would have loved to have been able to do something worthwhile.'

Isn't it extraordinary that the work we do is so often something that we barely ever value ourselves, while we waste time envying the lives of others?

Juliet

I HAD A PERFECTLY GOOD managerial job before I had my first

child. When I was pregnant, I had the intention of continuing to work full time and continuing to work as normal after my maternity leave, etc. But after she was born, I wanted to stay home and look after her and work part time. I wanted to be there in the early years of her life. You know what? Sometimes it is OK to say, 'I don't want the career' (although I do miss the money, etc.). It's OK to want to be with your children and you're not a failure if you choose motherhood over a career.

Julie-Anne, 34, mum, Derry, Northern Ireland

※

HOUSEWORK WILL always wait.

Anna, 41, avid gardener and horse-rider, County Dublin

※

LIFE IS LIKE JUGGLING a lot of balls in the air. These balls are health, family, friends and work. They're all made of glass and could get badly broken if dropped. The only one that's not is work – it's made of rubber. In other words, if something has to be dropped in order to maintain the others, make it work. It will bounce back!

Clea, 42, mum and part-time photographer, County Dublin

※

You don't have to answer a phone just because it's ringing.

Clodagh, writer, County Dublin

※

I got married, had three kids, he had an affair. He was sent packing. I, on the other hand, have three wonderful kids, work and I went back to college at night. At the moment, I have a four-, eight- and ten-year-old. I work part-time in an addiction service and I'm currently finishing my law degree on my path to being a barrister. This is my load and I do believe we get one that we can carry and try do it gracefully. Three and a half years ago, I never would have believed I'd come out the end of this better, but I did. So to everyone that has to juggle – we women can do it better than anyone.

Maria, law student, County Dublin

※

Do try this at home:

Do you spend most of your evenings watching TV? TV advertisers tell us that most people watch an average of four hours a day. If you take that out of the way, you'll find a whole heap of time you thought you'd lost.

SOME PROBLEMS CAN'T be solved by any action now – you need to wait until the future to act on them. So that frees you from worrying about them now. Put a date in your diary for when to worry about a problem and act on it when it comes up.

Susan, 38, computer software designer, UK

ℬ

I HAVE THREE DAUGHTERS – aged eleven, thirteen and fifteen – and I can't find the balance that everyone talks about. It's a Tilt-a-Whirl life. Trying to find balance while living in a house with a man and three teenage girls only frustrates me more. It's a hectic existence filled with unknowns and unexpectedness. I oscillate between service and sacrifice, and try not to lose myself in the chaos. Forget the balance, hormonally speaking, it's already lost. Learn to live the Circus Life, because you are the ring master.

Shelly, 40, palm reader, Texas, USA

ℬ

IT'S ALL ABOUT love and happiness. That's what it boils down to: a simple clichè. And you don't need to have the wisdom of septuagenarians or have spent decades meditating on one foot outside a shack in the Himalayas to reach this obvious conclusion. What's important in life is not the wealth you accumulate or the power you achieve, it's adjusting your outlook to find joy in the little things. I work full time as an editor and writer for three medical magazines, have three children and a husband whose work takes him away days and weeks at a time. It's bloody hard, I can tell you, but by focusing on those small and frequent instances that have the potential to bring a smile or a moment of happy distraction, I can see myself through the manic day and have something lovely to reflect on by the end of it.

Eimear, 39, journalist, County Kilkenny

Guilt-free Pleasure

After a long day at work, exercising the little grey cells, my guilty pleasure is watching wrestling on the telly. Not Greco-Roman wrestling, which is an Olympic sport, but the larger-than-life absurdly theatrical antics of the World Wrestling Foundation. Here, fighters go by charmingly evocative names like Hulk Hogan, The Undertaker or The Rock. Weapons include folding steel chairs or the StinkFace Manoeuvre (patented by Rikishi the Samoan, who squashes his opponents by sitting on them) and championship events are called 'Judgement Day' and 'No Mercy'. Splendidly barbaric, very amusing and absolutely riveting – highly recommend this for an evening's mindless relaxation.

Shireene (who also loves Jane Austen),
endocrinologist, Melbourne, Australia

CHILL OUT now and again. My mother works her ass off so I can go to college and not have to work, the same with my sister, so I want her, and any other mother/father doing that, to chill the frak out now and again. If you say you don't have the time to relax, then you don't understand relaxing. If you can put time aside for work, you can put time aside for sitting down with a cup of tea (or what-ever your hot beverage of choice is) and watching TV, or reading, or just messing around looking at the internet. The French have a philosophy that states work to live; don't live to work (*travailler pour vivre, ne pas vivre pour travailler*).

Molly, 21, student, County Dublin

✺

IF ANYONE KNOWS how to perfect a work–life balance, I'm all ears. I have to make an appointment to sleep sometimes!

Brenda, 37, psychiatric nurse, Northern Ireland

I am a woman and I aspire to get through my day in a peaceful, pleasant way. I aspire to be accepted for who I am, not who everyone wants me to be. I aspire to breathe and inhale the beauty hidden behind the hustle. I aspire to be myself in a commercially influenced world.

Shelly, 40, palm reader, Texas, USA

Myths
and multitasking

Women have a wider cortex at the base of the brain than men and this allows us certain gifts, such as multitasking, which were particularly useful during prehistoric times when the women had to fend off attackers from the family as well as cooking the stew while their men were out hunting. Even today, the wider corpus callosum in women's brains gives us super powers. Think of a busy woman answering the phone while stirring the Bolognese and fixing a toy for her child – after having finished a busy day in the office. She probably has to tell her husband where the butter is in the fridge, even though it is straight in front of him!

Just because you've got the ability to multitask doesn't mean you've always got to try to do everything at the same time. Juliet was cooking dinner for a party of ten while helping her children with their homework and doing the laundry and taking a phone call from work. She accidentally stirred a litre of chip oil into her soup instead of stock … it was revolting but her guests ate it anyway! Sometimes we are so busy multitasking that we aren't present with the job that we are meant to be doing.

Michelle multitasks all the time – like most women do each and every day. The older she gets, the faster and easier it is to pack her *children's lunch, make the breakfast and find coats for everyone in the house before they go out the door. But when it comes to being creative and writing her novels, she turns off the radio, puts her phone on silent and sits in front of her computer in her favourite place in her house. She has found that to be truly focused and creative, she needs to be task-oriented and absorbed in doing one thing at a time.*

Don't do it just for the sake of it. 🐚

READ THE manual!

Phyllis, 70, mother and grandmother, County Dublin

🐚

I WAS ALWAYS TRYING to enter data into the computer and use the phone at the same time, and I developed a terrible nerve entrapment injury in my neck which took months to heal. But women are always doing this, trying to get more than one thing done at the same time. We can't start one job without starting another, always with one eye on the clock. I've since learned that you just need to do one thing at a time, and if I run out of time, then it's not my fault. I'd rather do one thing carefully and get it right than try to do ten things half-heartedly and find myself all over the place. It's more important to feel that you've done a good job well than to have done a lot.

Augustine, 28, secretary, Germany

🐚

It's the hardest job in the world being a woman. You have to be all things to everyone and you are always the last person in the house to get your needs met.

Christine, 46, mother of four, County Dublin

ॐ

It's a gift and that's why we can do what men can't do!

I still don't have any experience in multitasking but my mammy is a super mum – she does a million things at the same time. When she travels or gets sick, everything becomes upside down. God bless mothers.

Aya, 22, medical student, Benghazi, Libya

ॐ

Remember there are days when everything won't get done. But that's OK. There's always tomorrow.

Mary, 50, author, County Cork

ॐ

I don't believe that women are better at multitasking than men. It's just a myth that was made up to try to get women to do ten different jobs at the same time!

Vivienne, 42, gardener and teacher, County Dublin

BEFORE CHRISTMAS I thought I had put the ring on under the spuds but I had put it on under the chip pan and set my kitchen on fire. Thank God no one was hurt. My new kitchen looks great.

Collette, 53, homemaker, County Dublin

🐝

THIS HAPPENED around three years ago. My parents were coming for dinner and I was in the middle of cooking when my husband asked what he could take for a headache. I went to the tablet cupboard (thinking about putting potatoes in the oven) and gave him what I thought were two Paracetamol. When he kept falling asleep, I realised that I'd actually given him two sleeping tablets instead! He felt really guilty about not being able to stay awake while my parents were there, and wondered why he had a worse headache than before. I only confessed to him recently!

Grace, 39, County Down, Northern Ireland

🐝

MY MOTHER WAS a consummate multitasker. I remember watching her in awe as she sat in the wing-backed chair in the middle of the living room, her glasses perched right on the tip of her nose to keep an eye on the pattern whilst she knitted, watching *Dallas* over the rim of her specs, an open Mills & Boon on her knees, the *Sun* crossword on one side of her chair and a glass of G&T on the other. Now *that's* multitasking!

Debs, 39, non-teaching assistant, Bedford, England

We just accept that we will feel unbalanced at times – it is part of the passion of living! Go create!

Successful women

To be successful at anything in life, we need goals, targets and rewards. Visions and dreams are vital for our world to be a success. These dreams are where the future of our world lies.

When Juliet was a little girl, her mother and father took her to Italy to visit her father's family. In the window of a shop were the most beautiful shoes she had ever seen. Her mother used her skill to mould Juliet's mindset at that early age. She leaned forward and whispered in her ear, 'If you want to be able to afford shoes like that when you grow up, you had better go to med school.'

When Michelle was a little girl, she was prone to daydreaming and although she didn't give any trouble in school, she certainly didn't stand out as a shining light of academia. Her mother didn't want her to follow in her steps automatically and become an art student. Apart from her concerns over Michelle's ability to provide for herself after becoming an artist, she also wanted her to have more options and to consider higher-regarded and better-paid professions. Needless to say, Michelle ended up in the very same alma mater as her mother and had a couple of very dodgy reports on the way. After one such report, her mother very coolly said to Michelle that if she didn't pull her socks up she wouldn't graduate. As it turned out Michelle worked in a sock factory designing socks the year she graduated from

Art College. She was fortunate to have a nice office, a car to get to work in and a job.

Somehow those little snippets of wisdom from our mothers helped to carry us to another place that we might not have got to. But not all women need role models to be a success. When we talked to women about our ideas for what makes a successful woman, what fascinated us was the variety of experience that women have in the world, and how different our measures of success can be. Whatever you do in life, do your best and be proud of what you do and you will always be a success. 🌿

I SAT MY SECOND-YEAR law exam five times but my mother was determined that I stick it out. She said she wanted me to be able to support myself. Now I'm running my own successful practice and realise how right she was!

Maria, 60, solicitor, County Tipperary

WORK IS WHERE WE SPEND most of our waking hours, so get it right. Choose a career in a field that interests or inspires you and don't over-plan your future in terms of stepping stones to financial reward alone. Don't even think of staying in a job where you dislike or feel uncomfortable with colleagues, cannot respect the ethos of the employer or, most importantly of all, do not feel valued by your boss; the satisfaction of a job well done is greatly diminished by feeling that you are taken for granted. A good workplace has a supportive leader who never fails to recognise privately and publicly the commitment and support of each member of her staff. You deserve nothing less.

Jackie, doctor, Melbourne, Australia

AMONG MY CIRCLE, I am famous for a couple of sayings, the most famous of these is probably 'show your workings'. This is very much in the context of work for me – it was one of the very best bits of advice a female colleague gave me and I pass it on at every opportunity. The ability to evidence our decision-making is essential (in life sometimes more so than work). If we can show that what we elected to do was sound, based on what we knew at the time and that we were acting in good faith, all will be well.

The important matter here is to go about our business conscious of the need to be able to show our logic. For many of us, the person we need to convince about the logic behind our decision-making is ourselves, so 'show your workings' can really help us organise our game, if not actually raise it. It is also a terrific way of cross-checking options to come to a conclusion. And in a world that can still harbour more chauvinists than a gal should have to negotiate her way around, being able to show your workings empties out another of their bogus arguments. Go ladies!

Geraldine, 50, management consultant, London, England

ONE THING I HAVE invariably found to be true is that men never sell themselves short. Women invariably do! Most men I've ever met or worked with always face a task believing that not only can he do it, but he will most likely do it better than anyone else in the room. Women not only hesitate, rarely taking the lead and jumping straight in, but when the problem is resolved they then spend most of their time thanking everyone around them for the solution! It is rare for a woman to claim the credit or acknowledge her own expertise. The tragedy is that this behaviour translates into an attitude where many women come to believe that they are inherently less capable, qualified or competent to address a problem. And, even worse, we punish those rare women who hold out against this trend, labelling them as 'aggressive', 'pushy' or 'forward'. We may well have come a long way, baby, but baby, we've still got a long way to go!

Marcelle, director of mission,
St Vincent's Hospital, Melbourne, Australia

❧

YOUR JOB AND STATUS now do not state how powerful or successful you are. What people remember of you in later years determines your level of success and self-fulfilment!

Ria, 35, manager, Derry, Northern Ireland

❧

I THINK FEMINISM has moved on to really finding out who we are as unique individuals and revelling in that expression and in our individual and personal power ... I love being me (but it was an arduous journey to get to the point where that is true). Role models come in all shapes and sizes ... including a little old lady I spoke to yesterday who told me the greatest love story I have ever heard (her life with her darling hubby and their trials and tribulations), or the girls living here from Moldova illegally who clean houses to support their families back home ... Sometimes, I just admire myself for being able to get out of bed in the mornings and get the kids to school on time!

Siobhán, homeopath, Baldoyle, County Dublin

IT'S HARDER FOR A WOMAN who is ahead of her time to be taken seriously than for a man who is behind the times … We usually make them the Prime Minister.

Frieda, 38, secondary school teacher, County Dublin

※

AT WORK AN IMAGE CONSULTANT once gave me the following advice – dress and act like you already have that job promotion you want. You can't afford not to buy quality. A few quality pieces and you'll get wear after wear out of them. Perception is important. If people perceive you in a certain way it's because of a reason, i.e. you're sending out that vibe. Or … maybe you perceive yourself some way … you can influence that. In those days, I was trying to 'manage' people, usually older than me/men and found out the hard way that frizzy blonde hair and pink tops and light colours didn't create the necessary professional image. Oh – and the successful woman chatters less and listens plenty. I'm still working at that one. Now success for me is changing as I go along, and I usually have a personal development plan (five-year plan) going on even in my head.

Looking after our family members and rearing children with good values is important for the world to be a better place, and promoting respect, for ourselves included. Plus not marching to the beat of a general drum all the time.

Jacinta, 35, development and outreach officer,
Bangor, Northern Ireland

Our friend Ger is an amazing woman who has had several very different careers in her lifetime and now runs her own company as a consultant to major industrial organisations in London. Something that has always helped her in times of trouble/doubt/fear/challenge is this:

Show up! Whatever we are facing, we are halfway there if we show up. Nothing is achieved by walking away. And while there are moments when a tactical retreat is entirely the right thing to do, we need to face matters before we can retreat. So whether it is an exam, a job interview, meeting an ex, some news we are quite legitimately dreading or any of the many and varied opportunities we women face where aspiration, esteem or dignity are at stake, showing up – the very act of stepping out to meet what's coming, great or small, real or imagined – is the essence of courage and truly represents who we are to ourselves.

Juliet & Michelle

A successful woman ...

... is stunning on the inside, graceful and at peace with herself and those around her.

Michelle, shamanic practitioner, County Dublin

... looks like the proverbial swan, calm and graceful on the surface but paddling furiously underneath.

Ciara, computer executive, County Dublin

> ... is a woman who gets to make her own decisions.
>
> *Eve, plastic surgeon, Chicago, USA*

WHEN I WAS YOUNG, my mother struggled to feed me, my sister and my brothers. My father had other women and other children and he drank a lot. When I finished standard seven school, I thought that was to be the end of my education and I looked around for some work to do – helping with housework, carrying water and firewood and cooking on the outside fire. Those were the only jobs open to me but I wanted to be a teacher. One day, I was fortunate to meet a Sister of Holy Union who must have seen some potential in me and she sponsored me through secondary school. After that, she sent me to their newly opened training college where they sponsored me to do my diploma. For three years now, I have been teaching Geography and Physics in a secondary school and they are further sponsoring me to do my degree this year. A dream come true thanks to the sisters at the mission.

Neema, 28, teacher, Dar-es-Salaam, Tanzania

*I am a success
at everything I do.*

Being creative

Creativity is what being a woman is all about. Survival may keep you alive, but to be creative is the essence of intelligence. What we believe is that creative women are stronger. Creative women make greater efforts with relationships. And creative women have greater happiness than women who aren't exploring the creative minds that nature gave them.

Being creative at work means that we are open to ideas, we are passionate about the work we do and that we want to do it well. Women work in different ways to men – we tend to be collaborative rather than competitive, we tend to be community-focused rather than individualistic, and we can be more holistic in our ambitions for our world. Now more than ever, women need to sit down together and solve problems in a creative way that improves outcomes for everyone. Work can cause a great deal of anxiety and stress if you let it, especially if you are met with brick walls every time a problem needs to be solved. If you are fortunate, you will find a job in which you can be creative in your work and use your talents to make the world a better place. But creativity is important in every aspect of our lives.

It's not just in the workplace where we need to free our minds. Having a creative life, a life where we are following our passions, *leaves us at liberty to be more content with ourselves in every way. Many women find they don't have the time to be creative in their daily lives, and spend all their days working and/or raising children. It's important to take back time from your life or to find the time to explore the gifts you have, to bring meaning into your life, to make your heart sing. We need to schedule time for our creative passions, just as we schedule our work day and our children's timetables. Picture yourself playing an instrument, painting a picture, writing a poem or a letter, building a garden ... see how happy that picture makes you feel! Women have always known the importance of beauty and creativity in our world. The important thing now is to find the time.* 🌿

YOU CAN'T IGNORE any creative talents or interests in your life. Women often put all their creative energies into bringing up children. Your children are separate people and they are very interesting – but don't forget to ask yourself every now and then: who, exactly, am I?

Justine, 32, psychiatrist, London, England

🌿

SOMETIMES, I'D WANT TO write a shopping list – but I write poetry instead.

Miriam, 31, poet, County Wicklow

🌿

THE BEST PIECE OF ADVICE that I ever received was this: No matter what your age is, or life circumstance, you can always reinvent yourself!

As I was dealing with the aftermath of a serious illness, and as a way of distracting myself, I thought of what kind of life I wanted if I had a second chance. Dreaming of this allowed me to get through the medical treatments with a plan.

I was going to access my authentic self and go for goals and dreams that seemed impossible. I was never going to give up on these goals!

I started with my first trip alone overseas and then some summer courses overseas. Then I applied for my first artist residency and met others who have become lifelong friends!

After a while, each time there was a blockade, I used the energy of my reaction to push farther along. I am still doing this. There have been many blockades!

I look to the other amazing and cherished women friends that I have met along the way to model strength and creativity. I discovered that I had organisational skills and could help others, so I formed a women's artist co-operative. There is truly strength in numbers and I feel the support from so many as I give it back to my creative circle of engaging, eclectic and brave, visionary women friends. They are in my heart wherever I travel! This is just the beginning!

Elizabeth, 55, artist, Canada

༝

After giving birth, the thing that struck me the most was – what had I done with my time? If only I could have that time back I would appreciate every moment and do all of those courses and visit all of those places that I couldn't now that I had the responsibility and commitment of a child. Of course we need to experience the loss of time to appreciate how precious it is. Also with that new realisation, you need to relish the precious time you are given with the wonder of a small baby – time moves fast for them too and before you know it they will be crawling and walking and running out the door! One thing I've learned is that you can't waste time because you don't possess it in the first place. So when you waste time what you're really wasting is yourself.

Michelle

❧

THE OLDER I GET, the more paranoid I get about wasting time. I start to actually resent having to sleep at night!

Deirdre, 43, general practitioner, County Dublin

❧

When my daughter was twelve, she entered a drama competition. She was quite good, and was in the running to be in the top three when the adjudicators had added up the marks. But there was one other girl who was spectacular. She stood out miles. She was a wonderful performer, she had amazing stage presence, she was a natural actor. During a break between acts, I got chatting to her mum in the loos – a nurse I knew through work. She and I talked about what our two girls planned to do at university. I told her my daughter wanted to study drama, to which she replied, 'And are you going to allow her to do that?'

'Of course,' I replied. I was just thrilled that she'd found something she loved to do. The other thing was that I felt that I had come from a

generation in which jobs, careers, money, status, permanency and pensions were all our parents cared about, and that had stifled my creativity and made me very unhappy. I'd wished I'd been 'allowed' to study something that I'd been passionate about, rather than something that was intended to 'lead to a good job'. So I was pleased to be able to give my daughter that chance. This woman then burst into tears. She admitted that she was just afraid for her daughter. She couldn't overcome the barrier she felt when she thought about acting as a profession. It was all about poverty, missed auditions, working as a waitress in between low-paid parts. It was all about failure.

Perhaps this woman was being very realistic. She wanted her daughter to succeed so badly that she was actually afraid of her daughter's talents. Her daughter's passion wasn't making her happy – it was making her feel afraid. Her daughter's wonderful gifts weren't gifts to her at all – they were holding her back.

I met this woman many years later – both our daughters are at university now. And my daughter isn't studying drama at all! But she has a very lovely life. And I do fear she'll never be financially independent. But I don't ever fear she'll fail.

The other woman's daughter is studying medicine now. I often think of her and hope she's happy. I hope she feels passionate about it too. I also think she's probably had to really change.

Juliet

☙

I DON'T KNOW how often I've met people who'll say, 'I'd love to do X, Y and Z, if only I had the time … I'd love to paint if only I had the time … I'd love to write if only I had the time.' These are people who then spend a great deal of time doing all sorts of other things. Things like watching creative people on television doing the things they think they'd like to do. I keep meeting women who've forgotten how wonderful it is to dance because they spend hours driving their kids to dance class. They've forgotten how much fun it is to sing or play an instrument because they've spent so much time nagging their kids to practise the piano!

Sarah, 47, food scientist, County Meath

I USED TO THINK that my kids needed to do a hundred after-school activities and I spent every day worrying about them not doing enough. When they grew up they admitted to me finally that they hadn't given a damn about all the ballet, soccer and piano lessons I'd made them do – they'd have much rather been hanging around street corners with their friends! Now, they seem to spend their lives lying in front of the telly just like everyone. I'm the one who wants to be creative now – I just wish I hadn't left it this late to begin with.

Rosie, 43, developing artist, County Louth

Do try this at home:

Women are always pressed for time. It's our greatest luxury, when we've got lots of it. But what we've discovered is that women spend a huge amount of time worrying! Wouldn't you just love to know how to quit worrying and find the time to do all the things you long to do?

Don't worry: Make a list.

Get out your diary and a blank piece of paper.

Make a list down one side of the paper, headed Problem.

Make a list down the other side of the page, headed Action.

List your problems, followed by an action for each one.

Then, make a date in your diary for each of the actions you need to do and tick them off as you work through your days.

What you'll find is that most people will have cleared their worry list in a matter of days! And most people have also discovered that there are several things that they have been worrying about, but about which there is absolutely nothing they can do.

Some of these worries will turn out to be problems that can only be solved by other people. So you are now freed up to stop worrying about them.

MY MOTHER'S MAXIM was 'be ye therefore as wise as serpents and as harmless as doves'. I think it is Matthew 10 verse 11. She was a lovely woman, kind and considerate, but she always knew what was happening behind her back! She worked for a time before the war at a rehabilitation establishment for ex-convicts, teaching them to be waiters and butlers. She applied this maxim with considerable success, always aware of what they were up to, but resolving it with a gentle hand.

Dinah, IT consultant, London, UK

❧

I USED TO BE SO UNHAPPY in my job. I felt guilty about that, because I'd worked really hard to get into college to become a pharmacist and then I hated it and felt I'd made a huge mistake. I was always getting sick. Then I decided to go back to art college and study sculpture. I started going to evening classes and studying for exams, and suddenly my daily working life didn't bother me at all. I was busy at my job, and doing it even better than before – I stopped getting sick, a whole winter went by and I didn't get one cold. And every day, I'd be working away, looking forward to the piece I would be working on that night, and to my art classes on a Tuesday and Thursday! I work part time now in the pharmacy and I've got an exhibition coming up at the end of the year – I feel my dreams have all come true.

Olivia, 38, pharmacist, County Dublin

❧

I CAN'T BELIEVE that when I was younger I wasted so much time doing absolutely nothing – and now I see my kids doing the same thing and it drives me insane.

Samantha, 52, interior decorator, UK

WORK TO LIVE, don't live to work!

We may have to juggle, but it's not the end of the world if a ball drops here or there – boys have to drop theirs to be men.

Take time out to recharge ... a flat battery simply won't work! There's no medals for martyrs in this world.

Theresa, 41, administrator for mental health services, West Cork

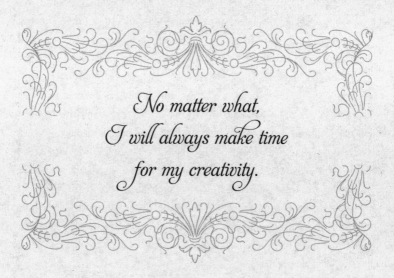

*No matter what,
I will always make time
for my creativity.*

In Work

I am a successful woman because ...

Money

*D*o we live to work – or work to live? How much money do we really need? These are big questions that many women are asking themselves now. In the 1960s, we got out of the home and into the workplace, earning our own money. In the 1980s, we were told that we could have it all. By the 2000s, we were running our own businesses. But the world economic crisis has taught us valuable lessons about the power and the powerlessness of money. Some women still earn less than men do for the same work, and most poverty is experienced by women.

For some women, money is all about independence. Having respect for money and understanding how it works means that you are free to be in control of your income and to generate the kind of wealth that you need. We have already got rid of the idea that women are always happy to be provided for by men. We also need to rubbish the idea that talking about money is vulgar, that being careful with your money makes you mean or boring. We need to dump the idea that having big credit card debts makes you a fun person to be with, and that saving and investing is too difficult so let's leave that up to the boys. All of these myths keep women from generating financial well-being, which is the ability to live well, independent of financial stress.

When we talked to women everywhere about what money meant to them, the one message that came out loud and clear is that money is much less important to women than love, family, friendship, health and happiness – and that women are quite often very prepared to tolerate poverty or reduced means in order to be free to enjoy these gifts. Living well is all about a balance between the freedom to earn your money and the freedom to spend it. Women now control 80 per cent of the consumer spending in the United States – and we control over half the inter-generational wealth too. As women continue to outlive men, and as our life expectancy increases, single women without children are destined to become the wealthiest demographic group in Western society. Spend wisely, ladies, because we shall inherit the earth!

What does wealth really mean to women?

When we talked to women in developing countries, we could see immediately that being in control of your own money is a vital part of women's power. Having your own income means that you have freedom, and you are free from fear. But how many women in the West still appreciate the huge battle that women have had to overcome in order to earn money for ourselves?

Having surplus money is a dream for most women of the world, so when we do find ourselves with money to spend, it's important to spend it wisely. We need to safeguard our future, provide for our children, feather our nests and reward ourselves for hard work. Having an income of your own is a woman's right, and it's a privilege. So you've got a responsibility to take care of it and to make sure you are getting what you really want from the money that you've earned.

Accumulating wealth is terribly important if you're going to fight poverty in old age, and women can't afford to be complacent. Nobody wants to end up poor and alone, but we have to get our values and priorities right.

Juliet once worked in a gynaecology ward, where there were patients *who were dying of cancer. She noticed that when the ladies were coming to the end of their days, they wanted very few possessions around them. They'd start to pare back, to get rid of things. They'd want their small room to be neat, clutter free. They'd often give away their belongings as if they were preparing for their final journey and they wanted to travel light.*

What she realised then, and what we try to tell women who worry about money all the time, is that the day you die, you don't want to look at your bank statements. You want to look at your photographs.

So invest in your friends. Invest in your family. But most of all, invest in yourself. 🌱❤

REAL WEALTH IS ENJOYING time with loved ones – it's precious. Think of the honeymoon period with your ex-boyfriends, the days with your teenage girlfriends window shopping or just going for a walk or eating Christmas dinner with family that have now passed on. The really special times that you would like to go back to probably didn't involve money, but people.

Jessica, 56, writer, Scotland

❧

WHAT IS WEALTH for women? Health is everything. When I was sick and poor I worried, when I then came in to money, but still was sick, I still worried. Health and a home and food and enough clothes to keep you warm and good people around you.

Sofia, 44, artist, Sweden

I WENT TO SCHOOL with a girl who had a very high-flying business-man for a father. In the course of his career, he made a fortune and lost it again. She had to move from palatial houses to ordinary semi-detached houses and back again to a mansion during her childhood. The advice she gave to me was simple: appreciate what you have because there will always be someone with more than you and there will always be some-one with less.

I have used this as my mantra and it has made me content with everything I have had at the different stages of my life.

Caroline, 44, mum of four, County Dublin

※

ENOUGH TO BE ABLE to pay the bills, put a roof over your head and feed and clothe yourself and your family – plus a little left over for a treat or two and savings for that rainy day! In this day and age, we forget about saving and it's so important. Money doesn't make you happy in itself, it doesn't have that power ... but I sure wouldn't mind a little lottery win because what I'd do with it would, for sure, make me and my family very happy indeed!

Honey, web surfer, County Dublin

※

MONEY MAY PROVIDE security and contentment somewhat, but honestly, I don't feel it provides true happiness. I think money and happiness are two separate things. No matter how much money you have, if you aren't happy within yourself, then money won't fix that. Look at all the celebrities who are really wealthy and their lives have fallen apart – being rich doesn't mean that you will be happy. Of course, you do need money to feel secure as I said and it may help towards feeling more content, but your happiness comes from within you and the love of those around you.

Geraldine, 19, student, County Galway

In business there is only one type of wealth and that is money. It's not clients or staff but cash in the door. This is also the value for most men. When you ask a woman what wealth is she will usually refer to health and happiness. If you talk to a man he will start with wealth. That's the whole divide between women and men and how we view money.

Janette, 42, solicitor, County Dublin

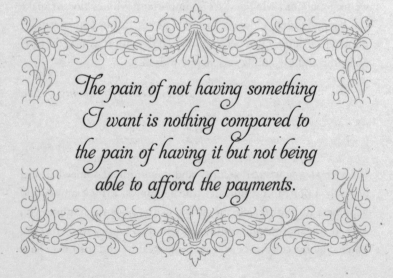

The pain of not having something I want is nothing compared to the pain of having it but not being able to afford the payments.

How much do we need?

Women worry a lot about money. How much time do we spend focusing on what we don't have or what we want, rather than what we do have and what we really need? Money is only as valuable as the cost of the item that you want to buy. It is simply a unit for measuring the value of a product or service. There is also a fundamental difference between what we want and what we need. We need to eat, we need to wear clothes and we need a place to put our heads at night to rest. But whether we cook a simple meal of vegetables and fruit or dine out in a Michelin starred restaurant, we are in both cases fulfilling the basic need to eat.

When we evaluate our accumulated wealth correctly — our health, our loved ones, the food on the table — then we will truly feel rich! When it comes to spending money, everyone loves to treat themselves. But if you really want to buy something and it's very expensive, do a cost-benefit analysis on it to see if it's worth it.

Michelle's friend Frieda wanted to get a family portrait of herself and her husband and two children. The cost of one large framed photograph was €700, so she divided it up into the length of time that it would be hanging on her wall and the cost per day. She figured that if she had it up for ten years it would cost 5.2 cent per day and that it was actually excellent value for something that she would appreciate for so long.

You can do this with almost anything – new clothes, shoes, bags, face cream – and see if the item is worth what you will spend on it. In other words, before you write the cheque, do the maths! ♐♥

YOU DON'T NEED every brand name going, you will not die if you don't have those €200 sandals, you don't need a huge SUV to drive yourself around (you do if you've got ten kids, but who can afford them these days?). You don't have to be a sheep and follow the herd. There are things that are important in life and they can cost money – good health care, a roof over your head, etc. – but there are things, such as paying €1,000 for the latest handbag and thinking it is a bargain, that are just simply crazy. Buy what's important, invest your money in your family, friends, health, education – not in trivial commercialisation dictated by the media.

Honey, web surfer, County Dublin

❧

STOP BUYING what you don't really need. If the food processor is fifteen or twenty years old but still works perfectly fine, you do not need a new one simply because the old one 'doesn't match' your new kitchen. This goes for pretty much everything, including clothes. I know women who are buying a different item of clothing virtually every week. Why? They rationalise this by saying they give the unwanted items to charities or to thrift shops, but really! The amount of money they spend unnecessarily on clothes is ridiculous! The list goes on endlessly, but as this is one of my pet peeves, I'll stop here.

Walk away. Give yourself a day to consider whether you really need the item, then go back if you must. Nine out of ten times, you'll discover you don't need it, and find you have more money in the bank as a result.

Frances, granny, Montreal, Canada

THE MORE WE HAVE, the more we want and most millionaires admit money doesn't buy happiness. As a matter of fact, money often leads to discontent, insecurity and unhappiness.

Shanti, Houston, USA

Guilt-free Pleasures

When you're really broke, spend your last fiver on yourself. Buy something new for your house. A new bath mat. A packet of fancy loo paper. A plant. A nice mug. It's your last fiver, so buy yourself something lovely that you can afford. When you're down to your last fiver, that's the very time you need to cheer yourself up.

SOMETIMES WE NEED to view what we have differently or make a small cosmetic change to something to completely transform how we feel about it.

I was so bored with my kitchen – it was a dark oak and although all of the drawers worked perfectly and it was designed exactly the way I needed it to work to suit me and my family, I was discontent.

I saw my friends getting their kitchens chucked out for modern, streamlined state-of-the-art models and questioned getting a large loan out to do the same. Then common sense prevailed. A very practical friend of mine gave me the phone number of a painter that she had found who converted her entire kitchen with a couple of pots of cream paint. So I followed suit and went all out and got some new floor covering too. My kitchen was transformed. It cost considerably less than a brand new one and I still have my good wooden presses which can be sanded and made like new should I choose to change them in a few years. For a while there, we were throwing out the baby with the bath water and rushing to get a fix of the latest thing – now I am delighted to see a return to valuing craft and quality and valuing things that don't need to be replaced.

Marina, 38, mum of two, County Meath

Do try this at home:

If you find you've got lots of time on your hands because of unemployment, learn to maintain your house. Dressmaking, curtain-making, plumbing, carpentry and car maintenance courses are all relatively cheap in your local community college. Having these skills will save you a fortune in the long run, introduce you to new friends and save you a lot of anxiety for the rest of your life.

I THINK A LOT OF PARENTS' money goes on unnecessary treats for their children. Paying for venues, food, entertainment for birthday parties when you can have a good old-fashioned party at home. Buying things for them 'because so and so has it'. Saying no to your kids is not depriving them, but teaching them values. Television, magazines, the internet all put pressure on us to buy, buy, buy. When my kids ask for something that is not really necessary, I simply say that I can't afford it! They get over it and the next week, it's something else! More times than not, I end up putting toys away for months without them being missed at all.

Breda, 49, home-help, County Wexford

❧

How MUCH do we need? That all depends on where you live. The cost of living varies from place to place and person to person. For me, it would be enough to own my home outright, have a buffer of savings that provides enough interest to live simply and give up my regular nine-to-five job and follow my dreams.

Alison, 29, Dundee, Scotland

It is OK to want nice things, as long as you don't let them define who you are!

Michelle, shamanic practitioner, County Dublin

Live well on a budget

Splashing money around just isn't possible for most women – but we shouldn't deprive ourselves if we can at all help it. Earning our own money means that we have the power to decide how we spend it – and yet children, bills, debts and our duties to others are always going to soak our money right out of our wallets. Living on a budget doesn't mean living miserably – but it means being very wise about your spending and saving. We need to be organised in what we do with our money. Every woman needs to provide for others as well as for herself, so make sure you set aside some money from your budget that is for your private use, no matter how small the amount. Saving is the key to protecting yourself against future crises. Debts will always mean interest payments, so make sure you are attacking your debts as vigorously as you can. Taking time to examine your spending habits is time well spent. If you can't afford the lifestyle you want to lead, you either need to earn more money or spend less.

It is too easy to be fooled by labels or brands. Buy what you like, what you can afford and the quality that feels right for you!

ONE OF THE POSITIVES to come out of the recession for me is that I am not feeling as much pressure to dress in designer gear/get the fake tan done, all that expense ... much happier being hippy me.

Susan, 42, full-time mum, County Dublin

🐝

WITH GOOD FRIENDS, there's no need to go to the trouble and expense of cooking an extravagant dinner when inviting them around. Especially if you all work during the week, then why not just order a pizza or Chinese and sit back and enjoy a bottle of wine together? Take the kids and then you won't need to get a babysitter! We need to simplify our socialising. For a while there, it had become competitive to do everything to a certain standard, but real friends are there for your company – not what you are going to serve up to them!

Mary, 44, librarian, County Mayo

🐝

I WORK IN THE BANK OF IRELAND and have seen many changes over the past few years. It's sad to see people having trouble paying their mortgages. My advice to them would be to contact their community welfare officer – but most importantly keep in touch with their bank and pay in whatever they can each month.

Lorna, 40, financial advisor, County Dublin

🐝

Since the recession, I am appreciating the simple things in life more, spending more time with family and friends, living life at a slower pace, kids realising there never was a money tree in the garden and treats have to be earned!

Jeanne, 44, unemployed, County Dublin

$\approx$

I live in Dublin and I think some of the best things to do with loved ones are free. There are lots of art galleries and museums if it's raining and kids love paintings and sculptures and make remarkable comments and observations when they are not hindered by the meaning or value of a piece of art. The beach is a favourite with the kids and we bring little buckets and spades and catch crabs (we always leave them back to their families at the end of the adventure).

Having kids, or falling in love, I always think makes you change your priorities and see the wonder of nature and the simple things in life.

Jade, 42, mum of two, County Dublin

$\approx$

I listed some old jewellery on eBay recently that had been lurking in corners of the bathroom for years gathering dust, then my mum gave me a few bits and pieces to sell that she'd had for years from her aunt – cute, vintage stuff but nothing I'd hang on to myself. However, one person's junk … so far, over the past two weeks I've made over €400 in sales. I've been bitten by the bug now and I'm starting to get rid of all sorts of clutter … old mobile phones, kids' clothes and toys, etc. So now, when I need to get face cream, for example, I go on eBay, pick up a bargain and pay with the money from my sales! I'm decluttering, making money and saving money while messing about and having fun on the computer. Don't you love technology?

Niamh, 30, County Kilkenny

Do try this at home:

There are times when shopping is good for you – the sales are an example – but they can also be times when it can all go horribly wrong.

Don't bring friends with you.

Make sure that your credit card is not at its max, because if it is, just stay at home!

Do have a list of items that you need – if you have thirty skirts and one pair of jeans, then make sure that you don't buy another skirt!

Don't go crazy by buying something that is not your size – your foot will only change size if you have just had a baby – remember Cinderella!

Same goes for clothes – you are the size that you are and don't buy something two sizes too small for the day when you lose the weight – it may be out of fashion by the time that happens!

Sales are only fabulous for getting bed linen, curtains and certain household items that you actually need, are too dear normally and only if there's at least 50% off!

KNIT YOUR OWN SOCKS. It takes so long that the main saving will be that you do not go shopping.

Mary Ethna, 52, public health physician, Serbia

※

HAVE PAINTING PARTIES with your mates when you decide to decorate/redecorate. Sweaty, hard work made lighter with many hands and a few well-deserved drinks after with a bite of grub. Who needs to hire a painter/decorator?!

Theresa, 41, administrator for mental health services, County Cork

※

I SAVE MONEY by shopping every two weeks and not doing the shopping in just one shop but going to the places where you can pick up bargains. Cooking up a batch of food and freezing it. Making gifts instead of buying them and using leftovers to make something nice for dinner the next day.

Collette, 53, homemaker, County Dublin

※

A WONDERFULLY elegant woman with whom I worked while in my twenties said to me when I was setting up house, 'Buy the most expensive saucepans you can afford. They will last a lifetime.' I followed her advice and now, some twenty years later, I still have all those saucepans and they're still in great condition.

Jacinta, writer and GP, Australia

CHARITY SHOPS are brill for getting cool vintage gear. I got a fab 'God Save the Queen' top for €5 last week!

Trish, 18, student, County Dublin

※

DON'T BUY convenience foods. Take the trouble to cook from scratch. It's cheaper and you get leftovers you can rejig later in the week.

Avis, 55, writer, England

※

IF YOU CAN'T AFFORD something or there is no money for doing things, there is no need to tell the children this. Instead, put a jar on the windowsill and throw change in it and tell them that you are saving for it. They will enjoy the treat even more.

Claire, 43, full-time mum, Holland

※

TRY OWN BRANDS, as they can often be cheaper and because they have to compete with name brands are of equal quality/standard. If you check the labels you may find they are produced by name branded companies and packaged for Sainsbury's/Tesco, etc.

Marie, 59, Derry, Northern Ireland

Stop worrying about what others have and you will cut your spending in half.

Sofia, 44, artist, Sweden

Always take a shopping list to the supermarket and never stay more than an hour! And always check the sell/use by dates on your purchases! Freeze any purchases that can be frozen if you think you won't use them soon.

Michelle & Juliet

Guilt-free Pleasures
Real wealth on a budget: stopping – literally – to enjoy the scent of flowers and trees blooming in the springtime, regardless of how many people are watching.

Lesley, Canada

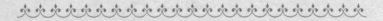

When the recession kicked in, it also brought relief to many people who had been having problems managing their finances. A couple of years ago, my friends and I would have thought nothing of going off to the cinema or a play centre to entertain the kids for the afternoon. Last year was different, so we went to the park instead. We were lucky to be entertained by a child's party that was on just beside us. It was the best day out ever and all it cost was making a few sandwiches and a couple of bags of crisps.

Fran, 27, mum, County Galway

ॐ

I HAVE RECENTLY completely forgotten my Visa PIN number – it's actually fantastic – very few shops will just allow a signature and I have definitely not bought frivolous purchases in the past month! Another thing I'm trying at the moment is to write down everything I spend – from the sneaky morning coffee to petrol in the car. At the end of the month it's a little surprising!

Suzie, sailor, County Dublin

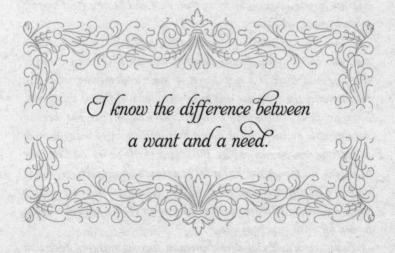

I know the difference between a want and a need.

Financial Independence

Financial independence means being able to support yourself. There is huge pressure on young women to be able to do this when they start to work. For some, they may be starting out with a debt that has taken them through college on top of the challenges of supporting themselves. However, there are also many financially solvent women who are hugely successful living on their own and being a great support to their extended family.

Money is at the root of many of the problems we have in our relationships. In some households, the woman is the only member working and there is a new breed of man undertaking what was traditionally the woman's role at home, which is fine if this works. Some women earn less than their partners and this can put them in a vulnerable position. We've found that this is why so many women suffer from jealousy, insecurity and a lack of self-belief. And the fear of having no money can put a lot of pressure on a marriage. Along with the fear of rejection, the fear of having no money is probably the main reason so many women worry that their husband is going to run off with somebody else.

Some women develop deep depression, anxiety and even addiction because of a marital breakdown and all that goes with it. If your husband has left you for somebody else, you can be eaten up with real rage along with a very genuine fear, a fear of poverty, a fear of not being able to cope.

When it comes to children, our prime fear as women is that we won't be able to provide for them. Unfortunately, money doesn't buy happiness, but freedom is definitely something worth working for.

Being in a couple often means that our incomes are pooled with our loved one. For many women, this is a loving expression of their union with another which may be for life. Marriage and life partnership brings with it a deep and reassuring trust, which is that from now on, our property and our assets can be equally shared. Equally important for many women is the reassurance that within a deep and loving relationship, they will always be able to earn and keep their own money separately. Sharing all of your wealth is a true expression of deep affection and absolute trust – and maintaining your independence is a wise and honourable choice as well. Making sure that you have independent savings and investments isn't a rejection of your life partner – it's a life choice that women are wise to make. The most important thing, the truly independent thing, is to be true to yourself and what you want from your life, your money and your partnership.

Everyone is different in their practices when it comes to money. For Juliet, it's very important to have her own money in her own account, a current account as well as savings. She doesn't like pooling her income just because she's married – she has worked hard to have her own salary and wants to be in control of that. Juliet and her husband both have very different values when it comes to money – she loves to spend and he loves to save – and she knows that if they only had a joint bank account, she'd feel her happy-go-lucky spending was being scrutinised by someone who has a very different attitude to money! But the most important thing is that nobody feels ripped off or hard done by and that they both get to feel independent as well *as making sure the house and children are taken care of and the bills are always paid. After that, her credit card debt is all her own work, and it's up to her to clear it!*

Michelle likes having a joint bank account with her husband – they both contribute to the running of the household and paying for the nice things that they enjoy as a family. It is important to have agreement with each other, as money is one of the biggest causes of marital disputes. The old days where it was men who controlled the finances and gave an allowance to their wives doesn't work any more – in most houses both partners need to be working together inside and outside the home to make the weekly budget balance out. It is time to realise that we need to pull together and be open and honest with each other – in an open relationship there is no 'my money' or 'your money' but only 'our money'. This is another way to prevent disputes about money as a couple. ℒ❥

WE WENT OUT with a couple recently who shared the cost of everything – the dinner, the taxi, the bar bill. Later, she told me that he was spending money on drugs and the only way to control his spending was to ensure that he paid equally for all of the household bills. I felt bad for her but admired her for the way that she was making her marriage work.

Suzanne, 46, beautician, Leeds, England

꙳

A LACK OF FINANCE can prevent women from the freedom to escape dangerous or abusive relationships. It is important to instil in our children, and especially our daughters, the need to be financially independent. It is up to mothers to ensure that their daughters plan for their futures and careers at a young age. We have fun in our house and discuss what our daughters want to be. My youngest daughter has difficulty making up her mind between being a teacher or a hairdresser but she is happy when I tell her that she can be both.

Joan, 38, teacher, County Louth

❧

MY HUSBAND IS dreadful for opening post and keeping records so I put all the bills into my name. It doesn't matter really because we have a joint account and the money comes out in a direct debit. Organising and forward planning is something I am better at than my husband and he recognises this so I take the responsibility. I also do all the hammer-and-nail stuff too – mind you, he is a great cook! Roles have reversed since my parents' time, but what is important is that our house runs well and we both do the jobs that we are good at.

Tanya, 49, receptionist, County Mayo

❧

WHY SHOULD A MAN pay if he is taking me out for dinner if we are both working and earning similar money? This is setting an old-fashioned standard where men felt they were due some sort of reimbursement later for paying. I think women should take responsibility for themselves and set the standard for how they want to be viewed should their relationship develop.

June, 43, artist, England

NEVER SPEND what you haven't got. You can't take it with you, so spend what you do have when you want to.

Keep a cushion handy!

Violet, 39, art technician, Upper Maelstrom, England

Financial independence is ...

... knowing you don't owe or have to borrow from any person or institution (bank, credit cards, loan sharks, husband, parents) and that you do not depend on others for you to live and keep living. In other words, would you end up on the street if you lost your job tomorrow without the help of others?

Kimberly, 35, pre-school teacher, Indiana, USA

... when nobody ever asks you in a concerned voice, 'How much was that?'

Sukie, 31, mum of four, County Dublin

... something you should never relinquish.

Keelin, 38, occupational psychologist, County Dublin

NEVER SPEND all your money ... be a giver and you'll receive in abundance (not the same as throwing your money away though), money is power, and, finally, don't mix business with pleasure.

Jacinta, 35, development and outreach officer, Northern Ireland

I grew up in the Dublin suburbs, and my best friend's mum came from the inner city – they'd done well in life and moved out to the suburbs. One day, she took the two of us aside and said, in her best Dub accent, 'Now girls, I'll tell yous one thing. Men are useful for some things, but you've always got to have your runaway money.' Then she showed us the lining of her curtains, into which she'd sewn stacks of banknotes. We thought it was absolutely hilarious – this lady with her nice suburban curtains and all the banknotes sewn into them!

When I went to England in my marriage, I never thought of it until something happened and I began to think it mightn't work out. I had never forgotten her advice though. I started sewing money into the curtains myself. I was very glad of it the day I left. I wouldn't have been able to leave without it.

My friend's mum and her husband are still married – they'll be together till they die!

I'm remarried now to a wonderful man and we are very happy. I still keep my runaway money though, and he knows about it too. It's in the bank now.

Linda, florist, County Dublin

❧

Money doesn't matter – it's the lack of it that causes all the trouble.

Anonymous

❧

What's my most valuable possession? My freedom – it's priceless.

Saniya, interior architect, Pakistan

*I will spend and share
my money with whomever I choose,
whenever I choose, but the choice
will always be mine.*

Gratitude –
bringing more into your life

Giving and receiving are very important parts of what we do as women – in friendships, in love, in motherhood. But very often, the gifts we have are nothing that anyone in particular has given us. Our real wealth is often something we have created ourselves. Our ability to work, to earn money, to save, to invest, our wisdom with the skills that we have means that we can reward ourselves. Being grateful for the skills and gifts that we have been given by nature is a vitally important way of bringing more success and financial freedom into our lives. If we don't recognise and acknowledge our skills, we will never have the wisdom to exploit them. If we don't realise where our talents lie, we won't have the ability to use them to gain wealth.

Being grateful for the money we've earned will bring a positive attitude to that wealth. We can feel proud of our ability to earn, grateful for the power that our money brings to us to make choices, and wise in our decision to save, invest and spend that money so that it brings us greater freedom and increases our wealth.

Juliet's friend Lynnette is very practical. Her house is minimalist and she's got great taste. When someone gave her a present she didn't like (a mug that was really very ugly), she immediately put it aside for the charity shop collection. Juliet was surprised – it seemed slightly ungrateful. But Lynette said to her, 'Someone else will really enjoy this and it doesn't suit my house at all.' And Juliet thought she had a point. How many times have you been in someone's house and they've pointed out something they hate that they are keeping just because it was a gift? That's real ingratitude! Now, whenever we give someone a present, we try to choose something that they can pass on themselves if they don't like it. And we don't keep presents we don't like – we give them away immediately to someone who will like them. We think gifts are made to be passed on. This saves money, and someone will always be grateful for a gift we didn't need. ☙

IT IS DIFFICULT to be unhappy and grateful at the same time.

Frieda, 38, secondary school teacher, County Dublin

꩜

GRATITUDE AND HAPPINESS are inextricably linked – to be happy you must have an attitude of gratitude. Grateful for the air we breathe, the earth we walk on, the food we have, the family and friends and love in our lives, no matter what state it's in, there are always those way worse off.

Ali, 34, County Cork

꩜

IT COSTS NOTHING to say thank you and really mean it – when someone says it to you, it lifts the spirits. My next-door neighbour is extremely generous – she's also very rich because she is constantly giving from her heart. It's no wonder her business isn't affected by the recession like so many others.

Kim, 35, IT consultant, County Dublin

※

LACK OF GRATITUDE and giving can make us feel very unappreciated – not a nice feeling to have when you have a family, though probably unintentional most of the time.

Barbara, 41, homemaker, County Dublin

※

I FIND THAT IF I give to a charity box outside the supermarket or store – even if I am a bit short – something wonderful happens shortly afterwards. It's like the cosmic energy created from giving is returned to you in some other way that you least expect.

Leona, 43, civil servant, Brighton

※

I LOVE TO TRAVEL and am always amazed when I go to Third World countries how happy the faces of the people are. The kids wear big smiles and may only have a ball made of string or a stick to play with.

Lucille, 31, air steward, France

GRATITUDE IS an important part of my day. The first thing I do in the morning is say thank you to the universe. I'm alive so that's a good start. I try to remind myself to continue to do this as my day unfolds, and if I get grumpy or curse at a driver who pulls out in front of me on the road, I find my day starts to take a downward slide. It's all about being in a positive zone and appreciating the good things. The happier I am, the better my day will be – the better my attitude will be towards those that I meet and vice versa!

Gaye, printer, 47, County Kildare

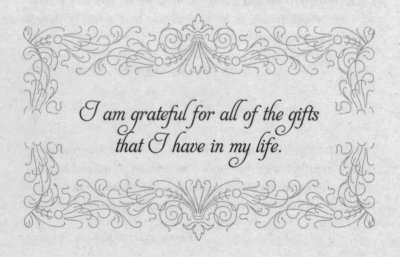

I am grateful for all of the gifts that I have in my life.

Giving money away

Women's affinity for relationships means that we are natural givers. We have a natural tendency to empathise – the average charity donor is a woman aged between fifty and seventy, and women give away twice as much of their personal income towards causes when compared with men. Women give because of strong feelings about a cause. We like to give in a 'hands-on' way – to beggars in the street, to a local community effort, to a fundraiser in a child's school, to an organised charity that has touched our hearts. Most voluntary work in the community is done by women. From school bake sales to large-scale international NGOs, women have always organised to give to others whom we see in need. We collaborate to ensure that wealth is distributed, that suffering is eliminated, that injustice is addressed. Giving to others brings great celebration and joy – not just to the recipient of the gift, but to the women who have given it.

There are many female philanthropists in history who have given their labour and their money to help the weak, the poor, the vulnerable, and women continue to be a force for change by giving our time and our money wherever it is needed. Making time to give to others is one of the most satisfying and life-affirming things that we can do. What we gain by giving is the deep knowledge of the real *change that our giving can make to the lives of others, and ultimately to ourselves.*

I'M WRITING THIS in my lounge-room in Australia in late January 2010, watching the news from Haiti, where over 100,000 people have died in the horrendous earthquake which has devastated their country. The screen shifts to an area of Port-au-Prince where supplies are available, but a woman talking to the camera shrugs her shoulders and says – 'but we have no money – we cannot pay for this food – we must wait and hope'.

Money is the only key to enable us to acquire and fairly distribute the means of survival for the disempowered families, those women and children of the world who do not have the wherewithal and skills to survive disaster. Surely we who are educated, trained, self-confident and secure in our ability to overcome such hardship have an eternal obligation to share our knowledge and resources to promote the well-being of our less fortunate cousins?

Rachel, 42, nurse, Perth, Australia

Women give differently to men – they plan differently and have different reasons for giving. Be true to yourself. Generosity has a boomerang effect, it always comes right back at you.

Mary, author, County Cork

WHAT WOMEN KNOW

I'D LIKE TO SEE MONEY go towards benefiting the teenage children of families who are not 'socially deprived'. My personal dream if I ever won the EuroMillions would be to set up a place where twelve- to seventeen-year-olds could come to socialise off the streets but moderately supervised, a place with a library and possibly a tutor if they wanted a place to study (coming from a large family, I always lacked the peace and quiet to get my homework done). A café/tuck shop, just something to do, but a place that doesn't exclude those children whose parents are both working. A total pipe dream, but it's what I'd love to do.

Angela, 33, stay-at-home mum, Omagh, Northern Ireland

❧

I WOULD LIKE TO HELP children in care, particularly to improve their access to good education, and would also like to include stroke foundations – some young stroke victims require lifetime support, and respite care or holidays would be such a blessing for them and their families.

Hilda, 53, bank clerk, Canberra, Australia

❧

GIVING TIME AND EXPERTISE, not only avoids giving money to administrate a charity but also encourages more people to volunteer. When I get approached on the street by charity fundraisers I always tell them that I give my time, which is chargeable at so much an hour! Also, if more people volunteered for charity work, then donations would go more directly to the cause, as the charity wouldn't need so many paid workers.

Jacqueline, 48, chief executive, Manchester, England

Yes, we should give what help we can to people in crisis but we should also be examining the reasons behind such need for charity. People are forced to fundraise for operations for their sick children, specialised education for their autistic children, housing for the homeless and many more things which should be basic human rights in a civilised society. In the short term, donations of time and cash benefit those in urgent need. In the long term, rectifying the inequities would banish the need for donations. It can be done. We are, after all, 50 per cent of the electorate.

Education is the key. Whether it's teaching people in a developing country how to increase crop yields or purify their water, raising public awareness on issues like domestic violence or being more proactive in changing the things we see as unfair, we can all have an input in making the world a better place in which to live. But that's a long-term goal and no help to someone in immediate need. That's why I think there has to be aid in the form of donations now but a longer-term plan to restore dignity and independence to those who are in need.

Carrie, 32, nurse, Nenagh, County Tipperary

Do try this at home:

Circle of giving. Lots of women are members of book clubs, bridge clubs or knitting groups – why not start a circle of giving? This works on the same principle.

Get a group of like-minded friends together with an interest in giving.

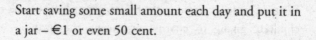

Start saving some small amount each day and put it in a jar – €1 or even 50 cent.

At the end of a month or six weeks, meet your circle and pool the money you have saved.

Now plan how you would like to spend it. Everyone gets a turn each month to nominate a cause or charity that they believe in or care about.

You will feel so good when it's the turn of your charity, and you will get to learn about other charities too.

This also works really well at Christmas in the workplace or in a large family instead of Kris Kindle – and it's much more fun than getting another scented candle.

My godmother is the most amazing, generous person I've ever known. Her whole house has always been geared towards her friends and visitors – always cosy with a welcoming fire, and tons of books to read when you go to stay. She's always lived on a very low budget but has been incredibly generous with her family and friends; if you admire a painting on her wall, she'd wrap it up and give it to you as a wedding present. If you were to remark on a lovely cardigan she was wearing, she'd give it to you for Christmas! I think that what I've learned most from her is that having nice things is only really a pleasure when you can share them with friends: the best thing about having money is when you get to give it to people you love.

Juliet

WHEN I'M DONE running the house, giving birth to and raising the children, giving to charity, organising the birthday, Christmas cards/pressies, gardening, looking after the family, I'll go and save the world.

Lonisa, 29, marketing executive, County Cork

No matter how small my budget, I will always give what I can to those less fortunate than me and I will save some money that I will spend just on myself.

In Money

I am grateful for ...

Love

*L*ove – the most powerful human emotion that there is. Falling in love is more than just a very deep level of affection – something happens to our brains when we 'fall' for somebody. We lose rationality. We devote ourselves beyond reason! Research by anthropologists into what humans are prepared to do in the name of love reveals that when we are in love, we will make incredible sacrifices for our loved one. We put our loved one's concerns and welfare before our own. They occupy our minds completely. We are more concerned about their feelings, their ideas, motivations, dreams, hopes and ambitions than we are with our own. No wonder love has been thought to make us insane!

Yet who would reject the opportunity to fall in love? Because despite the fact that we make all sorts of seemingly irrational decisions, we disregard our own well-being and we are prepared to make life-changing choices, all in the name of our loved one. The joy that these experiences bring can't be compared with any other happiness in life.

Lovers come and go – and possibly the most eternal love of all is the love that is unrequited. But one thing's for sure – women hold deep levels of affection for their mates. We don't give up easily. We forgive, we trust and we love and we want to keep on loving, despite the odds. Loving one partner at a time is what most of us do naturally – but life can throw us some very tricky situations that we aren't always prepared for. Loving more than one partner at the same time is a fact of life for many women – and living through the pain of rejection and infidelity can be hard on both sides.

As we approach the later years of life, most of us will become widows – a salutary thought for women everywhere who are destined by biology to out-live men. For many women, this is a time of loneliness, something to fear. Perhaps for others it's a natural part of the cycle of life, and we need to remind ourselves that the maturity and pleasure in our own company that we find in middle age is an essential preparation for a time when we will be free and single once again.

The single life

Being single is the best fun you'll ever have – and the worst. Single women are powerful – so powerful that they terrify their married friends! The beauty of singlehood is that we have such great friends, our friends are our family. Being single means that we are free to flirt, that our time is our own, that our money and our space are all about us – we are the envy of our married friends! But life doesn't always treat single women with the respect they deserve. The stigma of loneliness can make us uncomfortable about being single throughout life. It is important not to equate singlehood with rejection. Being with a companion can be a blessing, but no relationship is perfect and our experience of talking to hundreds of women is that married women spend just as much time fantasising about being single as single women do about being married! Being single becomes easier the older we become, because with singlehood comes great freedom and empowerment to be the woman that we choose to be. ✍

I AM A BIG BELIEVER in living alone before getting married. I lived alone for about ten years before getting married (at age thirty-eight). I loved it! Don't get me wrong, I love my husband and we get along great together, but I know I'll never be afraid of living alone again. It was one of the most empowering times of my life.

Hannah, 45, New Jersey, USA

🐝

JUST OVER A MONTH AGO, I was getting very down on myself for having been single for so long – at the age of twenty-four I've been single for nearly four years and am constantly surrounded by couples. I never seemed to meet anyone, and if I did, they'd end up being the same loser bloke who only wanted one thing. If someone was to ask me, 'Why have you been single for so long?', my answer would have been, 'Because guys aren't interested in me/I have no luck with men/I'm just not attractive to the opposite sex.'

Recently, I spent three weeks in Thailand travelling with a friend. It was a complete eye-opener – an amazing experience – I gained the confidence to speak to everyone I met, made lots of friends and learned to not be shy with the opposite sex – people liked me because I was friendly, open to new experiences and approachable. One of the guys I made friends with had feelings for me, although he didn't tell me directly, but I chose not to act upon it because I was having such a good time and didn't want to break the dynamic of the group. He asked me, 'So tell me, why have you been single for so long?' And then it hit me – here I was with a guy I liked but didn't want to evolve our friendship any further than it was because I was enjoying my time with him as it stood. I answered, 'You know what? It's because I choose to be. I haven't found anyone I've wanted to share my life pattern with enough to undergo a relationship. I'm perfectly happy in my own company and until the right one comes along I'm happy to stay that way for as long as it takes!'

The thing I hadn't realised was that you make a lot more decisions when it comes to relationships than you think you do – it's just convention that leads you to believe otherwise. And if you have been single for a while and think you're unattractive and not approachable – think again, it's quite the opposite – you are in fact a strong, stable, independent person who is so happy with yourself that you'd rather be by yourself than settle for something second rate.

Another thing I think is definitely worth mentioning though, something my friend always tells me: we're here for a good time, not for a long time. So never waste an opportunity!

Emily, 24, just starting her life

❧

OH MY! I love being single again … I loved it the first time and now I sit in the luxury of peace. I'm more skint, rushed off my feet and *so* much happier than ever. I love every second of every day … even when I am unplugging a sink or the loo, right down to digging the garden (well, I will when I get the urge) and to decorating every room. It's wonderful, brilliant and so exciting. I could not express how much I love it and the thought of another so-called adult sharing it makes my blood boil. I am the happiest I have ever been.

SuzDJK, 45, house-type person, Leamington Spa, England

❧

AFTER A TWELVE-YEAR MARRIAGE (in which I should point out that I felt very lonely in a different sense, for we can be lonely when in a relationship, not just when one ends) which ended when I was thirty-three, I was both delighted and scared to be single again. To be honest, I hadn't been single since my teens. I thought it would only be for a couple of years, though, then I'd be married again, so I should enjoy this 'single time' to the max. But as the first year drew into a second, I found that this freedom was tainted. I was lonely.

I realise now that I didn't even know who I was at that time: the real me, the me I had become.

I kept telling myself that I wouldn't be alone for much longer.

Five years have passed now and, finally, I am content being single. I have discovered who I am and I like me. It's not so bad being on my own after all! It took some time to get used to it, though! I have a loving home with my two young boys, a good job (albeit stressful and I could do with having another income coming in) and I have a good network of friends and a very close family. Now that I am used to the loneliness/freedom/bloody hard slog (of being the sole adult to pay for and run a home, having two wee kids and elderly parents to care for), whatever you want to call it, the thought of having a man back into my/our lives is now the scary thought! When, or even if, he comes along (I've stopped presuming that he will), I think it will take me another five years to readjust again! But if he's the right man, I am sure we'll be just fine. You see, a good relationship gives enough trust and respect to allow a degree of freedom, so being with someone shouldn't be at the detriment of 'freedom'. I believe you can have both.

I still hope that I will one day have a lifelong partner, but in the meantime, I am not going to mope about waiting for that day. I will cherish the single freedom I have, however lonely it gets sometimes. It makes me appreciate what I have (kids still at home and parents still 'going'!). Though lonely, I am not alone.

This whole thing has made me think forward to the older generation who find themselves truly alone. I hope it has made me more compassionate and understanding towards them.

Brenda, teacher, Scotland

*I am happy to be single and
enjoying my life with me!*

The habits of men

Some women carry around preconceived opinions about men and generalise on their bad points. We, however, are not afraid to admit that we love the opposite sex! It's in our nature as women to complicate issues sometimes instead of realising the simple way that men view the same issues. Michelle remembers when she was younger at certain romantic times with a boyfriend – wondering how he felt and what he thought of her and where they would be going in their relationship. Now, after many relationships and being married for ten years, she realises that he was probably just thinking about a match he had seen on the TV or feeling peckish and thinking about making a sandwich! What both of us wish is that we could talk to our younger selves and tell her to give men a break – but that is all part of the learning that women go through in the process of falling in love and finding a partner. Now that Michelle has a son of her own, she can see the way he views things so differently to her daughter.

We feel it is our duty to tell all young women out there to relax. Get in touch with yourself and get to know who you are first – you won't be ready to share yourself until you truly love and respect and know yourself. Stop focusing on the other person – especially if it's a man – as they have their own processing to do and the chances are that they will be much older than you before they realise that they have to do it!

Juliet has had two husbands and two daughters, so her house is one that's always been full of women – with just one outnumbered man! It can be difficult for men to adjust to a female way of living, and perhaps both genders need their own space to co-exist happily … sometimes women expect men to understand their ways of thinking, but perhaps men operate differently. Perhaps what women should remember is that we don't need to be everything to the man in our lives. It's important sometimes to just let men be and realise that they are different to us. Men need to have other friends, besides their wives, who will help them find the car keys! 🌿

HAVE YOU NOTICED that men can't find a sock in a drawer but can spot a blonde at 50 metres? They are programmed to see differently than women, literally! My mum told me very early on in life that you can't really change someone, particularly a man. You might just be able to influence them a weeny, teeny bit, but that's it! So why has it taken me till I'm fifty to believe her?

Lesley, 51, musician, County Dublin

Men are very different to women and the sooner women realise this, the better. One of the first occasions that I truly realised this was on my twenty-first birthday. I had been dating my boyfriend for four months! He was an accountant and very practically minded and while I had been chatting to my girlfriends and wondering if I would be getting jewellery or perfume, he had something else in mind. He produced a white radio alarm clock – I was devastated. I remember distinctly at my party going outside to cry and a few of my close friends consoling me.

I laugh when I think now about the way my young brain worked. My boyfriend had put a lot of thought into what I needed and, as he told me later, had written a list of things about me and I did find it difficult to get up in the morning. Ironically, I still have this clock – it is over twenty years old and now a dirty cream colour. It's not for sentiment that I keep it, but because it still works, and as it was a very good-quality appliance, it has stood the test of time design-wise. My boyfriend was obviously very good at his job! So because a guy's brain works differently, we should sometimes just accept it and see the merits of their different point of view. Our relationship didn't last, but the thought he put into my present meant that the clock has stood the test of time.

Michelle

❧

MY FRIEND DERMOT gave me a strong word of advice that he wanted to pass on to the women in this book: if a man says he can't multitask, he can. Take note, girls!

Linda, 43, mum, County Dublin

❧

MOST MEN can resist anything except temptation.

Carol, 67, retired, County Dublin

❧

WHEN GUYS GO ON TOUR they feel they have a pass to do whatever they shouldn't, but here's another thought – women do it too! When you are away from home with a group, you don't have the same moral compass!

Rugby wife, 45, County Cork

᷈

MEN NEVER, EVER CAN SEE what they are looking for in the fridge. They have problems with scanning and peripheral vision. This has more to do with the absence of peripheral vision than laziness. Women can scan a huge area in seconds – especially a room of beautiful women and spot in an instant which one her husband is looking at!

Nina, 38, psychologist, Manchester, England

᷈

MEN BELIEVE THAT they are the only ones who are qualified to use the remote control, but only pause for ten seconds as they flick through the channels. On the other hand, when you are feeling down, there is nothing better than an unasked for hug from them … it evens out the remote control situation for a day anyway!

Ruth, mum, County Clare

᷈

I was very cross with my husband once (for hanging the clothes on the line the wrong way), so he sent me a text message that read: 'You can change a man: if he's still in nappies.' I laughed so much I forgave him everything!

Juliet

I WANT EVERY WOMAN to know that you should never let your insecurities get the better of you, because that's how men get control.

Jessica, 18, student, County Dublin

Do try this at home:

If birthdays or anniversaries are important to you, then choose a date for your wedding that your partner will remember – a week after his birthday – the summer solstice – Halloween!

I'M FASCINATED BY WOMEN giving out about men not putting down the toilet seat after they have been for a wee. It may be a rational way of thinking about it, but they had to touch it to lift it in the first place – and isn't it considerate that they did lift it instead of peeing on it? And if they put it down, then they are the only ones who have to touch it, whereas if a woman puts it down each person is only touching it once!

Martha, 47, hippy, County Waterford

☙

A SON IS A THREAT for a man – especially his eldest. He may also treat him better then younger siblings, but there is always a fear that one day he will be conquered by him.

Kim, 48, photographer, County Louth

IF YOUR HUSBAND IS a good cook – cherish him. However, as is the case with a lot of master chefs, they don't cook economically with the kitchen equipment, preferring to use everything in the kitchen – get them to wash when they do cook and it will sort it out.

Kathleen, 37, waitress, County Dublin

🐝

IF MEN PURSUE EVENTS that benefit themselves, then please explain why he also forgets that he has planned to play golf, attend a stag and other such male-bonding events. It's a lack of function on one side of the brain if you ask me.

More to the point – have you ever seen your husband miss an important business appointment? Oh no, those are in the diary, but any social engagements and sure, that's what the missus is for! My husband rings me to see what he has on at the weekend!

Sarah, 37, senior project manager, County Dublin

🐝

WOMEN INSTINCTIVELY place a high value on activities that promote social and family cohesiveness, whereas men pursue events that benefit themselves, whether watching or playing a match, horse race, golf or doing business. It's all the same to them, a chance to identify and be part of a competition-based activity. It's all about winning, apparently.

Emma, 45, unemployed architect, Wales

I KNOW MORE PEOPLE that are married on or near their hubby's birthday so he will remember!

Susan, 38, manager sharehold services, County Dublin

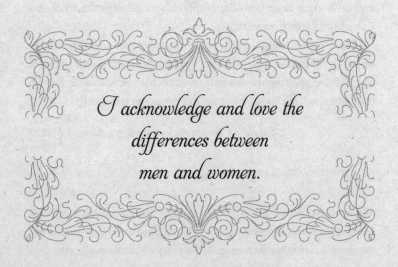

WE GOT MARRIED on my husband's thirtieth birthday. He can't forget that date!

Lisa, 42, hairdresser, County Dublin

> *I acknowledge and love the differences between men and women.*

Ways to find your lover

We all carry an inherent need to love and be loved and share our lives with that someone special. There are no hard or fast rules here, and everyone has a different journey of discovery to make. Many of us are looking for a person to co-parent the children we want. Others are seeking a friend, someone to share our interests, a collaborator, a comrade. Most of us are looking for all of the above — and with stunning good looks and a generous income too ... Mr or Ms Perfect probably doesn't exist and we would be foolish to think that 'holding out' for a prescription that we've concocted of the perfect partner is going to make us happy.

Meeting your soulmate isn't something you can always plan for. Arranged marriages sometimes work very well — but not many women are prepared to ask their parents to select a partner for them! In the randomness of humanity, and in all the ways in which we get to meet possible men, what are the chances of our finding someone who ticks every single box in our Prince Charming list?

What we have both realised from having loved different men and married two (each!) is that women change all the time. The kind of man we loved in our twenties is not the kind of man that we might love today. The boy we thought so handsome, so exciting, so irresistible that we would have done anything to be with him in our teens is now, in his *forties, someone pretty boring that we have nothing in common with.*

Being true to what you want in life is the most important part of any relationship. If you are lucky enough to find someone who wants to share your journey with you, tread joyfully! And remember that most women we spoke to told us that they met their beloved life partner when they least expected to meet anyone at all. Love is something that most of us find impossible to plan, but the most important thing is to invite affection and love into your life by showing the affection you are capable of. ❧

I THINK THE INTERNET will be the new way to meet. My son met his wife on a social site and they are a wonderful match. You know in the old days people used to use the matchmaker in the Irish countryside and he often came up with a good prospective partner. It was better planning than the efforts of young girls today who hang around bars and clubs trying to find Mr Right.

Bearna, 62, civil servant, County Dublin

❧

MY SISTER INTRODUCED US. That was a shocker in itself since she and I have exactly the opposite taste in men. However, this time she was right. Eight and a half years later and we're still perfect for each other.

Kathleen, 43, TV producer, Canada

❧

IF YOUR TRUE DESIRE is to find someone, a partner, a lover – stop looking. Spend time on you, and being the best person you can be. It is strangely at that time that opportunities present themselves.

Sammy, law student, Canada

❧

I MET IARLA in the Clarence Bar in Dublin. I was supposed to get the bus that stops near there – was even about to step on it – but my pal and I decided to grab a quick pint before the next bus. Iarla was having a drink with two of his brothers. He tells me he was like a man possessed when I walked in. Had to meet me, he says. He spotted my pal, who he happened to know from work years back, and made a beeline for us. During the next two pints, I remember he introduced me to a friend as the woman he was going to marry. Man of his word, my Iarla!

Eimear, 39, journalist, County Kilkenny

❧

I WAS VERY SLOW to try internet dating until my friend set me up with a blind date – she had put all of my details on a site and came up with a match. When she showed me the picture of the guy that responded, I was a bit nervous that the whole thing was a prank. It wasn't! He was a really cute guy and genuinely nice. We liked each other and dated a few times. There weren't any fireworks or anything, but we had good fun and even though we aren't dating any more we are still friends and meet up sometimes when we are at a loose end.

Carmen, 39, Liverpool, England

THE BEST WAY to catch a man is to give him a very long leash. When you fall in love with him, you have to realise he is not a possession. If things don't work out in love set him free – if he comes back he's yours, and if not, he was never meant to be!

Margaret, 60+, counsellor, County Wexford

🐝

I MET MY HUSBAND online. It was accidental, I wasn't on a dating site or looking for love. I was working as a web designer at the time and waiting for a site to upload (dial-up connection, before broadband). To pass time, I went into a chat room and got speaking to him and ended up chatting until the early hours of the morning. I knew that night that I would marry him! We spoke on the phone the next day and met in real life the day after. We've been together for ten years now, married for eight and have three kids together (plus my two from a previous marriage).

Madeleine, 38, self-employed, Hampshire, England

🐝

IT NEVER CEASES TO AMAZE ME when I hear single women in their thirties or forties complain that they can't meet a man. Then you ask them where they are going to meet them. If you are relying on pubs or nightclubs, forget it. Think practically – increase your odds. Join a club or night class which is top heavy with men – sailing clubs, golf clubs or take a class in engine repair. It's a no-brainer!

Laura, 38, scientist, County Galway

If you have an interest, go and do it and participate in it with joy and then the men who also enjoy your interest will find you. Always be true to yourself and once you are strong the universe will provide for you.

Mira, 38, interior designer, County Dublin

❧

I met my hubby online; we were on a forum together and I commented on a post of his. He emailed me on the Friday, by the Monday I'd asked him to marry me. We met in real life two weeks later and there was no doubt that we were meant for each other. We'll celebrate our sixth wedding anniversary in August – he is utterly and totally my soulmate and I am his. And I was thirty-six, he was thirty-nine, so we're not kids who didn't have a clue – we were just ready to meet the right person and we did. We were totally honest with each from the first second and it just felt like we'd always known each other. It was fate, we were destined to meet.

Honey, web surfer, County Dublin

❧

I know some very successful stories from the internet! One friend is engaged and expecting twins, and he is one of the nicest men I've ever met. Another person I know was widowed young and is now so happy with his partner of three years. And another girl I know never has to sit in on a Friday or Saturday night and enjoys herself immensely flitting around Dublin on dates, thinking maybe one day one of them will be her Prince Charming but she's happy kissing the frogs along the way to find him!

Ciara, 39, airline employee, County Dublin

శ్రీ

ALWAYS REMAIN A TINY BIT ALOOF – if you are too needy with any-body you will eventually push them away. Be confident of yourself!

Rose, 63, grandmother extraordinaire, County Dublin

శ్రీ

I WAS WALKING THROUGH Temple Bar the other night with my married friend – we are both over forty and were discussing a time when we were in our early twenties and scared that we would never find Mr Right. We concluded that if we could sit our twenty-year-old selves down, we would tell then to relax and be confident. That is the key to finding yourself and someone to share your life with.

Trudy, 41, receptionist, County Dublin

శ్రీ

YOU MIGHT NOT particularly like the guy that you are dating, but as my aunt always said, you never know who you'll meet in the process. As it happens, I did meet my husband that way, dating one of his friends. Wise words.

Suzie, 34, teacher, County Dublin

IN A DESPERATE ATTEMPT to save our relationship, a boyfriend once asked me to marry him. Everyone around me seemed to be tying the knot and, in a moment of madness, I actually considered his offer for about fifteen minutes. In dire need of some practical advice, and putting aside the fact that she couldn't stand the guy, I went over to my mother's house and delivered the good news. Taking my hand, she led me to the kitchen table and gave me a pitiful look. 'Sweetheart,' she started, 'life is very short. It comes and goes in the blink of an eye. That's the way it's supposed to be. But,' she continued with a grave expression, 'it's very bloody long if you pick the wrong person to spend it with.' Two years later, I met my husband and today I find myself wondering where on earth the time has gone.

Ger, novelist, Shankill, County Dublin

❦

IN MY TWENTIES, I had many relationships that lasted between one and two years. I spent most of this time travelling and doing things that my boyfriends wanted to do and not what I actually wanted. I was having experiences that I only realised afterwards I didn't want to have. Now I have turned forty and have the confidence to do what makes me feel happy.

Dee, 40, artist, County Cork

I am a magnet and attract the positive energy from a like-minded mate.

Falling in love

From the time we are little girls, many of us are constantly searching for our one true love. Well how about this for a proposition – what if there isn't just one? What if there are hundreds of people you have met in your life all eligible to be your one true love? Love is a wonderful feeling that is often confused as being something we get from someone else. A great idea – a bit like going to a fast-food joint and getting a fix when you are hungry. It will fill you up for a short while or provide comfort on your way home from the pub after one too many, but to really feel good after eating, you need to put good food in your mouth.

The real secret of love is to start with yourself. It's simple really and when you give yourself the right to love yourself, you will be amazed how many other people will start to love you too. Being dependent on someone else to provide you with love is putting a terrible burden on that person. Here is another suggestion – if everyone loved themselves truly, then they would not feel the need to be jealous of or hurtful towards others because they would be content with themselves. It's a good place to start! ✍

IT'S ALL ABOUT CHEMISTRY – if that isn't right at the beginning of a relationship, it doesn't matter how much you have going for you as a couple – it will never be right. We are put together with a partner to love and be loved and making love is one of the most important parts of being a couple. It's a fact that the cause of marriage break-ups are put down to one of two things – sex or money!

Barbara, 57, counsellor, London, England

BOTH OF MY GRANDPARENTS were not in the best of health, my grandfather living in a hospice, dying of cancer. My gran was also staying there, waiting for a place in a nursing home. It was a few days before my granddad's eightieth birthday and he kept saying that he was not going to be around to celebrate it, he would be meeting with St Peter then.

They decided to throw a small surprise party for him and first got my gran made over. Her hair was done, make-up put on and a new dress for the occasion. She was wheeled in to his room and Granddad said, 'My God, Cathy, you are every bit as beautiful as the day we married. And I still love you as much.' As you can imagine, there wasn't a dry eye in the place. That night, he passed away in his sleep. After sixty years of marriage, twenty-one children (five sadly passed away as babies), I've no idea of how many grand-children or great-grandchildren there are, that had to be the most wonderful thing to hear. My gran lived for another eighteen months.

Emma, 34, printer, County Longford

I MET MY HUSBAND in 1990 at a party in Seabright, New Jersey. He had long enough hair and a couple of tattoos, which I wasn't into. A couple of weeks later, he stopped by my sister's house so we could give him advice on places to visit in Ireland. After he left that evening, my sister asked me about him and my answer was, 'He's a nice guy, but not my type.'

A few months later, he came down to a BBQ in my sister's place, his hair cut, and looked cute. He told me that he had to go into hospital to have a lump on his neck tested. I said I'd visit him. I went into the hospital at 2 p.m. and stayed till 8 p.m. I went home and told Miriam that I must be a sick person because as he was sitting in the bed wearing a terrible pair of PJs his dad had bought him and with loads of tubes hooked up to him, all I could think about was, I wonder what he kisses like! Two weeks later, he came out of hospital and cooked me dinner one Friday night. After dinner, we lay on the couch watching TV and he told me he thought he was falling in love with me and I told him I felt the same way.

Long story short, we got engaged on 25 December (he proposed in front of my family over here). We got married on 25 June 1993. I guess the best way to describe Paul's feelings at the time were when his best man at the wedding made a comment in his speech that when Paul was going though the radiation for the cancer, Dave went to visit him. He asked Paul about the cancer and Paul's answer was, 'Cancer smancer, I don't care. I'm in love!'

Ruth, 45, special needs assistant and author, County Clare

FALLING IN LOVE is kind of like the feeling you get on a sleepover with your best ever friend when you are awake in the middle of the night and everyone's asleep and everything is so fun and magical and amazing and extra special. When I was falling in love with my fiancé, we both felt like this and also like being in a bubble – we were in the bubble together and it was amazing, like nothing could hurt us or bother us or get between us. I remember I felt like I was out of the bubble before him and he was put out by this, but we're still deeply in love and it still feels cosy and exciting and safe.

Rebecca, 32, teacher, Bolton, England

๕ঠ

WHEN YOU CAN hardly bring yourself to look at him, when every breath in your body rushes from you like a roar, when every touch feels like a burn, when every love song you hear relates directly to you, when a kiss takes your breath away, when you still can't wait for him to come home after a long day at work, when you realise this is the man I want to be my baby's daddy.

Margaret, 36, almost a first-time mum, County Donegal

๕ঠ

I FELL IN LOVE with my husband twice. The first time when I was seventeen and the second twenty years later – we had broken up and found each other later on in life. It's funny because I can't tell you when I fell in love with him, but I do remember the exact moments when I knew he was in love with me. Both times, when I did fall in love with him, it physically consumed me, it was like I could feel him in my soul and I really did feel like one with him. I have been in love with two other men during those twenty years and it never felt like it did with my husband. I really believe our souls found each other and we were meant to be. Next to my father, he is the best example of a man I have ever known, and I love how he loves me.

Hannah, 45, New Jersey, USA

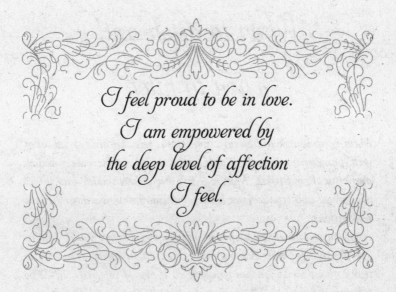

*I feel proud to be in love.
I am empowered by
the deep level of affection
I feel.*

When to ditch and
when to hitch

Making up your mind about a significant relationship takes a lot of skill! Some women make a pros and cons list, others take pot luck and cross their fingers. Marriage is a big commitment, but if you are careful and true to yourself, it's a decision that you don't have to make alone.

Be sure of what you want out of a marriage before you go into it. Pre-nuptial agreements shouldn't be just about assets. You need to think about what you are going to do if one of you gets sick. Who controls the money? Who will look after the children? What if your career doesn't work out? What if your career takes the marriage in a different direction? We can't plan for every eventuality, but most women we talked to told us that their marriages fell apart when children arrived. This is a very sad fact, because children are often the main reason we get married in the first place.

You can never be 100 per cent sure that any relationship will last – but trust your instincts, trust your heart, and most of all, trust your ability to love and be loved.

Getting dumped can be horribly painful, but having to dump someone else isn't any better – if anything, it's probably worse. It's important to let go of guilt and to have a plan for what you are going to do after a relationship. The end of a relationship doesn't mean the end of your self-esteem, your beauty, your intelligence or your ability to be loving and warm-hearted. We need to let people go and make sure that we don't lose our sense of identity when we've lost a love. And don't forget that losing a man means that you're free now to meet someone new. In every crisis, there's always an opportunity. ✍

IF YOU CAN'T IMAGINE living without him in ten years, consider marrying him. If you can't imagine living with him in ten years, lose him! Dead easy.

TW, County Cork

🐝

'PERSEVERANCE IS THE KEY to a good relationship. In other words: hold your nerve.

Jean, poet, County Kildare

🐝

I PROPOSED to my husband by fax. He kept me waiting for two days and then accepted by fax. I have both documents still, yellowing but still legible. Can the internet be quite as romantic?

Mary Ethna, 52, public health physician, Belgrade, Serbia

> ## When in doubt: the What Women Know hitch or ditch list of essentials in a man
>
> Make sure your man has genuine friends – ones that he can talk to when things go wrong – not just guys for playing football with.
>
> Make sure he likes women – not just page three girls. He must genuinely respect and admire women everywhere.
>
> Make sure he understands that love equals responsibility. Children, bills, anxieties and dreams all need to be shared.
>
> Make sure you have the same attitude to sex, money and children.
>
> Make sure he is passionate about something – not just you!

SHORTLY AFTER YOU START dating a guy that you really like, be sure to tell him that you have no desire to get married – he will immediately see you as marriage material. However, if you want to ditch him, start looking at engagement rings straight away!

Linda, 52, marketing consultant, County Leitrim

❧

WHEN I CAME SECOND to everything he did, that's when I knew it was time for him to go.

Angela, 39, single mum, County Longford

WHEN A GIRL OR MAN can't be bothered to have a tiff any more …
you just know it's over!

Valerie, author, County Kildare

✄

I had an auntie who was always saying, 'Never marry a mean man.' It stuck with me like a mantra and when a boyfriend proposed to me I kept thinking of my aunt's advice. My boyfriend was very exciting, ambitious, gifted, great fun – but I eventually turned him down and married someone less exciting but very, very kind.

Meanness isn't just about not spending enough money, either. Some men will shower you with flowers and chocolates but they can be possessive and jealous, they want to own you. The gifts are a way of maintaining your loyalty. Sometimes, a generous gift can be about control and owner-ship. My maiden aunt never got married though!

Juliet

✄

WHENEVER I GET DUMPED by a guy, the first thing I do is delete his number from my phone. It's really empowering and the wonderful thing is that if he texts, you genuinely have to ask, 'Who is this?' It's really empowering and helps you take back your dignity. He might be a bit shocked at how quickly you have got over him and beg you to come back – then it's up to you!

Christina, 26, secretary, County Dublin

When I was trying to get over an old boyfriend, a colleague in work gave me some great advice. She told me to make a time in the day to think about him and allow myself ten minutes to sob my heart out. She said I could pick a time later in the evening to do the same. I became preoccupied with counting the hours and minutes until I could do this and not thinking about him. Also I found when the time came to think about him, I didn't necessarily want to cry. After a couple of weeks, I was missing the daily time because I was too busy doing my work, etc. Eventually, I didn't want to think about him at all. Ironically, after three months, he decided that he wanted to try again, but I was so over him I realised that he was not the one for me.

Ciara, 43, teacher, County Limerick

I am confident that I know the right action to take with my relationships.

The secrets of
a happy marriage

We are still trying to figure this one out – if it was easy, we would all be living blissful lives sharing everything with the one that we love. But the facts are real – after the last piece of wedding cake has been handed out and the last present unwrapped, you are left with the reality that it is just the two of you – unless you have children already, of course!

Both of us feel that we have a bit of experience in this area but no two people when put together are the same and no two marriages are the same, so there is no golden formula. If it were that easy, it wouldn't be that interesting. We have found that communication as with most alliances and team projects, is probably the most important thing to get right. In any marriage, you both need to have your needs heard and to be able to get what you want, so that can mean learning to compromise. This is where it becomes difficult, as usually men and women want different things. But instead of focusing on those differences – focus on the things that you both want that are the same.

People get married for a variety of reasons – and if you want to live happily ever after then you should pack up and move to Disneyland. Being in a relationship is hard work and a journey that involves *constant learning. But we enjoy the companionship and love that comes with being in a marriage – if we didn't, we certainly wouldn't have done it twice!* 🌿❤

HAPPY MARRIAGE = compromise. Re-finding men – write out a list of what you want and what you don't want, then really focus on what you want and you will get it. Also, you need to write down what men you have attracted in the past.

Maria, Reiki master, County Dublin

🌿

ALWAYS MAINTAIN your independence!

Janet, 65, weaver, County Dublin

🌿

IF WE WOMEN spent half as much time choosing our groom as we do choosing our wedding dress, there'd be a lot less divorce in the world. Love is a truly wonderful thing, but to choose the person you are going to spend the rest of your life with without really thinking about who that person is and how you work together is naïve. Life can be really tough. It can be filled with challenges and tragedies. If you are going to spend sixty-odd years with one person, it should be someone who makes life easier, not harder.

The early years of a relationship should be the easy ones. When babies and mortgages and life's hardships arrive, that's when it can get tough. Your relationship should be the place you come home to after a hard day of life. My advice to any woman starting out on a relationship is: take off the blinkers. Choosing the person you are going to spend the rest of your life with and have children with is the biggest decision most of us will ever make, for ourselves and those children. It should be the one decision that we really put some thought into.

Dawn, 38, editor, County Dublin

❧

IF YOUR HUSBAND stacks the dishwasher incorrectly – or not the way you do it – leave him to do it his way. At least he is making an effort – never go and undo his work. It will get done just as well. Same goes for nappy changing, cooking and anything else involved in the home! The way you greet your partner when he or you come in from work in the evening sets up how your evening will go and, ultimately, your relationship. I'm not saying deny your own feelings but treat him the way you want to be treated and explain this clearly.

Grainne, 40, nutritionist, County Cork

❧

SOMETIMES, OUR LIVES can be crammed with duty – our work inside and outside the home, raising our children, fulfilling our social and community obligations (those endless cake stalls!). So much duty that we're at risk of forgetting how to have fun.

Sometimes, we feel there's no time for it or we're too old to bother with fun any more. But I've decided that making time to have fun is a requirement for a healthy, fulfilled life. Having fun is, to some extent, a state of mind: it means looking for the joy or amusement in any given situation and believing that your life will be enriched by it. Adopting a fun manifesto means believing 'you're worth it' (as the famous ad so succinctly says); that you deserve time off for a laugh or a get-together with people who make you feel good. So take your partner salsa dancing or book that balloon ride you've always dreamed of. And if you need any more justification, then how about this? It's not just good for you, but also for those around you! Someone who is enjoying life is always better company than someone who is not.

Jacinta, writer and GP, Melbourne, Australia

❧

MY MUM AND DAD are deeply in love and have a fantastic relationship. They have been happily married for thirty-two years. My personal affirmation is that anything worth achieving involves a challenge and you feel a greater sense of personal triumph when you can look back on all that you have overcome. And finally, a smile costs nothing!

Katie, 30, script editor, England

❧

SECRET OF A HAPPY relationship ... What I am searching for is a man who can bring to a relationship what I call my THRILL theory.

T trust H honesty R respect I innocence L loyalty L love – put all of that together and you experience the THRILL (I can also include Intelligence, H can include Humour and L Laughter).

I'm sure he does exist out there somewhere for me!

Marianne, 38, teacher, Scotland

HAPPY MARRIAGE = no secrets, a certain amount of compromise, being friends as well as lovers, listening as well as talking to each other. Does not work for everyone, but has for us so far.

Collette, 53, homemaker, County Dublin

჻

WHEN BUYING A BED, get the very biggest that your room will allow. You may not realise it before you have a family but you will need that extra space for your kids when they climb in in the middle of the night or the next morning. As you get older and grumpier, it is best to have more space between the two of you too. Remove bedside lockers if needs be to make space for the bed!

Cathy, 46, mum of two, County Dublin

჻

THERE'S NOTHING AS ANNOYING as being asked if, or when, you (or perhaps your daughter) are going to get married. It's a bit like saying, 'Has your son not left home yet?'

We women are encouraged to work hard at school, at college, in training for careers which often leave little time for social activities, for getting to know a man well enough to commit to a life together, that's it's perhaps surprising that anyone does decide to get married these days. Beautiful, intelligent girls no longer spend their evenings preparing for the weekly dance or party – they're too busy studying for the MBA or learning Swahili for that safari trip.

Marriage implies settling down, having a family, buying a sofa. The bride's parents are often on hold for the announcement of a grandchild, which doesn't help the working couple. A wise friend told me that it was a shame people bothered to get married unless they were expecting a baby because divorce was so disruptive if you find you're not right for each other.

I think she's probably right – I wonder how long you have to wait to find out if you're right for each other though? I read of a couple in their eighties marrying the other day and they looked delighted – the best reason for marriage is surely because you are so happy to be with each other!

Bernie, 64, Sydney, Australia

> *In my marriage,*
> *my main priority will always be*
> *to have more fun.*

When love hurts

Domestic violence and abuse are two of the most serious problems that can happen in relationships. It's a hidden pain, rarely spoken about, frequently missed by others. Women in developing countries with few social services are most at risk, but even in wealthy high society, men murder their wives, so great can the anger within a marriage become.

It's tempting to believe that women who live with abuse and violence are victims, or that the simple solution is just to get up and leave, but solutions to these problems are rarely simple. Love is very complex. Men and women who are indifferent to one another do not kill each other: what fuels these extremes of anger are deep and complicated emotions of jealousy, guilt, humiliation and fear.

Being in an abusive relationship does not make you a weak woman or a failure. Marriages become violent for all sorts of reasons, including addiction, poverty, mental illness or matters which are entirely out of our control. Having chosen a man who was once a loving friend who then changes to become an abusive and violent person does not mean you made a mistake. It means that the love you chose has changed into something completely different, and it is your choice what you do about it now.

Living with chronic violence and abuse will impair our ability to feel loved and worthy and cause ill health, depression and will put our lives at risk. The most important thing is that we recognise this and empower ourselves with the ability to know what to do.

Sharing our experiences of abuse and violence is not easy. We don't always get the support we need. We don't always get the answers we are looking for. Specialist services are there for a reason. Seek the right confidential service for you. Making a decision about an abusive relationship can take time, but make sure that you choose the right decision for you, and that you are true to yourself as a strong, powerful woman who has the world to live for.

THE ONE AND ONLY common denominator of domestic abuse is control. Having come out of an abusive marriage a number of years ago which was dominated by mental abuse (with the odd incident of physical assault thrown in for good measure), I can truly empathise with anyone in the same position. The thing is, I never would have taken advice from anyone. I knew better, or I was too afraid to do something until something clicked and I saw it for what it was. The victim has to have that 'click' moment to change things.

Martina, 37, psychiatric nurse, Northern Ireland

ITS' ALL ABOUT CONTROL and power, and the 'click' moment has to come from within, whether it is to save your kids or just yourself. I think if you have kids, the click moment comes quicker. I think the most prevalent abuse is definitely mental. Words torture and break you down from the inside out, beatings do it from the outside in. You have to keep your friends, and no matter how long it is you have to be there for your friends as they just might need you in their click moment. It may not last but it will come again for them in the future. I have learned to just be there.

Caroline, 37, retail manager, County Donegal

Something has to click and that abuse is about control. Men have it harder to prove, because people think that they should be able to handle what is going on. Either way, the abuse is very hard on whoever is going through it. It never goes away even after it is over. I know I was in that type of relationship years ago and still have issues from it.

Tina, 42, Wisconsin, USA

I think that the abuser doesn't always realise that he/she is doing it. If they do, then they are truly evil, for the damage they cause is left with the victims for always. It changes them for ever.

I would like to say that the work done by the Women's Aid organisation is tremendous. (I don't know if they support men who are abused, but I hope that there will be equal support for male victims.) It wasn't until I started talking to one of their workers that I discovered just what I had gone through. As an 'intelligent, middle-class, professional' woman, I thought that this kind of thing didn't happen to 'women like me'. Therefore I felt to blame for it all. I was wrong. Domestic abuse doesn't happen because of your brain capacity, social class or status, it happens because you are with someone who doesn't respect you, trust you or, ultimately, love you. You become their possession, to be controlled.

Ladies, gents, please speak out. This may be your time to have the 'click' moment. As scary as it is, remember you are not alone and there is a way forward for you if you have the support you need. Thankfully, domestic abuse is slowly becoming less of a taboo subject. If your friends don't want to 'get involved in your domestic issues', then I'm sorry, but they are not true friends. There are others you can turn to who will be there to support you in whatever way they can.

Brenda, teacher, Scotland

❧

I DON'T THINK MEN have a monopoly on anger, hatred and violence and I only wish that love did always win! I also know many men who are loving, gentle and calm, but I do think that men don't generally look after themselves that well, especially in later life and especially if they are on their own. I also think that stress is a big factor and women are much better at sharing their worries with family and mates. I think it's terribly sad that so many men find it so difficult to open up, definitely a genetic flaw, and for many men, it's not their fault, it's the way they are!

Laura, 40, journalist, County Dublin

Do try this at home:

If you are being hurt by your relationship, do something. You are not alone. Do not be afraid of being judged. You are the only person that can make the change.

*It is a privilege to love and
to have been loved.*

Divorce –

the chance to change your life

Almost half of all British marriages now end in divorce. Both of us grew up in Ireland – a country that didn't have legal divorce till 1995, when we were both already married! The legalisation of divorce in Ireland was one of the most important leaps forward for women in our history – and yet, most Irish people were very reluctant for a long time after the state was established to legalise divorce. People were afraid that if divorce was legalised, it would mean the end of the family. It's tempting to think that perhaps the Irish were always very romantic about marriage, but the sad fact is that because we didn't have legal divorce here until the 1990s, many couples stopped wanting to get married in the first place. Marriage had lost its place as a romantic, affectionate relationship for life, and became a messy, ugly bind.

Now, Irish people are marrying frequently again, but just as frequently, we are seeking divorce. Both of us were married and then divorced quite quickly afterwards, a decision that was painful and, at the same time, very liberating. Women who are divorced and separated are strong women. We have loved and lost but we are proud of who we are and we are ready to love again. Divorce means that one marriage is over, and that the rest of our lives can now begin.

The most painful part of any divorce is the effect that it has on children. But if there's one lesson that the women who have helped us in writing this book have taught us, it is this: no matter what crisis happens in your life, put your own oxygen mask on first. 🖤

🐝

ONE PIECE OF ADVICE I would give to anyone going through a divorce is to make sure everything legal is in the woman's name when the man leaves, like insurance and bills. Otherwise it could be very complicated if anything happened in the house – as I found out when my house was flooded.

Angela, 39, single mum, County Longford

🐝

A GIRLFRIEND TOLD ME once that the acceptable time to sulk over a man is one-tenth of the time that your relationship lasted. Of course, it depends on who ended the relationship as well. I think it's different if it's a marriage, especially if there are children involved. Then you will always have to be in touch with each other.

Clare, 34, hairdresser, County Cavan

🐝

WHEN MY FIRST MARRIAGE broke down, many people were shocked – from the outside we seemed like the perfect couple. But it was only then that I realised the important things in a relationship are not money, possessions and status – the most important factor is love and chemistry. You can get someone in to paint your house or mow your lawn. You clean your windows yourself if you want! But the most important exclusive activity you have with your partner is sex. Chemistry can't be made or forced, you either have it or don't have it with someone. So I made sure that the next partner I had drove me crazy with desire and, after thirteen years, I am pleased to say he still does. We do row about the lawn and the bins, etc., but it's fun making up!

Tori, 49, mother, County Roscommon

❧

I always remember as the end of my first marriage loomed over me at the age of thirty that feeling of utter fear of how I would feel when I was no longer married. I tried to get my head around how others would perceive me, and what a failure I was. Then one day in the gym, I met Siobhan, who I used to go to school with, and she consoled me. She had been through the same experience herself a few years earlier. She assured me that when the end comes, I would be surprised that I would still feel the same inside. Her way of explaining this was marvellous – she told me to remember what I felt like when I was single and how I felt the morning after I woke up after getting married. I had to admit that I was amazed that I still felt the same after going through the wedding ceremony. 'Well,' Siobhan said, 'you are going to feel the very same when you get divorced.' And she was right.

We are always the same and always a single entity, no matter what our marital status.

Michelle

❧

I WORK WITH A YOUNG WOMAN who is only twenty-seven years old, has three small kids ranging from seventeen months to five years. Back in February, her husband decided that he didn't want to be married any more and that they had kids too young (yeah, I know, don't even say it). She has no family around and is only working part-time. I told her that in every 'bad' situation in life, you need to look for the positive – I don't care what the situation is. I told her she may not see it right away, but eventually she would. I also told her to keep her sights on moving forward. She is allowed to have her moments and her own personal pity party, but not to let it get the best of her. To just keep moving forward. Now, when I ask how she is doing, she says, 'I'm moving forward, Joan.' She even has herself a hot male friend now – there's her positive!

Joan, 45, independent, New Jersey, USA

֍

I WAS MARRIED with a son at seventeen, four kids by twenty-four, separated by thirty-two and all fairly big events in the greater scheme of things. Yep, did the three jobs, four kids, crap hubby bit, but also retained enough of myself to go back to education, get a steady safe job, get a mortgage (on my own, thanks!) and am now the 'little mommy' in my house, with a wonderful partner who is also my best friend (and brings me coffee every morning!).

Did it hurt? Yeah, like hell.

Did I learn? Bloody right.

Am I a stronger, better person for my experiences? Bet yer arse I am!

Could I have done it alone? Probably, possibly, maybe … not definitely.

My friends were, and are, brilliant. They let me have my pity parties, told me when to cop on and, worst of all, dragged me out and made me live as well! Thanks, ye hoors!

TW, County Cork

❧

DIVORCE HURT, it hurt like **** (excuse my language), but, there again, it was liberating, wonderfully liberating. I was the one who ended the twelve-year marriage. I have since found me again, and you know what? I like me, even if he didn't respect me for who I am. Bear with the trauma of it all, ladies: happened to me five years ago and finally I am coming out the other side, albeit still single, but that is good, I've needed this 'me time'.

Brenda, teacher, Scotland

❧

I was devastated when we were going through our divorce. We were seeing a relationships mediator, and I kept bursting into tears. My husband seemed to be so cool and unruffled about it all, and I was so hurt because he wasn't more upset. The mediator asked me why I was being so emotional about things, and I lost my temper and said, 'Because this is the worst thing that can possibly ever happen to you!' To my astonishment, the mediator and my husband both replied unanimously, 'No it isn't.' I was just stunned. But it made me think. My husband was handling it much better than I was, and I had to start to handle it better. The thing I was most concerned about was the effect it would have on my children. But I realised that I was going to have to handle it well, because otherwise, how on earth could I expect them to handle it at all?

Juliet

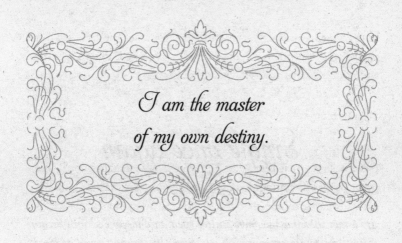

I am the master
of my own destiny.

Single once again

It's a fact that most women outlive men, so widowhood will become a natural phase in many of our lives. In the past, and today in developing cultures, widows can be viewed with suspicion: their bodies in ancient times were burned with their husband's on a pyre. Losing your beloved is probably the most painful loss that there is — some women we talked to told us that losing their husband was far worse than losing a friend, a parent or even a child.

Perhaps we need to prepare ourselves in some way for this eventual loss. Being alone is a challenge, but during our lives, we need to nurture and cherish children, friends and other circles of loved ones so that the end of a partnership will not be spent alone. Being alive means living every moment to its full, so that as life ends, we are not eaten up with regrets. The memories of a happy and affectionate partnership can be full of sorrow when that partnership is gone, but affection can deepen after death and acceptance is essential if we are to survive. It is vital to remember the joy that love once brought with gratitude and with peace. 🌿

LOTS OF PEOPLE told me to avoid older men because they would die before me. I didn't — and they did. But look at the divorce rates for same-age couples and it's the same difference. So follow your heart and never discount the fruits of experience. Women in age-gap relationships, don't knock them; and they last because it's the quality of the love that matters most of all.

It's amazing the status of widows. I've met separated women who wished their husbands had died. They don't think they get the same level of sympathy or support. They certainly don't walk into a pension but often have to fight for every last euro. If a husband walks, it's often assumed the level of hurt is minimal, or else that the wife is partly to blame, or is well shut of him. A man dies, and it's a tragedy. Indeed, it is – but all pain is equal when you're suffering.

People cling to each other like limpets. I know grown adults who don't want to go to the cinema by themselves. They want to sit in the dark next to someone they know – or stay at home. They won't eat by themselves in restaurants. They think everyone else is dismissing them as sad people. They won't go to parties alone, or on holiday. And yet they live in a big heaving world full of people, often also alone. What is it about people being unwilling to be with themselves? And to reach out to other people? To go out and reach out the hand of friendship to a stranger, widen the circle, take a chance? Too many people build cages around themselves. It's such a shame.

Why do so many people live as if they were on Noah's ark – two by two? Their whole social life revolves around meeting other people with their sexual partners in tow. Will men ever cop themselves on and realise that a woman without a man is like a fish without a bicycle? You keep on swimming.

Mary, journalist, County Dublin

❧

BEING ON YOUR OWN when you've been part of a long-term relationship and had it torn away from you for whatever reason, be it death or divorce, is a very difficult adjustment to make. There are nights when it's extremely lonely, when all you want is a hug from another person. To know that you love someone and that they love you back is more precious than anything. To have that person to give you support or just being there is such a gift.

There are certain aspects that I do enjoy and feel luxurious about my single life – the freedom to make my own decisions, I am the master of my own destiny and the creator of my own happiness, my money is my own to spend, I can sleep star-shaped diagonal on the bed by myself and I don't have to fight for the covers on a really cold night. Having been alone, I'm not afraid of it, but I can also appreciate the luxuries and benefits of being part of a couple.

Angela, 33, stay-at-home mum, Omagh, Northern Ireland

☙

I HAD A CLIENT who was an elderly lady who cried after getting a massage because she said that no one had touched her since her husband died. Since then, I never underestimate the power of a hug!

Sandra, massage therapist, County Tipperary

☙

MY DAD RECENTLY PASSED AWAY after he and Mom had been together fifty-five years. If I'd a euro for every genuine query about her since, particularly from other widows of that generation, I'd be loaded. The common theme is 'massive change for her' and 'it's fierce lonely'.

Being alone is a luxury if you choose solitude, it can be just plain lonely otherwise. We are all social creatures to one degree or another. However, women are strong creatures and adjust to any situation.

I think the trick is retaining your own identity as an individual while being the 'other half' of a partnership, or indeed while raising kids and only knowing yourself as 'Mom' most of the time, so when the time comes that you find yourself alone, by choice or otherwise, you appreciate your solitude and autonomy all the more.

Theresa, poet, County Cork

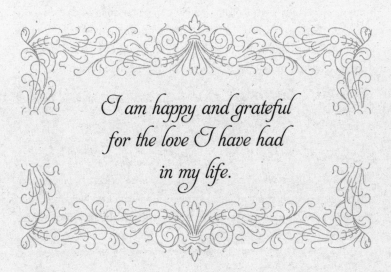

I am happy and grateful for the love I have had in my life.

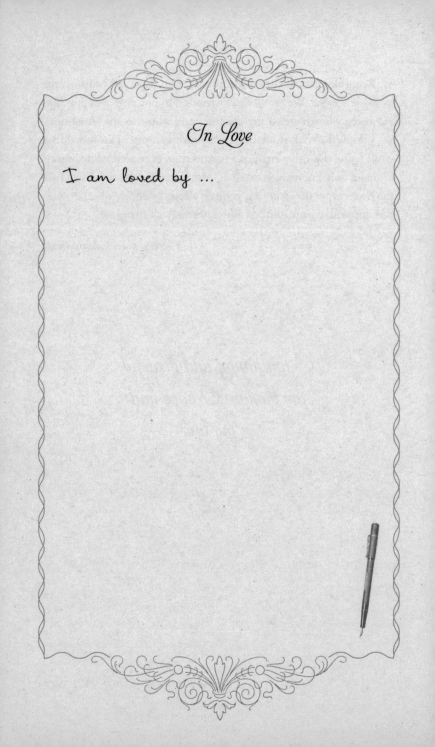

In Love

I am loved by ...

Sex

*S*ex is the basis for the creation of the species and it is one of the most important and greatest gifts that we have. Being sexually liberated can mean different things to different women, but what's really important is to value and trust our sexual feelings for others, and the gifts we have as women to enjoy our sexuality and the way in which we can use it to show and experience love. Who we have sex with, why we have sex, what kind of sex we have – these are all personal decisions and no one else's beliefs or attitudes to our sexuality matter apart from our own. On our journey through life, our sexual relationships are as important as any other and we should honour them just as much as our friendships, our children and our duties to our career. The vital thing is to take pleasure in our sexuality and feel empowered by the joy it brings.

While researching this book, we gathered some great stories. One woman wrote and told us about the time she was with her boyfriend in his high-rise apartment and just as she was about to climax a fireman burst through the door telling them to get out, as the building was on fire. Thankfully, no one was injured, but another friend suggested that it would be a fantasy to have a fully clad fireman arrive on the scene at the same time! Another told us of her time on a cruise ship when the captain took a break from the bridge and the ship broached – her cabin was under one of the swimming pools and water started to flood in through the ceiling of the cabin while ... you've guessed it ... she was in the middle of a little afternoon passion with her partner. It's wonderful to think that we all enjoy the same pleasures – sometimes in adversity!

We need to speak about sex in different terms with our young people and our peers to demystify it and take it out of the sordid and abusive way in which it is portrayed by the sex industry. For those who have been abused, it may be even harder to speak about it to your children, but we have to start somewhere and it is up to each woman to start with herself. Our sexuality empowers us and makes us loving, deepens our affection and strengthens our relationships.

Men and women seem to think differently about sex. Women tend to be romantic – to associate sex with love and commitment, which is a reflection of our practicality and desire to maintain a strong family. It is easy to feel disappointed with men who don't seem to share this depth of meaning, and many women find it difficult to untangle the differences in attitudes and beliefs about the experience of sex between men and women. In ancient texts, sex and orgasm are said to bring us closer to God. This is because we connect with another human at a very deep and spiritual level during orgasm, which can cause us to feel overwhelming love, profound affection and intense loyalty to our lover. Many people feel overwhelmed by the power of these feelings, but these are very positive feelings and mean that having sex is good for us!

Getting in the mood

We women fill our days with multitasking to such an extent that when we come to bed, it is difficult to sometimes switch off and concentrate on an orgasm. But concentrating on just one thing is something that men do very well, so it's no wonder that they reach orgasm so quickly. We owe it to ourselves to find out what we want sexually from our relationships. It is such an important part of being human that every woman should address the issue right away. Think about how much time we give to maintaining and looking after our houses and our careers and children. Sex is a basic pleasure, like eating or sleeping, and we need to address it to be holistic beings.

If you find that you are barely ever in the mood, or that your sex life has dwindled to nothing, do something about it, because lack of sex in a relationship makes love very difficult to maintain. And nobody ever regrets a night of passion with their loved one – no matter how tired they were to begin with!

Scientists all around the world are currently trying to make a drug that will do for women what Viagra has done for men. But what they are consistently finding in the trials is that women don't necessarily have a medical 'dysfunction' when it comes to lack of sexual pleasure. The scientists who are researching women's sexual pleasures have found that although most women don't go around in a permanent state of arousal, when we *start having sex, the foreplay rapidly leads to very intense and memorable pleasure. Whereas for men, although they may feel like having sex more often than women, when they are aroused they don't necessarily enjoy it as deeply as we do! It seems that for women, the pleasure is in having sex: for men, it may be more about the anticipation.* 🌰

TELL YOUR CHILDREN the facts of life, in a loving and open way, as soon as they understand. It is up to every woman to take this responsibility into her own hands and to tell her children to do this too. They will be getting in the mood before you realise they are ready to! Pregnancy prevention is better than a cure.

Keris, 47, public health nurse, Liverpool, England

🐝

THERE'S A VERY GOOD REASON to indulge your partner when he asks for oral sex – apparently it is the best way to exercise the muscle under your chin and help prevent it from becoming saggy and a double chin!

Goldie, 41, designer, New York, USA

🐝

WE WENT SKIING a few weeks ago with a large group and we picked up a new friend who was travelling alone. He was recently separated from his wife and had that west of Ireland charm that men from there are famous for. One of our group lost her wallet and coat in the middle of the après ski and was distraught. With his charm, our new friend suggested something to take her mind off the upset.

'Would you like me to go down on you?' he asked.

She was speechless to his suggestion, so he continued, 'for an hour and a half?'

It was a very male way of taking her mind off the matter and we all fell around the place in stitches laughing. It worked. She replied, 'I think we'd need towels for that!'

Sasha, 40, tennis-playing mum, County Dublin

※

WHEN I WAS ABOUT THIRTEEN, my friend and I were walking the beach and trying to work out what a blow job was. She said to me that someone had told her that it was oral sex. Problem was we weren't sure what that was either – but as it was oral that meant in the mouth – so we concluded that it was just talking about it!

Karen, 44, special needs assistant, County Dublin

※

MY MOTHER AND FATHER sat me and my sisters down when we were young and did detailed drawings for us and told us everything they could about sex. When my periods became painful at the age of sixteen, my mother was very quick to suggest I start to take the Pill. She admitted years later that she was worried that I would get pregnant and I am so glad that she did what she did. My parents were ahead of their time but I will ensure that I do the same with my children.

Giselle, 41, County Dublin

Do try this at home:

Oral sex – it's all about communication.

When a man loves your vulva with his lips, mouth and tongue, he is worshipping the sacred female inside of you. It takes time and patience – tell him where to move his tongue – hold your partner's penis at the same time as you are receiving to complete the circle of loving energy between you.

The cleaning will wait, in fact I find it stubbornly patient! Find something more interesting to do that isn't stubborn but maybe is dirty!

Sukie, 31, mum, County Dublin

※

WE DON'T NEED VIAGRA, we need men to understand that it takes more than a quick grope of our breasts to turn us on!

Bev, 42, delivery driver, Worcestershire, England

※

WATCHING HIM do the ironing and cleaning the floors does it for me!

Frieda, 38, secondary school teacher, County Dublin

WOMEN DO NOT NEED medication to turn them on. They just need to understand what it is that makes them 'tick' – and communicate it effectively to their partner.

Kathleen, 43, TV producer, Canada

⁂

GOOD SEX is all about communication and it's not the destination – it's the journey. Some men need to be told this and the sooner, the better.

Helen, 49, artist, London, England

⁂

THE MOST IMPORTANT sex organ is your brain.

Anonymous

⁂

WOMEN ARE MUCH more interested in having sex than in our parents' time – it is partly because of the freedom, since contraception and vasectomies have become more common. Sometimes, our husbands might not have the same sex drive as us – I find my husband likes to be the one to initiate sex and is more reluctant when I initiate. I found in the past that it is confident men that like women to initiate – or grateful ones!

Sandy, 38, financier, Tyrone, Northern Ireland

DON'T DO IT on the beach because the sand gets everywhere!

Anonymous

⚘

WE HAD BEEN READING a book about Tantric sex – it was coming up to a significant anniversary and I felt that it would be good to spice things up in our marriage. My husband was delighted to participate in a win–win project like this! The philosophy involves the building up of energy and connection between the two people making love and is taken from Eastern books like the *Kama Sutra*. One Sunday morning, we had left it a bit late to start foreplay as I had to collect the children from their sleepover – my husband asked, 'Can we have a Western one then?' I laughed out loud when he suggested it because I thought he meant the Wild West – but, of course, he meant the way it is practised in thousands of households across England!

We need to take stock of how we practise our love-making and the signals about love-making that we send to our children. It has to be regarded in a new and open light and taken out of the sleazy way that it has been portrayed in media and by the Church. It's a wonderful transference of energy between two people that should be made time for – when the sexual side of your relationship is going well, it is easier for all the other parts to fall into place – and best of all it's free!

Sheena, 38, researcher, London, England

⚘

THERE ARE ONLY TWO kinds of sex – good sex and bad sex!

Dee, 64, counsellor, County Dublin

WELL THERE WAS THE TIME that my fiancé prepared a surprise for me ... a room full of lit tealights, Marvin Gaye playing, sparkling wine, massage oil and decadent sheets. But I came home stressed out and so tired that I just wanted to go up to bed to sleep! That was three years ago and it's not really any surprise that he's never tried all that since!

Catherine, 32, student, Northern Ireland

❧

THE NEXT TIME you have a group of girlfriends gathered together – preferably with a few glasses of vino added – ask this question: 'Where is the most interesting place you have ever had sex?' We guarantee it will change your perception of some of your friends. And it's great fun!

My party piece was always to answer this question with, 'Well, in the second decade of the new millennium, the DART [Dublin's rapid train system] seems like a very daring place to have sex. But this act was initiated a few yards after rolling out from Bray station where there were no CCTV cameras installed and no other passengers until Booterstown. And it was in the 1980s so it was far from the daring escapade that it would be if practised today.' Since then, I have been outdone by two other stories.

One of my pals was dating a med student and they needed a lift down the A69 in the UK. They were given a lift by an ambulance and herself and her med student boyfriend decided to put the time to good use ... excellent way to travel by all accounts. But I think even that has been surpassed by another friend of mine who told me about her friend who was travelling very cheaply around the United States on the skinny dog (a colloquial term for the Greyhound bus!).

Apparently, it is a notoriously slow mode of transport and she got talking to the guy in the seat next to her. Over the course of eight hours, they became very familiar and got very well acquainted between the seats of the coach! There is this sense of excitement in us all and if you are in the middle of rowing with your boyfriend or husband, why not throw caution to the wind and spice up your love life a bit … go on, use your imagination! He will love you for it.

Simone, County Dublin

🐾

I WAS SKIING with my family earlier this year and it was towards the end of the day. My husband and I had a ski gondola to ourselves and there was no one in the one ahead or behind. The trip was a good ten minutes to get to the top of the black run and we looked at each other wondering how to fill the ten minutes – the scenery was stunning and the thrill of making love in such an open place added to the excitement! Definitely one of our favourite different places.

Bianca, 38, County Dublin

🐾

MY HUSBAND WAS WORKING abroad on a contract and would be away for a three-month period. We weren't long married and were both anxious about how the separation was going to affect our sex life. Before he left, he handed me a box and said that it would help while he was away. I got a shock when I opened it and found a vibrator inside. He rang me when he arrived at his new place of work and home for the next three months. So after a good deal of hot and heavy sex talk he had me worked up into a frenzy – he told me to get the vibrator out. Then, it all went horribly wrong – he hadn't bought any batteries to go with it. However, our vibrator has become a useful toy and now that he is back home it still gets taken out on occasions.

Kylie, 36, County Dublin

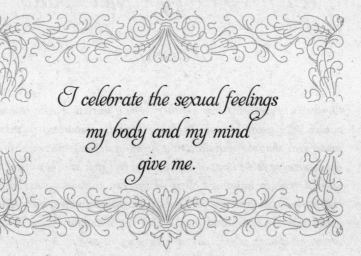

I celebrate the sexual feelings my body and my mind give me.

When Harry Met Sally

orgasms

Orgasms are overrated – or are they? Why is there so much preoccupation with them in women's magazines? It's important to teach young girls that the sexual act is a deeply spiritual experience. It is not something to be jumped into lightly. But girls and boys need to be told how to enjoy sex. Part of the fun is 'finding out' and exploration and everyone has a different journey of discovery. But apart from the basic mechanics of intercourse taught in the sexual education class in school, nobody tells you how to have an orgasm.

The sex industry is full of images and harmful signals that degenerate sex. Nobody sits you down and tells you how to enjoy your body and offers suggestions about how to make it feel better or make sex more enjoyable. It is no wonder that so many younger women and men have distorted ideas on what sex in meant to be like.

When it comes to orgasms, the best advice we've got is: have plenty! ✒

THESE LITTLE BURSTS of pleasure are so important. We don't give them the same attention that men do and are prone to fobbing off amorous attempts from our husbands when we are not in the mood. A woman takes a long time to build up and achieve an orgasm and if your partner does not realise it – tell him, or look for another one.

Sally, 37, pharmaceutical representative, London, England

꙰

MEN AND WOMEN are different in the way they view life and the way they react to situations. Men tend to be impulsive – act quickly – demand instant gratification. A woman takes in the big picture – the long-term view and works things out with a consideration of all parties. Translated into sex, we see a parallel too. Men are like fire – quick to ignite and quick to extinguish. Women on the other hand are like water – you can't rush a kettle to bring it to the boil. When these facts have been established, men and women can mutually agree on how they are going to enjoy their sexual practices. But this fundamental reality needs to be considered and worked out by both partners when making love.

Martina, 38, psychologist, County Dublin

꙰

I WISH I COULD TALK to my twenty-year-old self and tell her how to enjoy sex – show her how to make the most of having a young man with the energy for her …

Caitlin, 48, Canada

MEN MASTURBATE a lot, as I discovered when my son turned four-teen – he was at it all the time. I found his little hand towel that was crusty under his pillow when I went to change the sheets. I didn't want to embarrass him about it but he admitted to me that some strange white stuff was trapped under his foreskin – and it hurt to pee. I told him that he needed to go to the toilet after this – he knew what I meant. It's difficult to discuss some subjects with your children but they need to know that it's a healthy part of life and not something that they should be afraid to discuss. They also need to be warned not to overdo it!

Jenny, 38, nurse, County Dublin

❧

AN ORGASM is much more fun than pelvic floor muscles excercising.

Ann, women's physiotherapist,

❧

Do try this at home:

Straight after orgasm is the best time to have another – multiple orgasms are best achieved with practice and can even be better than the first one. Try it next time!

I COULD NEVER HAVE an orgasm with my boyfriend – he just hadn't a clue how to make me come. But, eventually, I masturbated in front of him and that really helped! Now we do this a lot – and we love to watch one another masturbating, it's become a really sexy part of our love-making.

Greta, 32, Carlisle, England

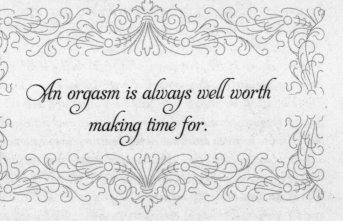

An orgasm is always well worth making time for.

Love your vagina

Why do women in the West worry about how their genitals appear? They are beautiful if they work and aren't infected with anything. Think of all of the women who have been mutilated without their consent through female circumcision as babies and little girls. We really need to heighten awareness of this heinous crime against women and stand up for each other. Circumcision of baby boys does not stop their sensation of orgasm the same way as the circumcision of girls. This is not something that reflects a religious belief – it is a crime against women. Perhaps if every woman in the West wrote to her prime minister and insisted that the abolition of female genital mutilation became part of the constitution of developed countries, they might put enough pressure on nations where it is condoned to do something about it.

It is a basic human right to grow up with your body intact and without the torture and pain that goes with this barbaric act. Become aware – these little girls need your voice as they have none of their own and it is often forgotten that many die in the process of bleeding.

Juliet has worked for many years in the area of women's health and she never ceases to be amazed at how dissatisfied women are with their bodies, especially their genitals. Over the years, she's had many patients complain that they hate the look of their sexual organs, hate their breasts, hate their labia, hate the way their inner labia stick out past the outer ones. Most men have very limited experience of women's genitals, and most of the ones that they have seen a lot of are the ones that have been photographed for porn. Women in pornographic photos have shaved, infantile genitals, with small inner labia that have often been surgically snipped to make them look like a little girl's. But this is not what real adult women look like.

Yet this is exactly what we decry as female genital mutilation when it happens in Africa and Asia.

Meanwhile, here in the West, women are volunteering to try to make their genitals look more like the genitals they know are only available in porn mags.

A lot of women like to shave and rip out their pubic hair in the hope that this makes their vagina look prettier, but don't forget this increases your risk of infection and ingrown hairs. Is it worth all that just to have genitals that look like a little girl's?

Love your vagina!

I MET MY HUSBAND very shortly after breaking up with a long-term partner of eight and a half years – the last three of those were very lean on the sex front, so I made up for lost time. After about three months of going at it like rabbits, I found myself getting cystitis regularly. It was infuriating and painful. I went to an urologist and without looking up from his desk, he pencilled me in for a general anaesthetic and a cystoscopy! I was horrified and was shaking as I left the practice and went to a different consultant. This woman was wonderful and asked me about my history and was very concerned at the fact that I had broken up from a long-term relationship. She asked me if I was having intercourse more frequently – when I answered yes she smiled knowingly. 'Are you going to the toilet afterwards?' she asked. I shook my head and she informed me kindly that all women should go to the toilet after sex because the urethra is shorter. My life was liberated and I haven't had cystitis since – probably not having sex as often either, but at least my kidneys are in good shape for when I am in the mood.

Olga, 47, teacher, County Dublin

Do try this at home:

Always go to the toilet after making love – no matter where you are or how much you want to curl over and fall asleep. This will prevent urinary tract infections and cystitis!

If you use a tampon try to use an organic one that does not have chlorine added.

Your vagina deserves only the best. Don't clean it too often or use strong chemicals or perfumes – the vagina is self-cleaning and water alone is the best and safest way to keep it clean.

If you find you are getting lots of vaginal discharge, check that you are wearing underwear made from a natural fibre and not synthetic, which can make your vagina sweat and cause thrush.

If you have thrush and a sexual partner, make sure you are both being treated at the same time or you

will continue to reinfect each other. Put a few drops of lavender essential oils into a small bowl of warm water, dip cotton wool into it and douse your entire vulval area with the cotton wool. Put a few drops of the oil onto a wet tampon and insert it, changing it three times per day. Don't scratch! Natural yoghurt also prevents thrush – eat it or put it into your vagina on a tampon.

PERIODS ARE A PAIN. Every girl remembers when and how they got their first period. Thankfully, today, women prepare their daughters and tell them what to expect. My mother thought that she was bleeding to death when it happened to her, but thankfully, sex education in schools has seen to this issue. There is a terrific homeopathic remedy called sepia that helps. (This remedy is also useful when you have PMT or feel like killing your husband for no apparent reason!)

Rita, 47, nurse, County Waterford

❧

ONE OF THE QUICKEST ways to rectify a dry vagina is to go to the chemist and buy a lubricant. There are, of course, other, more fun ways – but not every woman enjoys their partner giving oral sex as part of foreplay. Another alternative is to use your own saliva and apply while love-making. Let sex be as hot and sticky an affair as you can make it.

Tamara, 47, sexually liberated, London, England

WE NEED TO LOVE our vaginas and our breasts and everything that is feminine about us as women.

Judith, 47, estate agent, Florida, USA

My body is beautiful and sexual and perfectly made to bring me pleasure and give love.

Why do men and women have affairs?

Affairs only really happen when you are bored, not having sex or not in love with your partner any more. If your husband or partner is having an affair, it is usually easy to know. Your feminine intuition will tell you and it's possible you will know when they are about to before even they will.

A friend of ours – let's call her Kate – was reporting to us about an affair she was having with a man when her marriage was going down the rocky road to divorce. She told us how she would hop in her car and be shaking with excitement inside at the prospect of meeting her lover. Her lover wasn't exactly the most handsome or the most entertaining – he certainly wasn't a more attractive package than her husband, but Kate told us that the drive to see him would leave her with her heart racing and pulse pumping. She was so aware of her blood flowing through her body and could feel her lips and muscles swell up with the anticipation of meeting him. Another thing that struck her, she said, was the speed that she would orgasm with him. Initially, they used a hotel room but they found that too time consuming and used to just drive off somewhere quiet and do it in the car – in the middle of the day. She said that she couldn't wait.

Kate wondered how much of this fabulous love-making was the result of the excitement she had built up in her own head before doing the deed at all. The affair didn't last long but it served its purpose and helped her decide that she didn't want to be with her husband any more.

Kate got us thinking about the positive points of her actions. Maybe we could all ring up our partners and lovers and meet them in a secret place every so often and pretend that we are forbidden lovers?

From talking to hundreds of women, we have come to realise that the only time women ever contemplate having an affair is when they feel unloved by their husbands. Most of us want to remain true and be faithful to the one we love, and so we barely look at other men. If you find yourself falling for someone else, it's almost always because you don't feel loved enough by your partner. Maybe we need to watch out for the warning signs, feeling lonely, left out, disconnected, unappreciated. An affair doesn't need to end a marriage and it can be a strong boost to the ego when you're otherwise feeling very left out. The important thing is not to let it hurt anyone and to be true to yourself and your needs as a woman. ✑

MY PARENTS will be married fifty-seven years come this November and my father cheated in the past. It was a very difficult time for my mother, for many years following. It was also difficult for myself, my brothers and sister. I had idolised my father my whole life. I had him set up on a pedestal, but when he cheated, he fell off that pedestal. I was only about fourteen when it happened and was not forgiving towards my father. It was years later that I realised it wasn't fair that I put him on that pedestal, it's not fair to do that to anyone and expect them to live up to your expectations. I also realised that he was human, and we all make mistakes. And when we make mistakes, we want to be forgiven. I forgave my father many years ago and I'm thankful that I did. I love my father so deeply, he is my best man – as a matter of fact, before he walked me down the aisle, that was the last thing I said to him as a single woman: 'Daddy, you're still my best man.'

I'm also thankful that my parents stayed together and worked it out. I can honestly say that my parents are truly in love with each other, they are my proof that true love does endure. I have been asked if I thought my husband would ever cheat on me. I always answer that I would like to think he would not, but he is human. If that ever does happen, I pray my marriage is strong enough, like my parents', to endure it. If not, I'll move forward and I know I'll be OK.

Tina, 47, Maryland, USA

🎴

I THINK IT DEPENDS on the nature of the affair. If it was merely a sex thing, I could probably forgive. After all, we all are human and make mistakes. However, if it was a love affair, even if it never became a physical affair, that would be much harder to live with and forgive for me personally. The idea of my other half letting someone else into their heart – a space you are supposed to occupy – is unforgiveable. Or do I just have really high ideals?

Edel, 37, buyer for health service, Derry, Northern Ireland

THERE ARE MANY different reasons for affairs: boredom, circumstances, abusive relationships, etc. I would never judge affairs as I believe there are two sides to every story.

Liz, 41, part-time secretary, County Cork

🎐

I FORGAVE AN AFFAIR because, at the time, we had too much to lose, but it turned out that I couldn't forget. I don't think you ever really can forget.

It's not necessarily the end of the relationship, as long as he is truly sorry and willing to make amends.

Poppy, 24, data analyst, England

🎐

WHILE I THINK that some relationships can survive an affair, personally, it would end it for me. I would always be wondering when he is with me if he is thinking of or comparing her to me? As far as I know, no one ever cheated on me and I would like to keep it that way.

Mary, 46, doctor of criminal,
forensic and developmental psychology, Northern Ireland

🎐

MY HUSBAND HAD AN AFFAIR. I divorced him. Twenty years of marriage down the drain because of his lies. Not the sex you'll notice, it wasn't the sex that bothered me at all, it was the betrayal, the blatant lies, the deception and abuse of the absolute trust I had in him. That can never be fixed. Even if you can forgive, you never fully trust them again.

Bev, 42, delivery driver, Worcestershire, England

I enjoy the mutual trust and respect that I share with my partner.

Enjoying sex as your life changes

After middle age, lots of women lose interest in sex – sex with their husbands, that is. But if you were to ask the same women whether or not they'd turn down a date with George Clooney – well, you can predict what their answer would be! Losing interest in sex with your life partner is a part of growing old together, and familiarity makes excitement difficult to maintain. But for many women, it's important to feel loved and to show affection, even if sexuality has changed. And, it's important to enjoy your sexuality at any age.

We shouldn't feel guilty about wanting to play around with our ideas for sex. Fantasising about another man doesn't mean you don't love your partner, nor does masturbation or using toys. We can enjoy deep, loving, sexual experiences with another person while our private thoughts may not be shared – the most important thing is to share the love and the intention of the moment as it comes.

I WAS HAVING A GOOD CHAT with two friends the other evening over dinner. All three of us have been through divorces. I said if I was to be honest, the chemistry was never right in my first marriage.

One of my friends agreed – she said that they were great pals, but in the sack, he didn't have the same needs as she did. My other friend said that her sexual relationship with her first husband was wonderful and special because he was her first love. The conversation continued and after a while she confided in us – she was recently back from a week-long holiday with her new love who she has been dating for a year, 'If I am to be totally honest our sex life wasn't great,' she said. 'It's just that I didn't know any better. The sex I had last week was amazing and I never had it like that with my husband.'

KF, 39, County Dublin

꙳

I WAS AT A GATHERING of a group of women varying in age from thirty-five to forty-five and we were all having a good heart-to-heart about our sex lives. We all agreed that sex was definitely much better after we had settled into our relationships with our life partners. It was also much better now that we were all of an age where we had our child-bearing over and sex was just for pleasure.

Bianca, 38, County Dublin

꙳

YOUNG WOMEN are more interested in pleasing men – older women are more interested in pleasing themselves.

Emma, 45, unemployed architect, Wales

I AM GOING TO TALK to my daughter when she is of an age where she is going to be sexually active and ensure that she has her priorities right. After working with teenage girls as a counsellor for many years, I would be very concerned that they are having sex with boys to be liked or to fit in with the crowd. A friend told me recently that the only reason she had sex was because she thought all of her friends were having it – she later found out that they were all boasting and talking about it but not doing it. If she hadn't resorted to peer pressure her first time would not have been behind a tree in her school uniform!

Maria, County Limerick

꙳

WHEN YOU GET INTO YOUR FIFTIES, it's all about whether you want the desire of an older man, or the confusion of a younger one.

Beth, 50, make-up artist, County Dublin

꙳

WHEN I WAS A TEENAGER, I recall how my vaginal juices would turn on like a tap at the sight of a guy I fancied – a lot of this is Mother Nature kicking in and getting you ready for motherhood, ensuring the propagation of the planet while you are at your fittest and best to conceive. Of course, this doesn't necessarily fit in with the social and economic set-up of most women, and as you get older, you may find certain factors affect your vagina lubricating as quickly as it once did.

Sheila, 47, psychologist, London

THE MENOPAUSE doesn't mean the end of your sex life. For me, the menopause came along at the same time as our kids left home and I was initially really upset. What I didn't expect was the wonderful freedom of my time and space that came with the empty nest. My husband and I experienced a sexual awakening that we couldn't have had while the kids were living with us. We started to make love on the living room floor and even on the stairs. It was like being teenagers again. And we didn't have to worry about contraception!

Denise, over 50, County Dublin

My sexuality is a gift that I cherish and nurture, to give me pleasure throughout my life.

In Sex

What my sex life means to me ...

Children

hy do we have children? What is this maternal instinct? Is it real or is it something that we have nurtured in us by the expectations of others? Having a child can be the most traumatic, uplifting, heart-warming, heart breaking of journeys.

Between the two of us, we have four children – in two different generations! Michelle's children are pre-teen and in primary school, Juliet's are at university. But one thing we know about children, no matter what generation, is that children never become the people that we imagined they would be! Our children never cease to amaze us every day by being so different to anything we could possibly have expected. So many parents spend all their time trying to 'shape' their kids – worrying about school selection, pushing them through extra-curricular activities, banning all sorts of dangerous TV and websites, determined that the image they've created in their heads of what their child will be as an adult will come to fruition.

But the sooner we realise our children are completely independent people with their own thoughts, ideas and dreams, the easier it will be to support them. Spending all your time hoping that your children will be just like you is bound to fail. Instead, we need to feel excited to have the opportunity to get to know these strangers, and to welcome them into our lives.

Pregnancy, miscarriage, abortion and childbirth

Pregnancy, miscarriage, abortion and childbirth are all events that can severely stress a woman. Much of this emotional trauma is thought to be as a result of the hormone progesterone and the effect it can have on mood. When we give birth or end a pregnancy for any reason, our hormone levels can fluctuate dramatically and this makes us particularly vulnerable to extremes of emotional well-being. If you have recently been pregnant and your mood is suffering, talk to other women who share your values and who care about you. Seek professional help when your sadness is more than ordinary. These mood problems are temporary but they are painful and can cause you to suffer greatly. Your body is strong enough to become pregnant, but your mind is very powerful, and your emotions are the most important part of who you are.

What we found most inspiring about all the stories about childbirth and pregnancy is the amount of suffering that women endure for babies – pain, loss, fear, bereavement – and the emotional strength we have to transcend all that suffering with such power and joy, to give life to the world ... no wonder we are goddesses! 🌿

Pregnancy

A wise obstetrician we know told us that there are two kinds of women in the world – women who want to become pregnant, will do anything in their power to get there, and women who don't want to become pregnant, who will do anything in their power to avoid it. But most of us know that you can be either, both or neither woman at any one time!

Women nowadays have lots of problems with fertility. But at the same time, couples in their thirties and forties are often very busy and don't have enough time and energy to have a lot of sex. Make sure you are having sex at least five times a week if you're trying for a baby. Enjoy it – that helps conception too. ✑♥

I LOVED THE EXPERIENCE and that is something I *never* thought I would say. I spent all of my twenties and a lot of my thirties thinking that I did not want kids. Then the body clock ticked loudly at age thirty-eight. Then, after giving up on conceiving, I became pregnant at age forty-one, quite out of the blue. I had loads of energy and felt happy and positive. Didn't even realise until I was three months on. The pregnancy was a great experience for me and the end result the best thing that has ever happened in my life!

Claire, 44, administrator, County Dublin

✺

I NEVER HAD THE CRAVING to become a mother, but I thought I'd better try or I may regret it later. I hated being pregnant and the invasion of my body. I never expected to get pregnant straight away. Having a baby changed me more than I thought possible. Never again, I swore. But I didn't want him growing up alone and the first couple of years go so fast. Again I was pregnant straight away. At eleven weeks I had a scan. Twins. The shock was horrible. The pregnancy was fantastic. I was as fat as I am tall and could hardly walk. I hadn't seen my feet since I was five months gone. At thirty-six weeks, I had a boy and a girl. Both perfect. And about six weeks later, I felt more like my old self than I had in three and a half years.

Claire, 43, full-time mum, Holland

🐝

BOTH MY PREGNANCIES were different and seemed to mirror the two different little people they produced. My first pregnancy was quiet and easy, without much movement, which of course was a huge concern at the time, and the child I was carrying has turned out to be a quiet, shy, creative person. My second pregnancy I was aware of, even right from the start this little person likes to make her presence known! Constant movement at all times of day and night. This little person has turned out to be a constant dancer, a mover full of go. They bring out the best in each other. I often think back and it seems as if the spirit of these children was so strongly engrained right from the start.

Áine, 39, former post-primary teacher, County Dublin

🐝

ENJOY THE REST you get and fuss that's made over you before you have your first child. You will be so busy running around after it, and when you are pregnant the second time nobody will be telling you to sit down!

Kerry, 34, musician, County Dublin

＄

IN BRAZIL, the silhouette of a pregnant woman is seen as something beautiful. Women get their photographs taken with their partners showing their naked bellies. Fathers constantly touch and kiss their partner's stomach and show love to their unborn baby. I have never seen this type of expression since I moved to Ireland.

Nayane, 25, student of life, Brazil and County Laois

＄

WE HAD ARTIFICIAL INSEMINATION for our second child. Both pregnancies went well, but I had post-natal/post-partum depression after the second one. Extremely tough going and not enough room to put in here. This little lad was diagnosed with autism late last year, which puts us into another area of discussion. Motherhood can be many of the adjectives both good and bad in the mixing bowl, each stir is a surprise.

Ruth, 45, special needs assistant and author, County Clare

＄

I'VE NEVER BEEN PREGNANT, tried to get pregnant a few years ago with fertility treatments, but God said no. However, I did have the honour of witnessing my friend Tracey give birth to her daughter. It was the most amazing thing I have ever witnessed. I was on such a high from it for about a week. It made me realise how incredible a woman's body is. A woman's body can create a life, let that life pass through itself at just the right time and then her body can feed that life. I have such an incredible respect for women who have children … and I have just as much respect for a woman who doesn't have a child, but is still considered a mother by her actions and her love.

Joan, 45, independent, New Jersey, USA

※

BEING PREGNANT was flipping marvellous! I wasn't sick once, I did the whole 'glowing' thing. I was very bold and did have my glass of wine/pint when I wanted. I stuck to five cigs a day – which I know is really bad, but it's true, I worked up until the Friday and went into labour on Sunday. It was a lovely, lovely time. After two miscarriages (both of which made me very unwell), this one was obviously meant to be – and she continues – every day of her life – to make me grateful for that experience and fill my life with joy!

Aisling, 41, teacher, County Cork

※

I DISCOVERED I WAS PREGNANT and my sister had just given birth to quads! So as you can imagine everyone I told the news to said, 'Oh, maybe you'll have more than one.' Having heard this from so many people, I finally asked my gynaecologist if I could have a scan (this was pretty uncommon in 1986). My gynaecologist agreed but told me in his wonderful West Brit accent if there was more than one, he would 'eat his hat'. While lying on the table having the scan, I recounted to the nurse the story and, at that, she pointed me to the little head and the little heart and then to another little head and heart. I just remember going into hysterical laughter! My wonderful mother within eleven months became the proud grandmother of six beautiful babies!

A baker friend of mine baked a pastry hat which was presented to my gynaecologist! Strangely enough, there were no multiple births in our family and a first cousin of mine went on a year later to also have a set of fraternal twin boys like myself!

Jeanne, 47, unemployed, County Dublin

I AM BLESSED with five lovely children and am about to become a grandmother for the first time and am so excited. Just wanted to add, enjoy your pregnancy, it's yours and the baby's alone, the most wonderful, special and privileged state we can be in. My only regret is that most of mine arrived early, impatient buggers, but that was a warning of how things were going to continue!

Ber, 39, mother and community worker, County Cork

When I was pregnant with my first child, I was concerned, as most new mothers are, that the pregnancy would go well and that my child would be OK. Whenever I felt anxious, I would quietly put my hand on my

stomach and repeat a few words that I had made into a mantra to help focus on my child: 'My baby is healthy, happy, kind, clever and beautiful.'

These were my priorities and the order in which I had them in. I am truly blessed to able to say that when my son was born he was all of these things and he still is!

Michelle

Miscarriages

From the moment a pregnancy test is positive, we know what we want for our bodies, our children and ourselves. For women who are longing for a child, a name is picked, a school selected, a future planned – almost before the dipstick is dry!

But one in every five pregnancies ends in miscarriage, and this is the commonest emergency in gynaecology. For many women, a miscarriage can be a devastating experience. What we found from talking to women who have experienced miscarriage and early pregnancy loss is that the overwhelming feeling is one of failure. A feeling that your body has let you down, and that the prize of motherhood has been lost, snatched away.

Most babies who are miscarried were incompatible with life and this is why nature has let them go – but to a woman who is mourning her lost infant, this is no comfort. The grief we feel after miscarriage is a reminder of the investment we make as women in the future of the next generation through our bodies and the decisions we make. Losing a baby is a challenge for any woman and we need to face it with strength and great courage. But our bodies are not just for babies and so the most important thing is to know that our lives can be just as rich and fulfilled whether we do or do not give birth to all the children that our body can conceive.

I GAVE UP SMOKING shortly after a miscarriage. I was very upset and resorting to a quick drag from the dreaded weed whenever I could. My two little girls were in the playroom and calling to me to come and play with them but I was intent on sticking my head out the back door and smoking instead. I was in a sad state because I had recently been told by a specialist that I would never have any more children and I was perimenopausal. As the rain poured down, I had a light bulb moment and realised that instead of being upset about the loss of the baby, I had two wonderful children that needed me instead, so I put the butt out and went in and played with them. I am still off them to this day and have a lovely baby boy now who arrived as a complete surprise shortly afterwards.

Jenny, 42, sales director, County Dublin

THE SIDE OF PREGNANCY that people don't openly talk about is miscarriage; it does sometimes feel like a 'dirty secret' we should all keep quiet about. I've been pregnant twice and we lost both – the last one we managed to see the heartbeat (on my husband's birthday) but, in the same breath, we were told that it probably wouldn't go on any longer. We had to wait two weeks to find out that they were, sadly, correct.

So many women have suffered miscarriages and have received very little support with the physical and emotional trauma surrounding it. You get well-meaning people saying things like, 'Well it wasn't a real baby, was it?' and 'Sure you can try again'. Most comments are totally unhelpful, some might as well be daggers in your heart. I don't think, however, there is a right thing to say at the time, just being there and giving a shoulder to cry on helps more than anything. At this stage, we have decided not to try again, but it took us years to get to that stage – however, it still hurts a lot but life is to be lived, not regretted.

Celine, 42, County Dublin

🐝

MY FIRST PREGNANCY was great, I was full of energy and it was trouble free. I had several miscarriages after that and then my last pregnancy, twenty-two years ago, was going well, I thought, till I got to the fifth month and it went wrong and I lost the baby. I remember the doctor saying to me when I was crying, 'Pull yourself together, you are still young enough to have another baby'. I stopped trying for another baby. Now our son is going to be a dad in November.

Collette, 53, homemaker, County Dublin

🐝

I've had two miscarriages. After both, I was very upset. The babies had names, they were real children to me. You feel as though your body has done something wrong, has let you down and killed your baby and you feel very guilty. But you do get over it and the sadness passes with time. Women are very resilient and our hearts are very strong.

Juliet

Abortion

Don't carry guilt – too many women are left to feel negative and you have the right to choose what happens to your body. Let's get away from the feelings of guilt and blame – they have already been identified as tools and weapons put upon us by religions in order to control us. ℒ♥

MY FIRST PREGNANCY was memorable as I was homeless, in a disastrous marriage, I was severely under-nourished and suffered from really bad morning sickness which lasted all day and stopped me eating anything but new potatoes and baby tomatoes. When she was born, I totally rejected her. I didn't receive any help with my post-natal depression, so when I recovered it took several months get her back in my care and I have had to live with the consequences of this ever since. Seventeen months later, I had my second child. The pregnancy was completely trouble free – no morning sickness, no post-natal depression, a trouble-free birth and I returned home the next day so I didn't have to be away from my daughter. I was again in a disastrous relationship.

My third pregnancy was terminated as I knew I would not be able to take care of my two living children. I have never regretted that decision and I have never forgotten that child and think about her/him fondly from time to time. Since then, I have found my perfect partner. We have been married for over twenty years and I have had three ectopic pregnancies, each one a totally different experience exposing different levels of gap in the medical knowledge, leading to my nearly dying twice.

Debz, 52, independent mental health advocate, England

I HAD AN ABORTION when I was seventeen. When I told her that I was pregnant, my mother was mortified and worried about what the rest of her family would think of her. I didn't have a choice. She brought me to London and a very clean and businesslike clinic where my baby was terminated. I was so young and still in school – the whole experience was like a dream. I wasn't with the baby's father for long and the abortion finished it for us both. I thought about that baby for at least ten years – it haunted me. Then, one day, I felt a wave of forgiveness flow over me. It was just before I met my husband. It was like my baby that I had terminated set me free and I was able to go on and love again. I have three children now and they are healthy and wonderful and although I do think about my first baby, I don't beat myself up about him any more.

Veronica, County Wicklow

❧

MY FIRST CHILD was born when I was thirty-five and I couldn't believe how lucky I was. My husband had been married before and he'd had other children but I didn't think I'd ever love anyone as much as I loved Polly, my baby girl. When Polly was three months old, she got meningococcal meningitis and nearly died. Our world was turned upside down. She was in hospital for two years, during which she became blind, her hearing is very bad, and she lost two toes on one foot, four on the other, a thumb and two fingers and she's got a hole in her face instead of a nose. She's had lots of plastic surgery and she looks much better now, but she'll always be handicapped.

While Polly was in hospital, I discovered I was pregnant. I

couldn't believe it. It was the last thing I could cope with. I went to England to have an abortion because I absolutely had to make sure that I could be there for Polly 100 per cent every day for the rest of her life. We weren't even sure how long Polly would live, but I didn't want anything to be a distraction for even a moment from all the love I needed to give her.

Polly is ten now and she lives in residential care. I am so proud of her that she fought so hard to stay alive. I don't regret my abortion because it was what I had to do at the time. Polly's my only child. I wouldn't want it any other way.

Anonymous

❧

WHEN I WAS SIXTEEN, I was staying in my friend's house for the night as I regularly did before going to a local rugby club disco. She had an older sister who was twenty and meant to be staying with us and minding us while her parents were away. When I arrived at my friend's house, she said that her sister had to go away for the night but would be back the next day. We were both very naïve but excited at the prospect of being on our own in the house. We went to the disco and had a great night.

When her sister returned the following day, she was visibly upset. She had been to London and back with her best friend who had a very quick abortion. I can still remember the cloak and dagger exercise and the shock of hearing what her friend had done. But over the years, I have heard this same story more and more. How many women are now living with the regret of an abortion because they had no choice or the guilt that was thrust upon them by the Catholic Church and the closed society that represented Ireland until recently? I think a lot more than we would like to admit and maybe we need to take responsibility for our young women and support them in the choices that they make.

Zoe, County Dublin

Whatever choice we make, we do it with courage, determination and joyful abandon for whatever nature has in store for us on our journey through life!

Childbirth

Modern obstetrics and midwifery means that women should be more empowered than ever to enjoy childbirth – but are we? So many women talk negatively about their experience of giving birth. Despite all the advances of pain relief, the epidurals, general anaesthetic and all the drugs and acupuncture we can take, very few women come out of the labour ward with memories of anything except pain! How astonishing that something that can cause such terrible pain can also bring such joy. But that's the strength of being a woman, isn't it?

When Juliet worked in midwifery and ObGyn, it was very fashionable to write up a birth plan, which was a sort of recipe for the midwives to follow, listing preferences for pain relief, music and lots of expectations – which were rarely met! What Juliet began to realise is that the more elaborate and explicit the birth plan, the more unpredictable and badly planned the birth seemed to go. The truth of the matter is that babies and our bodies are unpredictable. And nature has such extraordinary power that even medical science can't always get it right.

Michelle found while giving birth that the most important thing was for her to trust her midwife. Be confident in what you want during your labour. Be careful to speak your mind but at the same time acknowledge that your midwife is at work and very unlikely to see things exactly the same way! But most of all – enjoy your delivery. It's a very special moment, you won't have many, and you'll always want to be able to remember it joyfully.

IT'S A HORRIBLE FACT that if you don't have a Caesarean section there is a good chance that you will never see your perineum again after giving birth – enjoy it while you have it!

Monica, 36, make-up artist, County Carlow

❧

CHILDBIRTH? Yes, it's awful, but you do forget – if you didn't, you wouldn't have any more!

Jenny, scriptwriter, 47, London, England

❧

IF YOU WANT DRUGS to help you through labour – do it. If you want to go it alone you should be let do it also – only listen to people whose advice you agree with. Don't take on board anything that doesn't sit with you. Trust your gut!

Roisin, 47, chef, Birmingham, England

❧

CABBAGE LEAVES are a great cure for mastitis on the first few days after giving birth. Nobody tells you that after giving birth you are going to need wads of massive sanitary towels like your granny used to wear and will possibly need to use them for up to eight weeks while getting used to getting up in the middle of the night to feed your baby!

Carol, 48, domestic goddess, County Dublin

Raspberry leaf tea before giving birth and rubbing almond oil on your vulva helps the contraction and retraction of the area.

Majella, 42, Amsterdam, Holland

※

Rub bio oil into your skin while pregnant and afterwards to help relieve stretch marks.

Harriet, 34, pharmacist, County Carlow

※

Just relax, is the best advice I got, no point in worrying yourself silly, women have been doing childbirth for a very long time, trust your instincts.

Fran, 39, County Carlow

※

Even though your method of childbirth may be the same as others, your journey will be unique. I found birth plans are a great way of preparing for the event, as they gave me a sense of purpose and control. However, don't panic as your birth plan may go out the window when events unfold in a different manner. Remain flexible and roll with it.

Áine, 39, former post-primary teacher, County Dublin

DON'T LISTEN TO other women's tales of woe when it comes to labour and birth, some folks make it sound epic and like to lay it on thick: 'I was in labour for three days, my waters broke and people thought the dam up the road had collapsed, the nurse came at me with a ten-inch needle, there was blood up the walls, the midwife passed out with exhaustion,' etc.

I have had two experiences of labour and birth. Yeah, the first one was fairly long drawn-out, but hey, this was new to my body. We hadn't done the push-the-large-thing-through-the-small-opening bit before, so it wasn't going to be a walk in the park. I opted for an epidural as my travelling companion on that journey. Felt nothing from my bust to my toes. What can I say, it does what it says on the tin. All in all it wasn't so bad so I decided to do it again.

My second birth was a different one. Different, good. I listened to my body. I was calm, relaxed and enjoyed every minute. From when the drip kicked in and I rocked gently on a rocking chair, to when I stood up with my elbows resting on the bed and did something resembling a hula dance. Until finally making a sound like a grizzly bear on an electrified fence giving it my all and delivering my beautiful baby girl with the aid of gas and air (wonderful stuff) and a shot of pethidine.

My babies came into the world, Abby to the sounds of Charles Aznavour singing 'She' (from *Notting Hill*) and Eve to the sound of James Blunt (can't remember which song). I cried. Not with pain but with pure joy and that you have to experience for yourself because I'm sure the greatest poet could not put into words how you feel at that heart-melting moment. When the little person who you first saw as something the size of a kidney bean on an ultrasound is placed in your arms and you realise, I'm a mum!

Deborah, 37, technician in computer company, Northern Ireland

IF YOUR LABOUR has to be induced with Petocin (oxytocin injection, USP), get the epidural! I wanted a natural childbirth, but in America there's really no such thing. I'll tell you, like, the fourth nurse on duty during my sixteenth hour of excruciating labour told me, 'Honey, no one is going to give you an award for having this baby without the epidural!'

Shelly, 40, palm reader, Texas, USA

༄

I THINK IT'S IMPORTANT to be fit prior to pregnancy, it helps with the labour – and get the epidural no matter what anyone says.

Sophie, teacher, County Wicklow

༄

DON'T IMMEDIATELY LIE FLAT on your back when the hospital staff tell you to – find your own position. My best one was bouncing on my haunches like a frog about to leap – helped the pain go away – but it all came back big time when they made me lie on the bed. No way! Oh, and don't expect to 'fall in love' immediately with the wailing creature that caused you so much pain and falls out of your body. And don't feel guilty about it if you don't. It will come.

Basically just don't listen or expect your experience to be like anyone else's. It just won't be. And don't read too many 'how to' books. Even breast-feeding is a minefield for some.

Debs, 39, non-teaching assistant, Bedford, England

DON'T HAVE A RIGID BIRTH PLAN – it never goes to plan! Play it by ear and you'll actually feel more in control than you would if a plan fails to come to fruition. And despite the pain, try to enjoy … it's a scary but wonderful experience.

Martina, 37, psychiatric nurse, Northern Ireland

❧

YOU WILL KNOW when it is real labour – really.

Accept the epidural – we really have nothing to prove about how much pain we can take.

If the doctor offers hypnosis, take it. It's great!

Say no to Petocin! Tell them in advance and be forceful about it! You still feel the pain but it makes you too stupid to complain – that's why the nurses like it!

Ask ahead for no internal monitoring. It is unnecessary unless there is a risk.

Sit up during birthing. It is much easier, less painful and a better experience.

Let them take the baby to the nursery when you are tired! They will take good care of the baby and you will appreciate the rest later!

There is no right or wrong way to birth your child – hospital, midwife, in water … your body and your will can guide you and it is your experience. So, choose wisely and enjoy.

Kirsten, 39, office manager and director of communications, Illinois, USA

❧

LISTEN TO NO ONE! Every woman is different, how they cope with the labour and birth depends on that person. I had a really bad time – three days of slow labour, I was left too long to have any kind of pain relief. It was scary. Even now when my friends are having babies I don't mention too much of what I went through because I wouldn't want to put them off. If you really knew what you were in for, would you go through with it? I love my son with every breath I have but there is a reason for small families – birth!

Elaine, 36, stay-at-home-mum, Derry, Northern Ireland

✥

DEMAND AN EPI on arrival.
Arm yourself with a TENS machine and an iPod.
Use a bouncy ball to move to music.
Breathe.
Take gazillions of gas in the labour ward and hopefully the epi will work.
Breathe lots more.
Push hubby away and curse at all and sundry.
Push until your veins are protruding in your face.
Gape in wonder and awe.
Puke.

Susan, 42, full-time mum, County Dublin

✥

DON'T LISTEN to other women's stories, yours will be different. Trust your own instinct, you will know when the baby is coming. Above all other things, stay calm.

Jennifer, 47, outreach/case worker, County Dublin

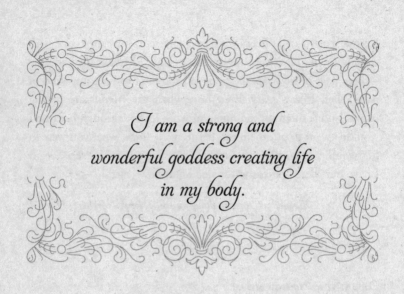

I am a strong and wonderful goddess creating life in my body.

Now that I have it, what do I do with it?

Coming home from the hospital with a new baby – and an enormous shopping list! Nobody can be prepared enough for all the twists and turns of new motherhood. But many women are so caught up with preparation, getting all the equipment in, preparing the nursery, that they're too tired to enjoy the baby when it arrives. Our grandmothers and our mothers didn't have any of the modern equipment that we have now to feed, change and transport babies – they had much larger families and they got by famously.

Be careful about putting all your energies into your changing station, your diaper genie and your microwave steriliser – and none into singing a song to your baby in your arms. Don't forget to rock your baby. Sing to her. Tell her stories before she can speak. Read her a story every night before she goes to bed. And tell her every minute how much your love her! And don't forget, you don't have to get everything right. Babies are much tougher and much stronger than you think.

Michelle remembers arriving home from the Rotunda Hospital with her bundle of joy. It was the third day after giving birth and together with the euphoria of discovering that she was the proud bearer of the most beautiful boy that was ever born, she was drained and experiencing the worst period and discomfort from her stitches and sleep deprivation. Her husband propped her up against a pillow on the couch in the living room. He was so proud and delighted and had put the three days that she had spent in hospital to good use by painting the living room. The fact that he had broken her favourite vase in the process didn't matter as she had different priorities now that she was a mother, and what would have been important a few days before was no longer. A programme came on the television discussing the starving millions in some unfortunate part of Africa and the flood gates opened. Michelle was inconsolable. Her mother rushed in from the kitchen and nodded knowingly. She had crossed a threshold – she now knew what it meant to feel all the pain and joy and responsibility that go with being a mother. She was changed that day forever.

Juliet was twenty-two when she had her first baby, and very inexperienced! She was working as an intern, up all night running around the hospital and then going home to a very cranky baby! One day, she had been shopping in the supermarket and put the baby on a wall asleep in her carrycot while she unpacked the groceries from the car. She went up to her flat, put the groceries away and decided to lie down for a nap. After a couple of hours her husband came in. They sat and chatted for a while and then he asked her, as they were eating dinner, 'Where's the baby?'

Juliet had left her on the wall.

They raced down to find her still there – fast asleep. She'd never guessed.

Today, Juliet's baby Molly is twenty-one. She still loves to hear the story about how her mum came home and forgot she had a baby! 🖤

THEY KEEP CHANGING THE RULES with what you should do and shouldn't do with babies when they are small – my children were born over a twenty-year period and I stopped listening to any advice – you know best.

Ciara, 45, mum, County Dublin

Do try this at home:

Now that you are a mother you have an instinct and knowledge of your baby that nobody else in the world can possibly ever have. You know what your baby needs and when she needs it. The biggest thing you have to do now is to trust yourself and your inner voice – take on board only the advice that you feel suits you. If you want to breast feed, that is fine – be firm with those around you and say this is what you are doing. In the same way, if you choose to bottle feed, be clear and happy with your decision – there is no need for guilt or doubt with this either. Be true to yourself and your baby.

WHEN THE CHILDREN were babies I used to have the beds made, the kitchen floor washed and the house spotless by nine o'clock or else I felt like a failure. New mothers put terrible pressure on themselves. You can get into a rut with things that don't matter – so do what does matter to you. Now, my kids are all over ten and all I worry about is checking my emails by nine o'clock – I haven't washed my kitchen floor in weeks.

Niamh, 41, engineer, County Dublin

I THINK YOU HAVE to be prepared to leave your brain in the maternity hospital after you have a baby. It took me a full year to recover physically after each of my babies – emotionally I don't think I will ever recover. Young mums, there is hope, though, and you do get to the stage where your life becomes somewhat normal again, but after kids, your priorities will never be the same.

Jane, 47, IT consultant, County Cork

Do try this at home:

Pinch yourself every day to remind yourself of this: your children don't belong to you. They are a gift that you are given for a short, short time. They are on loan to you and very soon you'll have to give them away to someone else … so make sure they still like you enough to call by every now and then!

I was sitting in a fast-food restaurant with my husband and our new baby Jessica needed a feed. So I opened my anorak about an inch (this was Galway, West of Ireland, mid-winter!) to let her snuggle in. The weather was freezing so there certainly wasn't any flesh on display that day. A man came over to me from the next table where he was sitting with his wife and seven children and asked me to stop. 'You shouldn't be feeding her in here,' he said. 'You should go into the toilet to do that.' I politely explained to him that the baby needed feeding – and that he wouldn't be expected to go into the toilet to eat his lunch. He got his entire family to get up and leave the restaurant, food uneaten. I felt so sorry for his kids and his wife. What a shame that the mere thought of a woman very privately breast-feeding her baby at the next table was enough to put him off his lunch!

Juliet

ॐ

MY FIRST DAUGHTER was sick when she was born. I couldn't feed her and my milk was pathetic, so she was admitted to the special care unit. I cried and cried – I felt such a failure. Then one of the nurses came along and spotted me crying and asked me what was up and I explained that I thought my baby had got sick because I couldn't feed her. She showed me that my breasts were full of milk – I just hadn't the first clue how to get it out! She was an intensive care nurse and it wasn't her job to teach breast-feeding, but the midwives had all been very busy so they'd left the baby with me and gone away back to their work. This intensive care nurse sat there with me for hours that night and just by encouraging me, got me feeding the baby. She'd breast-fed twins and seven other kids herself. After that, I always made an effort with any of my friends who had babies to sit with them while they were breast-feeding to encourage them. It can be very lonely otherwise.

Sallyanne, 35, librarian, County Dublin

ॐ

I CAME TO TANZANIA in 2007 at the age of sixty-seven to help at our Mission here. One thing that surprised me then was that a grandmother well past the age of child-bearing could actually breast-feed again. Did you know that? It seems that with constant suckling, lactation can begin again. In our area, small babies are often left without a mother due to AIDs and other horrific diseases and the grandmother or other older woman is often left to look after these little children. Happily, they can breast-feed.

Frances, Holy Union Sister, Dar es Salaam, Tanzania

ॐ

THERE IS NO RIGHT and wrong when it comes to breast-feeding, but after a year is generally a good time to stop. The nutrients are minimal after that and it is generally more a form of comfort as the child should be eating a variety of food at this stage. Some women advocate breast-feeding up to the age of four and older and I have to ask who is the breast-feeding for when it is carried on this long?

Kim, 41, nurse, Birmingham, England

ॐ

NEVER EVER wake a sleeping baby (advice for new mums).

Laura, 28, mum, Waterford

ॐ

WHY DO SOME PARENTS feel it necessary to boast that little Johnny or little Sue was staying dry all night by the age of two? Every child is different and it's unnecessary boasting and sometimes downright lying. It only serves to undermine and make women feel inadequate in their job as parents.

Fran, 36, teacher, County Galway

%

You HAVEN'T FAILED as a parent just because your kids take ages to potty train!

Jane, 39, surgeon,

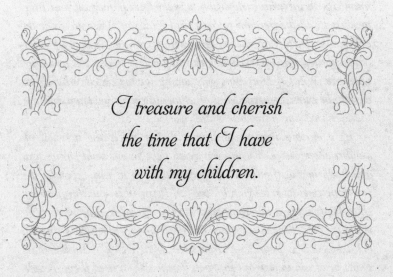

I treasure and cherish the time that I have with my children.

Being a mum

When do you stop being just yourself and start being someone else's mum? It's an incredible transition to make from having all your time to yourself, all the freedom to come and go as you please, to suddenly being completely responsible for another person. And with that responsibility comes a terrifying and fragile love that scares us to our very core. What if something goes wrong for my child? What if he were to be hurt? Injured? Most of us would rather lie down and die than let anything harm our child!

It's a curious instinct for survival that places the survival of another above our own – and yet, we all fight for our children's welfare and happiness as if our own lives depended on it. Little wonder we can sometimes let it all go a bit too far! Being in love with your own child is probably a necessary part of their early life. The important thing is to see it for what it is – an affair to remember. And like all great loves, it is bound to come with anxieties, fears and dreads. Don't be afraid to seek out supports whenever you need them. People are happy to help. You aren't a failure if you find mothering difficult – you are a success if you recognise how hard it is and harness the support you need.

Women are tribal when it comes to rearing children. We are good team players and we know what works. Build a support network of *other women in the same situation as yourself. Don't try to do it all on your own.*

It's extremely important if you have come from the world of work and are now at home minding children to keep in touch with the outside world – this can be done easily with technology and the internet or by joining a community group or class for your baby. This gives you a chance to meet other mums in your locality.

If you have parents or in-laws that live nearby, nurture them – appreciate and accept any help they are willing to give. Children thrive with a supportive family network.

It can be so hard to learn to let go of your children when they hit their teens. People tell you children grow up too quickly and it's such a cliché, but it's so easy to forget to just sit back and enjoy your kids every day. We spend so much time worrying about our children – their future, their school results, their employment and marriage prospects – that we can forget that they are going to be growing up in a world that's very different from anything we experienced and so we can't possibly prepare them for it. The only thing we can do is to love them, every day. Never stop telling your children that you love them, that you're proud of them and that you are lucky to have them in your life. ✍

ONE DAY WHEN I was in my local shops a little old lady stopped to admire my seven-month-old. Where I live is populated with lots of little old ladies, so this was a pretty regular occurrence. But then she said, 'Oh, he is lovely. Enjoy him now, just enjoy him!'

And to be honest, up until that point it had never actually occurred to me to enjoy my own baby. I was so caught up in first-time mother nerves that all I had concentrated on was just keeping him alive! I was totally focused on feeding him, washing him and making sure he slept that I just sort of forgot to enjoy him! But it really made me think and after that I did try to relax and just enjoy him and it is so true; they are little for such a short time and you can get so engrossed in trying to get them into a routine and making sure they do all the right things that it can be easy to forget just to enjoy them for the great little people they are. Since then, I've gone on to have a little girl and from the moment she was born, I have just really enjoyed her and it has been wonderful!

Ciara, blogger, writer and mum, County Dublin

Do try this at home:

Cherish the early years with your baby and young child – they are hectic and exhausting but very brief.

Don't compare your children to those of your friends and family. All children are individuals and will reach their milestones at different ages.

Make a special box to keep little mementos and reminders of your child's early years.

Take too many photos – you will be surprised how quickly your little one changes by the week. (Keep this practice up with each child – often families have too many of the eldest and very few of the youngest child.)

Don't forget that this child is yours and your partner's and nobody else is going to be as interested in it as you are!

DON'T WASTE TIME limiting the amount of TV your kids want to watch as toddlers – enjoy the peace that it brings. In a couple of years, you will be begging them to stop wrecking the house and sit down and watch a movie.

Vicky, 41, physiotherapist, County Dublin

❧

DON'T KNOCK YOUR CHILDREN – the world will deal them enough setbacks. Encourage them to try, praise them on what they do well, express regret when they make mistakes and give them strength and comfort them when they have disappointments.

Karen, 53, sales assistant, London, England

❧

BEFORE I HAD CHILDREN, I thought motherhood would be filled with picnics in the park, Saturday afternoons baking muffins with my little helpers, all that fun stuff. I now have three children, a husband, a dog and a full-time job, and things are a far cry from the Utopia I imagined. If someone had told me back then that there would be days when I would be a screaming lunatic trying to juggle a dozen things at once and failing dismally, I would have said they were crazy.

There may well be women out there for whom it is all so easy but for most of us it's a chaotic dash through the day trying to get as many boxes ticked as possible. As women, we can be hard on each other and even harder on ourselves. There are days I feel like a complete failure – as a mother, a wife, a daughter, a friend, an employee and so many other things. It's OK not to be perfect. It's OK to feel overwhelmed sometimes. You'd be surprised how many women are feeling the exact same way.

Dawn, editor, County Dublin

🐝

I WAS THE ELDEST in my family and my mother had four boys after I was born. I remember one day we were in the living room and my youngest brother, who was about four at the time, picked up a picture of my parents with all his siblings. He was quick to spot his absence and asked, 'Mummy, where was I?' 'You were in my tummy,' she replied. My brother looked at her with utter shock. 'Did you eat me?' he asked innocently. We still remind him of that story!

Jenny, 42, auctioneer, County Dublin

🐝

I WOKE UP LATE for work one day, not so long ago, and thought: this day could get worse or I can alter it now. So instead of running around the house trying to get three kids to school – up, dressed and lunches made – knowing everyone would have been in bad humour, I decided to go down and bring three bowls of cereal up to the kids in bed. Told them it was a special day. They woke up laughing. I ran back down, prepared the lunches, brought up toast and juice. They were so happy when they were finished that they got dressed did their teeth, faces and hands without having to go downstairs until we were all ready to leave. We got out of the house at the same time as usual. They are still talking about it because they usually only get breakfast in bed on their birthday.

Maria, 36, health worker, County Dublin

 ୬

OUR BABIES ALL THINK that we are all Yummy Mummies, and we probably are – but the common definition is probably a description of an impossibly perfect, youthful glamour-puss, placid, talented, socially active, with the assets of a Stepford wife. Her child/children are also perfect physically and seen as a sort of accessory resting on a hip. Her child will probably be superior mentally also, as the Yummy Mummy undoubtedly played Mozart during and after her pregnancy and has French tapes playing while they stroll round the art gallery.

I wasn't actually a Yummy Mummy, I must confess – just a very hassled working mother who never seemed to have the right clothes for any social events – but I knew some Yummy Mums. We had an adorable next-door neighbour who looked like the goddess Diana – tall, athletic, blonde with beautiful tanned skin and the mother of four delightful children, a handsome, successful husband and the sweetest nature. She played tennis daily, did the (large) garden, went to coffee mornings – and told me once that she envied me because I had a job where I could make a difference. I assured her that she made a difference too! Another Yummy Mum, an incredibly beautiful brunette with two beautiful, talented children and an equally enviable social life but no career, was hoping to persuade her businessman husband to let her train as a teacher of handicapped children – perhaps she wanted to make a difference too.

Now I think my daughter, daughter-in-law and their friends were, and still are, all Yummy Mummies, in my definition of the expression. They are completely enamoured of their children, but don't spoil them; they are obviously proud of but not boastful about their children; they cultivate their cultural, artistic and sporting interests, dissuade their children from aggression and praise their achievements, but don't stifle them with ideas. They are working mothers, the equals of their spouses, very comely and self-assured – what could be yummier?

Jaclyn, endocrinologist, Victoria, Australia

⚭

WHEN MY YOUNGEST grew out of her first pair of little pink Wellingtons, I didn't have the heart to pass them on – so I put them to good use and filled them with fertiliser and planted bedding flowers in them. Wellingtons make great flower pots of all sizes!

Rachel, 43, anaesthetic nurse, County Dublin

⚭

TREASURE THE PARTIES you have for your children while they are small – soon enough they won't be interested in celebrating in their own house, and before you know it, they won't want you involved at all!

Leanne, 45, set designer, County Dublin

TAKE A MOMENT whenever you can to just look at and cherish your children – those of us who have them are blessed in a way we should always remember.

Elizabeth was eight weeks old when she had her first operation. She was suffering from liver failure and had to undergo three more operations before we were told that she would have a chance of survival. I was walking down the corridor of Our Lady's Hospital in Crumlin and overheard a woman in convulsions telling someone on the other end of the line that her little girl was going to lose the top of her little finger on her right hand. I remember thinking that I would gladly give the tops of all of my daughter's fingers to keep her alive and swap places with that woman. I keep this thought with me always and realise that your problems are as big as you allow them to be. Elizabeth is now four and doing really well living a normal, happy life – we are very fortunate.

Suzie, 34, teacher, County Dublin

❧

DON'T GO BUYING expensive toys for your babies – most shop-bought toys are plastic and not very interesting to touch. Babies love putting things in their mouths and we have become so obsessed with safety we have forgotten about things that are everyday objects and safe. Put a brown paper bag, a large orange, a comb with strong teeth and an avocado into your baby's playpen next time instead of a plastic toy. These are all things that your baby will find amazing. The smell and texture and noise that they make will fill your baby's senses in a way that a shop-bought toy can't – and prepare them for the real world.

Karen, 37, child psychologist, England

MAKE THE THREAT REALISTIC!

I once threatened my son with dumping his PS2 if he insisted on coming in past the agreed time. Needless to say it happened again, so I dumped one of the PS2 games and made him believe that's what I had said! He hasn't pushed that boundary since.

Always follow through with threats! When I was younger, my brother and I would always fight and Mum would always say, 'I'll tell your father.' Both of us never pushed boundaries with him so it was a good threat until we realised that no matter how bad we got, Mum never told him. Because of that we always played up on her.

Sorry Mum!

Brenda, 37, psychiatric nurse, Northern Ireland

To be a good mum
I first need to be me.

teenage kicks

There isn't a parent anywhere who'll tell you that they look forward to their children's teen years. And for parents of teenagers, the incredible cruelty that your teens can pour on you can be frightening! But it's important not to let the hostility your teens express get you down.

Teenagers feel as though they are adults – from the age of around fifteen, they feel as mature and capable and independent as you do. You may not see them that way, but it is vital that you acknowledge your teenager's rights to an adult life because otherwise you will alienate him completely and cause yourself unending stress as well. Children do become adults at fifteen and yet they still need our support – just because your daughter is having sex doesn't mean she doesn't need her teddy bear at night. It's this complexity that makes our teens such fun, and the most important thing is to keep loving them. ✒

ADOLESCENCE IS A TIME fraught with challenges, when young people go through many changes at a physical, emotional and social level. Somehow parents have forgotten most of that themselves (thankfully, you might say). In my experience working with parents for many years, a useful exercise is to get parents to reflect on their own teenage years – were the friends very important? What was on their minds? Was it anything about their parents' well-being or was it, more likely, something to do with friends, fashion, sport, the opposite sex and a crush, etc?

Teenage boys are not renowned for their conversation skills, especially around parents. The little boy who wanted to go everywhere with his mum doesn't want to be seen anywhere near her in public now. This can come as a shock to first-time parents, but it is perfectly normal and will change again in a few years. It is an important stage in development when they need to develop a sense of who they are and who and what they identify with.

Teenagers are often preoccupied with the range of changes they are experiencing. Can you recall what it was like to feel your body changing and developing or if you were falling out with friends, sure of yourself today and thinking everyone is talking about you tomorrow? Then add in a few hormones to the mix and see how that plays itself out.

The above is a way of understanding teenagers but it is not a reason to condone bad behaviour. So when do parents need to get involved?

1. If they are really disrespectful (this does not include a grunt or a look, etc.).
2. If they are involved in anything that is a risk to their health and safety, including hurting someone or damaging property.
3. If they compromise their education, e.g. mitching school, poor behaviour in school, etc.

In these instances, parents need an appropriate discipline plan which they can both agree on and which they carry out assertively.

Raising teenagers can be difficult, but remember, they need more than ever to know that you love them and they are still the beautiful children you had before – if you remember to notice that.

Margaret, 57, parenting advisor, County Dublin

Do try this at home:

Get to know your teenager's friends, their favourite bands, the books they like, buy in their favourite foods, respect their culture. Their teenage world is so important to them and they'll respect you more if you show real interest in their world and care about it.

I HAD DINNER with my mum tonight and over a few glasses of wine told her about a few parties we had when we were kids behind her back! But the funny thing was we were so naive – our grandparents lived behind us and although we thought our parties were unsupervised, not so. Pop (my granddad) had a shotgun and when the noise level got too loud he would silently arrive out of nowhere into the kitchen with the shotgun over his arm half cocked and the fifty local lads and lassies would scarper within thirty seconds! I wish he was still alive he would make a fortune now on a fire drill that takes my office three minutes! Oh, the memories!

Karen, 42, business centre manager, County Dublin

DON'T BE NAÏVE and think, My son or daughter is not having sex. Remember they are crossing thresholds that you didn't even know about before they hit puberty.

Yvonne, 45, interior designer, County Dublin

TELL YOUR CHILDREN to never go up the stairs empty handed – it will save hours of cleaning!

Vicky, 41, physiotherapist, County Dublin

I don't have to understand my children to love them.

Mothers and daughters

The eternal love–hate relationship – the mother–daughter bond. What is it about mothers and their daughters that can cause such frustration amid the joy? Perhaps as women we sometimes try to mould our daughters a little too much. It's tempting to see our daughters as a second chance to be ourselves. But the quicker we forget about this, the better. Our daughters are very different people – the joy is realising this and cherishing every moment of discovering it.

Women often try to reinvent themselves through their daughters. Michelle's mother always wanted her to have short hair – she said that her mother made her wear waist-length plaits until she was twelve. She didn't want Michelle to be burdened with the same affliction, so she used to have it cut short like a boy until Michelle was of an age where she would take care of it herself. But Michelle wanted to be like other little girls with long, flowing hair!

So when her daughter Nicole was born, she was delighted to have the opportunity to watch her little girl grow her hair nice and long. Michelle discovered that it wasn't easy to keep because her daughter hated having the knots taken out and the constant care needed to ensure that it looked good, but she had her flowing mane and Michelle was very proud. Then shortly before turning six, Nicole took it upon herself to change her hairstyle and didn't tell Michelle.

Using nail scissors, she hacked into it, taking chunks off and leaving herself with a mullet and long tail down her back! When Michelle went in to look on her later that night she found mounds of her hair in the sink. She ran in to see Nicole sleeping peacefully with her new hairstyle. Michelle was devastated. The next morning they went to the hairdresser, who said that the best Michelle could hope for was a smart bob. It did look sweet but wasn't what Michelle had wanted for Nicole. When Michelle said sadly that 'it was lovely', her daughter put her hand up to comfort her and said, 'It will grow back, Mum. It's only hair!'

Wise words from a five-year-old! And the wisdom of generations had come full circle.

Our daughters are different people and it's so important to remember that your daughter's world is very different to your own.

TELL THE PEOPLE you love how you feel about them at every opportunity. You never know when will be your last chance. My mother died at forty-one. My sister died at thirty-nine. The last time my sister and I spoke I kissed her on the cheek and told her I loved her. When I saw her three hours later she was unconscious and hours away from death. I have a lot of regrets about my life, but if I hadn't had a chance to tell her how important she was to me, I'd have a lot more regret.

Dawn, newspaper editor, County Dublin

I WAS PANICKING about deadlines for assignments and was so tired from pulling all-nighters, and I broke down crying. My eleven-year-old daughter told me, 'It's OK. What's the worst that can happen?

Tell your teacher you'll have it for next week. I'll ring Granny to have us for tea and you have a wee sleep.' I felt really guilty that she was taking 'care of me' but I thank my lucky stars that I have such a loving daughter and I did what she told me. I felt so much better after my sleep, and I emailed my tutor and it was all OK!

Catherine, 32, student, Northern Ireland

❧

Baby girls take less time to be delivered than baby boys. Even in our infant years with our most primal instincts we have the edge!

Louise, 42, midwife, County Dublin

❧

My mother always said that she learned her hardest lessons from her children. She had a wonderful singing voice and had sung in choirs and musical societies all her life. So when my sister, Sarah, began to show signs of becoming a promising little songstress herself at the tender age of nine, Mum wasted no time in arranging an audition with a prominent voice coach in Dublin. However, as the big day approached, Sarah showed no enthusiasm, much to Mother's annoyance. At the audition, Sarah made no effort and croaked her way through the pieces.

As they made their way up Westland Row afterwards, Mum tried to conceal her fury. Holding Sarah's hand firmly she asked her why she'd made such a mess of her big chance. Sarah simply replied, 'I never wanted to do it.' With this, Mum abandoned her calm demeanour and began to rant and rave about singing and talent and how she had wanted Sarah to be just like her. Sarah immediately let go of Mum's hand and stopped dead in her tracks. 'But I don't want to be like you,' she said innocently.

I'm happy to report that thirty years on, both mother and daughter are best of friends, but my mother always said it was her most levelling experience as a parent.

Ger, novelist, County Dublin

᙮

MY NINETEEN-YEAR-OLD daughter and I have a special bond. We communicate several times daily, even though she is living away from home to attend college. We are honest and supportive of one another. We may argue about a topic but we always listen to the other's point of view. When taking big steps forward in life, we are there to cheer each other on. We provide a good balance for each other, with love and open communication.

I cherish my relationship with my beautiful daughter.

Elizabeth, 55, artist, Canada

> *I acknowledge that my daughter and I are two very different and special women.*

Mothers and sons

Mothers and their sons – are we tempted to spoil the men in our lives just a little bit too much in the hope that they'll never love another woman quite like us?

Michelle's son used to hang on her breast as a baby when she fed him. He was and is still so cuddly and affectionate. Her daughter was a very efficient feeder and never spent more than ten minutes on each boob – she didn't want to miss anything in the process. Maybe it was just personality or maybe boys just can't get enough of our boobs!

To be a mother of sons is a great opportunity to develop a deep relationship with a man. And it's a great opportunity to help young boys grow up to be thoughtful, caring and considerate men. Talk to them about the qualities that women like and do it in a fun manner. If there's ever a man you can hope to have a strong influence on, it's your son. So make sure you give him strong messages about women, and that you encourage him to be a man who admires and respects women just as much as he admires and respects you. ✿

LITTLE BOYS are totally wrapped up with their mums until they reach about six and then they want dad's attention – it's really important for your husband to realise this. I know that when my son was very small, my husband was jealous of the attention and time that he took from me – I sometimes felt that my husband was the child by taking his resentment out on our son. He used to look at my breasts and grimace at the pleasure our son received from suckling. But now that he is old enough to kick a ball and shoot a basketball hoop and go diving in the swimming pool, he wants his dad. I don't mind but wish that my husband had realised that he was only mine for a little while. Enjoy your sons – this stage doesn't last forever.

Patricia, 54, teacher, County Dublin

❧

WITH MY SON I live in fear of the day when he is too big for mammy kisses and cuddles, so I'm getting a lifetime in now just in case. I get very emotional when I think that one day I won't be his be all and end all – while the girl I'm proud of every independent little move she makes. Girl power! A true Irish mammy, or what?

Claire, 34, author and journalist, Derry, Northern Ireland

❧

IT'S REALLY UNFAIR but most children look like their father – someone once told me that this was so that the father would bond with the child.

My son loves to hear about what he was like as a baby. How beautiful he was and the story of the man who walked up to us in the street and gave him a €10 note for being so lovely. He takes it on himself now to give a euro or whatever he has when he meets a new baby for the first time. He is genuinely interested in newborns and has said that he wants to make a good father some day. He is only nine so I did tell him not to rush it!

Noelle, 37, mother, County Cork

Do try this at home:

Avoid repeating the mistakes you saw in your house growing up by spoiling your son or treating him differently to his sisters. You are responsible for how he behaves with the opposite sex, as your relationship sets the standard.

LITTLE BOYS ARE DIFFERENT – it's hard to explain why they like contact sports or read adventure rather than fairy stories, or why they shout so loud. We used to live in a semi-rural area and didn't have a TV. My daughter had Barbie dolls called fairy princess names, but my son somehow acquired two military man-dolls complete with camouflage outfits who were called Fierce-o and Toughie and who beat the living daylights out of each other and the girlie dolls. We were an anti-war sort of family so this was a bit daunting at the time! But these aggressive tendencies didn't persist, and our son is now a very courteous man, terribly kind to women, respectful to old people and doesn't even think of kicking the cat. I think that some men are more likely to become violent but the reasons are the community failure to provide appropriate occupational advice and training. We should be out there canvassing for positive support for our sons. Let's hear it for the mothers of sons!

Philomena, 72, physician, Australia

SONS REALLY NEED a strong male mentor from the age of about nine – this person may not be a close relative – even an older cousin can be a wonderful influence and person that offers security from the judgement of parents.

Francesca, 42, mum, County Limerick

🐝

LITTLE BOYS LOVE COOKING just as much as little girls and they can weigh out ingredients and stir and do all the things little girls do – my husband rang me once a short time after we moved in together while I was away for a night. He wanted to know how to cook a pizza that was in the freezer. I will ensure that my son is better equipped for his future partner!

Sandy, 43, cabin crew, Luton, England

🐝

I HAVE FIVE CHILDREN and they each are different in their own way but all were excellent when it came to school – all, that is, apart from my youngest son. He was a dreamer. He went from one bad report to the next and when he got to Leaving Cert and his studies were only causing him and the rest of the family frustration, we let him leave school early. He wanted to travel the world and find himself. He was always interested in different things to my other children and while living in the UK, he found a topic that he loved while working as a gardener – he decided to go back to college as a mature student and study bugs. This degree brought him to a master's and, in a few weeks, I will be attending his conferral as a doctor. He is currently a university lecturer. So my advice is to let your children be true to who they are – they will find their own feet in their own way.

Jackie, 68, bridge player, County Dublin

*I will give my son the support
he needs to grow up to be
the best man that he can.*

Parenting isn't for everyone

Having children isn't for everyone. During our journey to write this book, we were especially empowered by women who are child-free and whose lives have been made powerful and fulfilled by being able to devote their passions to what is important to them. We were also fascinated by the number of women who told us that if they were to live their lives again, they might choose to remain child-free next time.

Children are a huge responsibility and a burden as well as a joy, and there is a tendency in our century to overrate children, which can make women without children feel left out, like a failure or depressed. Your body is your body. If it is fertile and you want to procreate, that is your choice. If you want to become a mother where nature has not provided for you, there are many opportunities available to you to be a mom, aunt, guardian, or carer of children in any number of other ways. Being a parent isn't just about having a positive pregnancy test, a bump and a day in the labour ward. It's also about school bullies, Maths you can't figure out, smelling smoke from a locked bedroom door, finding drugs, getting a door slammed in your face and spending all your money on a designer handbag for a teenager whose gratitude will last as long as it takes to read your credit card statement!

Everybody's life is different and parenting isn't for everyone. Be true to who you are. If you desperately want to parent, there are countless ways that modern science can help, but if you can't easily reproduce or even foster children of your own, don't let this destroy your love for children and your ability to be a wonderful aunt, lover, sister, daughter and friend. Your sister's/brother's/friends' children will benefit hugely from your unrivalled love. And finally, remember, all children become adults very, very quickly. There are many experiences that parents miss out on. The important thing is to live a rich and fulfilled life first.

I DON'T THINK it's society that puts pressure on women to have children – it's women themselves wanting to look like they have it all. Sorry, but I've never felt the need to have children or be married or to have a brilliant career. I have a brilliant career, I was married, now divorced and never had children as I don't connect with children. I have friends who, to be perfectly honest, seem to want children in order to fit in. Women put the pressure on themselves. If we are truly free then we decide what we want and are proud of that choice – sadly, I think many of us do things to look successful to other women.

Victoria, 45, scriptwriter, Tasmania, Australia

DEFINITELY, SOCIETY PUTS THE PRESSURE on you to have children. I didn't get married until I was thirty-eight and all I heard (or my parents heard) was, 'Why isn't she married?' It made me crazy! Do we seriously need a man/partner to be complete? Why can't a woman just stand on her own – alone? Plus, I never wanted children, but when I got married, I changed my mind because that's when I was ready for it. I wasn't able to have a child on my own. My, that doesn't mean I'm not a mother. There are many children in my life that I have been a mother to.

Joan, 45, independent, New Jersey, USA

❧

I WAS NEVER MATERNAL. Didn't like kids. Still don't. Love my own obviously, but tolerated my friends'. Hated the 'baby years'. Needed to be able to communicate. Very stressy time.

Debs, 39, non-teaching assistant, Bedford, England

❧

SOCIETY IS FULL OF PEOPLE looking over your shoulder to see what is going on in your life to see if it is better or worse than theirs. They measure their own lives by seeing what the person beside them has. So if the only reason that someone is getting married or starting a family is because they feel that this is what society expects of them, they are mad. Find your own happiness. Don't measure your life by the standards of people around you. I believe you don't truly mature till you are in your thirties. You begin to see life differently as you mature and what people think soon becomes very far down your list of priorities. When you are content in your own life, that is all that matters. If marriage and a family fit the bill, go for it, but it is not the only thing in life. Don't waste time seeking a partner. You will get obsessed. Sit back and let life evolve!

Lynda, 38, mother of four, County Clare

※

WHEN I WAS YOUNG in my twenties, I was like, 'Come on up to the hill of happiness!' I wanted to bring everybody with me but I was considered to be a freak because I was so positive. In my thirties, I chose travel and freedom while everybody was having babies and I felt bad about that. But now I'm in my fifties and I'll tell you, baby, it's all about me!

Beth, 50, makeup artist, County Dublin

Respect your children, trust them and let them go.

In Children

What I want for the children
in my life ...

Spirituality

*S*pirituality, for many, is the word we use to describe the connection with God. How often have you heard God being described? He is ever-present – He made us in His likeness. He has no beginning and no end. He is the essence of all that is good.

These may seem like abstract concepts and difficult to understand in our time–space reality. However, they are all really very simple – God is energy – She is all around us – She is what made us and all living things from the smallest spec of stardust to the elephant.

What if God wasn't some great omnipotent soothsayer as the religious doctrines – that were all written by ordinary men – would have us believe? What if God really was inside us? Then She would be the energy that is us. Science has proven that energy cannot disappear but must go somewhere – so the energy that makes us human will continue on after we are dead.

Spirit and the Universe

Women have always had a sacred connection to spirit and part of this reason is because of the natural spirituality and intuition of women. We feel things differently to men. Often we feel these things in our gut. We grow the seeds of life itself inside our wombs.

Perhaps it's our innate psychic abilities that most women can connect with so easily that sets us apart from men. Through history, we have had to be more intuitive and work in unison with our environment in order to produce and survive.

Michelle used to have difficulty sleeping at night as a child, wondering when the universe started and where it ended. After years of pondering, she is happy to conclude that we may never know the answer to these questions – nor need to. Everyone is part of the great creative consiousness which is the universe. What Michelle believes now is that with the passing of time and the experiences that have brought her to where she is, as a woman and a mother, comes the acceptance that we are all the same. We are each other. We are all made out of the same energy as the universe. And at some time in our future we will all return to being one.

Last year, Juliet started going on astronomy field trips, seeing what astronomers do, looking at the stars. One damp November night she got to see Saturn through a giant telescope in the Phoenix Park. It was the most beautiful thing she'd ever seen, and looking at that giant ball of *gas with its amazing rings, watching over us, she almost cried. It made her realise how much the universe is guarding us, and how very insignificant and yet incredibly fortunate we are to be a part of all of this. These stars. This solar system. Now, whenever she gets upset about something, she thinks of planet Saturn, how beautiful it is watching over us, how fortunate we are to be a part of this universe, and she instantly feels better!* 🌱

I DO BELIEVE there is something there. When I pray for something, my wish is never granted at that stage but it is mostly granted at some later date. When I contemplate this it usually happens just when someone else thinks I need it most rather than when I actually prayed for it. So this leads me to think there is something there bigger than ourselves.

Mary, 46, doctor of criminal, forensic and developmental psychology, Northern Ireland

You are the centre of your universe. Nobody else in the entire world knows how it feels to be you. You are unique and your perception is completely different to everyone else's.

Do we need religion?

Spirituality is an area that is important to us all – if it wasn't, there would never have been so many religions. The strong have used the God-need in people and manipulated it – why else would religion be the cause of so many disputes and major wars since history began? We already know that religion has been used by governments and societies to control people, to horrific effect for many women in the world today. If Jesus, Mohammed or Buddha or any other prophet walked on earth today, they would not possess an ounce of the judgements and dogma that humans have managed to put on each other – and especially on women. This is an area where women have been truly oppressed and in many ways, again, it is because of our power that we have been kept this way.

Not too long ago in Catholic Ireland, a woman had to be 'churched', which was a type of blessing given after she had given birth – a way of cleansing her of the sin she had committed to conceive her child. There was no such ceremony performed on the fathers after the delivery. Why is this? Why do man-made Churches continue to feel the need to keep women in as limited a role as possible and not full members of their Church?

In the Jewish and Muslim faiths the sexes are segregated for prayer. Why are women regarded as inferior? We don't need a religion to tell us how to be or dress or think or love. We have the power of God and we have gut instincts that tell us what is right and wrong. If we trust in this, we are on the road to real spirituality and moving away from the old outdated doctrines on life and how man, not God, wants us to be.

I GO DIRECTLY to my dad – my personal direct line to Heaven – when I want to connect with a higher level. He's never let me down. Believing in something higher than this life is spirituality to me, depending and relying on something we can't touch, see or feel – simply belief.

Mary, author, County Cork

RELIGION IS WHAT we were force-fed from the cradle all the way through school. Spirituality is the personal connection with a greater power than oneself – you don't need to be in a particular building at a particular time to experience it. My mum is big on praying to saints, but I've always said, 'Go to the boss if you want the job done properly!'

Theresa, poet, County Cork

I WAS BORN AND RAISED in Sri Lanka for thirty years, lived and worked in Dubai, United Arab Emirates for five years and emigrated to Australia in 1996. Married for twenty-six-plus years and have two adult daughters still living working/studying at home. My thoughts are as follows:

The experiences one has as a child, teenager and young adult are vital to the individual achieving his/her full potential in later life, so we mothers should do our best to create a conducive environment. It's easy enough to say, but most difficult to do. I find that the faith instilled in me by my own mum and dad and the loving relationships of an extended family with lots of aunties, uncles, grand-aunties and grand-uncles, loving us through good times and bad, make us who we are.

It is good to look back at your own parents' life and see their strengths and weaknesses. While learning and imitating their good examples, we are in a unique position to spot their errors and learn from them. Also we need to be brave enough to discuss our own faults and shortcomings with kids, so they feel they are in a unique position to look and learn (never to be like Mum, who is a maniac about eating veggies and being so neat and tidy).

We women must learn to forgive and it starts at home. It may be a partner who is unfaithful, a friend who has hurt you deeply or your own child forsaking your values and ideals and bringing you disrepute. There is something liberating about forgiving someone and starting afresh. Also we women need to take responsibility for our own body/mind/spirit balance. There is no point in blaming genes, bad habits you inherit/pick up, weather, etc.

Being physically fit is as equally important as learning something new to expand your mind as well as developing your spirituality. We tend to focus on the physical aspect too much these days. We need to remind ourselves that we mums need to be at peace with ourselves first before we bring that to the world through our husbands, children, friends, neighbours and colleagues.

How do you develop a good balance of body, mind and spirit? I think practising your faith enriches you to have the awareness that you are not a mistake but a loving creation put together by God and you can overcome all your weaknesses and shortcomings if you trust Him. I have lived and worked with Buddhists, Hindus and Muslims and have learned much from their faiths and how it helps them to be the people they are. Another important aspect is living in a spirit of thankfulness.

Miriam, 41, Melbourne, Australia

Do try this at home:

We all essentially have a spiritual dimension. Access and foster your ability to imagine, create and share ideas about the wonders of the universe. Belief in the existence of love and essential goodness, whether related to God or humanity, is a rock on which we can base our lives and which will sustain us all our days.

I NEVER THINK OF RELIGION and I don't like it at all. I am spiritual, though, and feel incredible when I do something to help someone – I really try to feel the moment and appreciate myself for reaching out to people. That is my religion.

Vicki, screenwriter, Australia

I DON'T THINK you need religion to feel spiritual. I believe if you are a good person and do good things then you can feel spiritual.

Helen, designer, County Kerry

❧

PERSONALLY, AROUND TIMES LIKE EASTER, I reflect more on the control mechanism that the Catholic Church is and I feel sad. Every day is spiritual, when the daffs trumpet spring is here, or my daughter tells me she loves me!

Alison, 34, owner of marketing company, West Cork

❧

When my husband and I lived in Oxford, just before the turn of the millennium, we met a lovely guy from Singapore – his family were Indian and practised Hinduism. He was studying the same course as my husband and we became great friends. The study desk in his lodgings had a picture of Jesus hanging on the wall beside his lamp. When I asked him about it, he said that Jesus was a Hindu prophet and he spoke about the time that Jesus had spent in the Himalayas practising yoga. This was news to me as a Catholic. It is remarkable when you think outside the doctrine that you have been taught how similar all religions are in basis and even with the prophets that they use.

Michelle

❧

I AM THE CHILD of a mixed marriage. Today, this could mean that I'm a beautiful café-au-lait colour, the female equivalent of Barack Obama with brains to match and a wonderfully diverse cultural heritage, but in my day, it meant that my parents and maternal grandparents were from different religious backgrounds. This wasn't really a problem for me as my father converted to Catholicism, though he did tend to provide feedback on the sermons, with biblical references, to the alarm of the homely local parish priest.

But my Catholic mother had never been inside the Church of England which her own mother had attended until her mother's funeral. During the service, she learned from the vicar that her mother had played the organ, taught at Sunday school and was well-known and liked by many parishioners. While this was comforting, my mother regretted that she had been inadvertently excluded from this important part of her parents' life, that they had never discussed their beliefs, their diverse thoughts about spirituality, life and death.

We often fail to talk to our loved ones about our deepest thoughts, our beliefs, our spirituality I suppose you could call it. Religious (and racial or social) intolerance is largely a thing of the past, and I'd like to affirm that we should embrace our diverse beliefs and not hide them till death do us part.

Philomena, 67, Salford, England

༄

MOST PEOPLE CELEBRATE holidays, not even knowing the real reason behind the celebration. If you ask what the Rabbit or the Egg represent, or why we refer to the holiday as Easter, most will admit they don't know. It's about Christians celebrating pagan rituals, completely unaware of how it began or why! Blind followers of a Financial Faith, not about spirituality at all.

Shelly, 40, palm reader, Texas, USA

꙳

RELIGION AND SPIRITUALITY are two very different entities, and both are thought of very differently by every individual. Feast days, like Christmas and Easter, do bring these elements to the fore for some, especially non-church-goers, but if you're a strong believer, then these are occasions to celebrate and enjoy your faith and not just reminders.

Martina, 37, psychiatric nurse, Northern Ireland

꙳

RELIGION IS THE BUSINESS END of spirituality and unfortunately, as in commerce, predominantly patriarchal. As far as I'm concerned, these boys' clubs have little to do with true spirituality. That's to be found in hearts and minds, in flora and fauna, in sun and rain. It's the helping hand given and received, the beautiful sunset, the moral compass that always points in the direction of unity and peace.

Mary, 50, author, County Cork

*I believe in my own faith and
I am true to myself
and my belief in Spirit.*

the spirit inside of you –
gut instincts, your inner voice

Your inner voice is your truth advising and guiding you. If you don't listen to it you will inevitably wander off your path. We are holistic beings connected by mind, body and spirit. To stay centred and focused on our life's journey we need to respect and listen to our inner voice.

Our gut is located in the same place as our solar plexus, which is the centre chakra and if that is open or damaged or denied we will invariably end up sick.

As women, we are blessed with strong centres and instinct and we have had to use these to survive and look after our families.

We have other signs that help us realise when our gut instinct is talking to us. One of these is the power of coincidence. There is no such thing as a coincidence – it would be too difficult to create the condition of a coincidence, so there has to be some meaning. Be aware – to do this you must be awake first. So many people go through life in a kind of daze, accepting things as they appear and not questioning or developing their own gut instinct. ✍

OUR EMOTIONS are the means by which our higher self communicates with us. To deny these feelings is to shut off important information from our souls.

Trusting our feelings strengthens our psychic ability.

Michelle, shamanic practitioner, County Dublin

࿐

FOLLOW YOUR INNER GUIDANCE and don't mind what other people say.

Anita, life coach, County Dublin

࿐

WHEN I STARTED HEALING, it was like an underground movement. Those who practised alternative therapies dressed like hippies and cooked chickpeas. Now ordinary women are experiencing their own connection with spirit through themselves. They are attending courses about angels, receiving Reiki and practising yoga. You could walk around the supermarket and wouldn't be able to tell who was and wasn't in touch with Spirit and the new way of thinking.

Cara, 37, mum, County Dublin

࿐

LISTEN TO YOUR GUT instinct and act accordingly and look after yourself as you can't look after anyone else unless you do.

Mary Ann, jewellery designer, County Donegal

I BELIEVE THAT WHEN I go off the path that is for my higher good, I am, in subtle ways, guided back onto the right path; when on that path, I believe I am supported in that in an effort to keep me there. I have learned to listen to my body and my soul and have discovered it is only my insecurities that take me the wrong way. I know this from the heaviness of heart and the gentle persuasions from 'above' that lead me back. My body and soul tell me when I am back on track by feeling happy and light and more and more positive things come my way to reinforce to me that this is where I should stay.

As for evidence – last year I took my photography hobby to the next level and turned it into a small business, charging next to nothing as I was too insecure to have the confidence to ask clients for more. I got very little work. A series of events, too long to note here, but too coincidental to mean nothing, have led me to increase my prices. I have felt better within myself and the work is now coming in.

Angeline, 36, photographer and mum of four, Hampshire, England

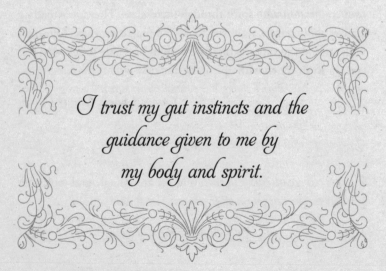

I trust my gut instincts and the guidance given to me by my body and spirit.

Yoga, prayer and meditation

Yoga, prayer and meditation are all ways of slowing down and stopping the normal survival methods that we use to get through the day and reflect on what it means to be human. It is wonderful to focus on the power of life itself and the forces and energy that make up our essence. We are all divine channels for the mind, body and spirit. Yoga, prayer and meditation help us to live in the moment and feel and visualise what it means to be alive.

Michelle was sitting in the waiting room of a hospital clinic and watched with wonder an old lady who was sitting opposite. She seemed extremely calm and serene before going to see her specialist consultant. She didn't make eye contact with anyone else who was sitting in the room but quietly took out her rosary beads and without moving her lips or a muscle she began her prayers.

Michelle also noticed that the beams of early spring sunshine had changed their positioning since she entered the room and were now falling on the spot where she sat. She felt that this woman radiated a positive energy of love and light.

Her Catholic beads could have easily been substituted for the numerous others used in religions all over the world. They all do the same thing and this woman through her prayers was really just meditating – which is the most direct way to connect with Spirit.

Praying and belief in spirituality can make a big difference when following the path of healing, because it gives us hope and consolation, as well as making meaning out of what is sometimes a very complicated life.

Juliet often has to break bad news to patients in her job as a doctor. When she is trying to console or talk to a patient about a difficult diagnosis or a very sad situation they're in, she finds it always helps if they have some sort of faith. What she is finding increasingly is that although many people reject conventional religion, people do want to believe in spirituality of nature, in the power of the universe and in a meaning to our lives that transcends the boundaries of man-made institutions of power. There is so much power in the universe, there is incredible power in the human imagination and there is wonderful power in the spirit of human nature. We certainly don't need man-made organisations to harness those powers any more – we need to be free to explore them and glory in them. ✐❤

A SIMPLE START to the day is the sun salutation sequence of asanas. It takes very little time and is an excellent practice – it is also an excellent way to finish the day.

Joy, homeopath and yoga teacher, County Dublin

WE ARE ALL where we are meant to be, on the way to where we are meant to go. Just breathe, relax and let the rivers lead you where they will.

Grace, 34, Northern Ireland

※

YOGA IS FANTASTIC for keeping a body fit and supple. Meditation for a healthy, connected mind. (I would highly recommend Yongey Mingyur Rinpoche's book, *The Joy of Living* for the latter.) But for either to work it has to become a part of life, like brushing your teeth – has to be done! The benefits are many but you can really only experience them by following the path yourself. My prayerfulness is the practice of both of these and the gratefulness I feel from the experience they give me.

Mairi, 47, ceramicist, County Cork

※

I PRACTISED YOGA for some time when I was experiencing difficulties in my life. For me, it was useful to help me to tune into and allow myself to feel the things that at the time I was suppressing in an effort to be strong and carry on. Opening up the heart chakra meant I had to face and deal with all of the things I needed to examine so I could grow and move on.

Prayer for me is a daily event but not in the traditional ways – I mostly thank God for all the things I have in my life, I am grateful for the opportunities I have been given and especially the ability to bounce back from the difficulties I have faced and see the positives and not wallow in self-pity or allow the events of my life to define who I have become. Occasionally, I ask for assistance, but nothing specific – a simple 'help me' has proven to be the strongest prayer possible and I have faith enough to believe that the right things will happen.

Edel, 37, buyer for health service, Derry, Northern Ireland

❧

I COULD NEVER HAVE PLANNED for my life to have turned out the way it has and it's been extraordinary. What surprises me most is that the very things I thought were the worst invariably turned out to be the best, albeit in the very, very long run. The other big shock was that when things were at their worst, God's presence made itself known in the most palpable ways – even though I thought I had closed myself off from it for years. Best advice I ever got? Pray. Even if you don't believe, pray anyway. The rest will come.

Sue, 49, journalist, County Donegal

❧

FOUR YEARS AGO, my life went through the toughest change I had ever experienced. The reason for this change was a broken marriage which led to a broken heart and broken self-esteem and a lot of questioning. Suddenly, everything I believed in changed. It was devastating, but it brought me down a path I perhaps never would have taken had I not gone through the experience. For this I am grateful (I can say this four years later!); however, I feel saddened that it took such a major change to force me to look at life in such a different way. I now see that everyone would benefit from looking at themselves and life from a different perspective. Don't wait for a major life change to do it!

My story is that I was forced and also determined to turn what I saw as a very negative experience into a positive one and push on – primarily because I had two small children depending on me. I knew I had to work on myself, i.e. find a way to get through this in as positive way as possible, for my kids, because I felt that if I was OK, then they would be OK.

This path started with seeking out a life coach for myself. I found one in the Golden Pages, and rang the number. I was suddenly speaking to a stranger about my life, which was very new to me, but ended up being very positive. A life coach is someone who can be there not only to support you but to challenge you too. They can help sift though all the excess thoughts running through your head so that you can be clearer about what you want. She taught me that we all need to take responsibility for our own actions/feelings and not to blame others.

A few months after this, I decided to go to a hypnotherapist. This aim was to have a bit of self-analysis. I was not looking to analyse my marriage or my ex-husband but look deep within myself to see what had brought me to this point. Nearly everything relates back to our childhood and the labels we have placed on ourselves – usually by others. Unfortunately some of these labels we carry around unnecessarily, many of them untrue to who we really are deep down. This then led to some sessions of Reiki. This is a form of energy healing that works in a holistic way. I found it very powerful. I became open to angels, guardian angels, numerology and manifestation. Having never really been on my own for most of my life, it gave me great comfort to think that we all have angels protecting us and that if we need help we just needed to ask the angels.

I have since gone on to study and now practise Reiki and also Aura-Soma, which is a form of colour therapy that helps to see who you really are – not only from a personality point of view but from your soul. It helps to peel back the layers of consciousness. As an artist, I have always found colour to be very powerful and Aura-Soma to me combines my love/interest of colour with something a lot deeper/spiritual. Basically 'we are the colours we choose', each bottle has a story, each colour a meaning and the order chosen, a significance.

I was told once that change is the ever constant and it's the one thing that we can always count on, which is of course true. Most of us (myself included), however, fear change. What I try to remember is that while it can be tough when it is unplanned change, even that won't last forever and there is always something positive that can come out it. There is a reason for everything and we all have the power within ourselves to achieve anything we wish for. The trick is to let go of fear and replace it with faith. Easier said than done, of course, and it's an ongoing journey for most of us but when we are taking baby steps forward at least that's a start. I find relaxation is a big player for me – yoga, walks outside in nature, appreciating the small things in life and Reiki sessions are all helpful.

Cathy, 37, Reiki and Aura-Soma healer, County Dublin

You don't need to be sitting with your head to the East and your feet smothered in oils with incense burning to pray. I do my best mantras and affirmations in the queue at the supermarket or when I am filling my car with petrol. For me, that is living with spirit.

Sheila, 42, yoga teacher, County Dublin

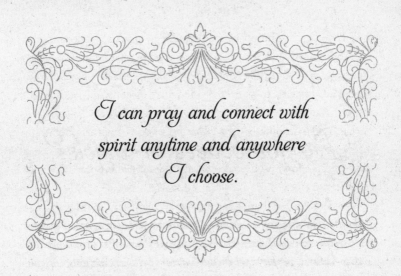

I can pray and connect with spirit anytime and anywhere I choose.

Do you believe in angels?

It's ironic that angels are suddenly becoming popular again. Perhaps many truly spiritual people are feeling disillusioned by the use of God to control people and build barriers between nations. Angels have been present in every religion in some form or another. In Western society, they have been painted with beautiful feathery wings and golden halos. These halos are merely our auras – a space of energy that our body radiates around itself. Michelle had hers photographed at a beauty fair in the RDS a few years ago and some people can actually see auras with their naked eye – so nothing mystical or magical about them! Whether you choose to call them helpers or spirits or energy, it doesn't matter – they are there. All they want is to be acknowledged – they help unconditionally and whenever they are needed.

JUST BECAUSE YOU TALK with angels doesn't mean you can't have a bad day. It doesn't mean that something difficult or bad can't happen to you. Don't get involved in spirit as some kind of insurance policy, like joining a gym doesn't mean you won't get fat! Healing is about facing your issues and dealing with them in a healthy way and not about everything being rosy. They can, however, prove useful if you trust in them as my story illustrates.

My daughter had an evening class that usually ran on a Tuesday but last week it was changed to Thursday – the same day as I had organised a family celebration night out. She told me that she couldn't come as her class was more important, so I just let it be and didn't fuss. Shortly after our conversation, she received a call to say that her class was changed yet again to the Wednesday, so she would be able to attend.

'I knew as soon as you mentioned it that your angels would organise it!' she said.

I had to agree because I leave decisions like these to them now and it cuts out on stress between us as a family.

Angela, 50, healer and artist, County Dublin

❧

I LOVE THE ANGELS and ask for their help on a daily basis. My son can see angels, I encourage both my children to thank the angels every night and ask the angels for help while trying to find things in the house. I do angel nights were I do angel meditations and my friends love them!

Maria, 38, Reiki master, County Dublin

❧

I BELIEVE THAT THERE IS A HIGHER POWER out there. I wrote an article a while back which I titled 'The day my life didn't change forever … or maybe it did?' It was a reflection on my life and the paths I've followed since that day. The day was 17 May 1974. I was ten at the time, going to school in Dublin city. My sister used to go down to Dad's office after basketball practice a couple of days during the week and he'd bring her home. I used to get the bus home earlier on those days. On 17 May, Mum was away, so Dad left the office early to take care of my brother Barry, so Miriam got the bus home. That was the day of the Talbot Street bombing. Dad's office was right across the street where the bomb went off.

The next day, when he went into his office and looked at his desk, a large sheet of window pane that had blown in lay across his desk jutting out about two feet from the desk towards his chair. If he had been there he definitely would have been killed and perhaps Miriam too. When I reflected on this and looked at my life since then, I knew it would be completely different to what it is now.

Ruth, 45, special needs assistant and author, County Clare

❧

THERE IS DEFINITELY a higher power guiding and protecting you through your life. I personally believe that God/Higher Power assigned two guardian angels to be with you through your life from the moment you were born until the moment you die to guide, protect and help you. My personal evidence of this is twofold. I was in Omagh in 1998 the day the bomb went off. I was knocked to the ground by the blast and one of my colleagues landed on top of me. There was glass and debris falling all around us, but I felt at the time as if there was something protecting me from harm at that point. My work shirt was covered in glass but I never got so much as a scratch. The injury I did sustain was from the impact of my colleague landing on my back.

The second evidence I have of guardian angels guiding and protecting me is a bit of a long one, but I will try to be brief. I had been trying for a baby for three years without success and my soul was crying out in pain and frustration. I had been off work for several weeks with depression because of these issues and I had fallen into a routine where I watched a certain TV programme at a certain time in the morning. On this particular day, I couldn't settle to watch the TV programme at all and switched over to ITV's *This Morning*, where Gloria Hunniford was talking about her daughter Caron Keating and her belief in angels. I believe that this was my guardian angels' way of telling me that they were there and that all I had to do was ask.

After some tears and a lot of reflection, I decided to ask God and his angels to help me get pregnant and left my worries and stress in their hands. That was at Christmastime in 2004. I was pregnant by the middle of February 2005, without any medical intervention, and I can definitely say that my son is a divine gift from God. He is the most precious, good, loving, gentle little boy and I'm blessed to have him.

Edel, 37, buyer for health service, Derry, Northern Ireland

Do try this at home:

Imagine a secret room. This is a space in your head where you visualise something that you really want and put it into it – it can be an emotional outcome, a material object or even an achievement. But to get something into your life, you must first visualise it. Long ago people would have carried out a novena to a certain saint – this is essentially the same thing. The essence of Spirit or goodness or God – whatever you want to call it – is inside of you. All you have to do is ask.

I WAS STAYING IN THE COUNTRYSIDE for a weekend break and visiting my parents. When it was time to go, I packed up the car and put my three children into the backseats. But before I said goodbye to my dad, I got a strange feeling that I should check my tyres – I had never done this before and wasn't sure what was making me do this. I couldn't believe my eyes when I saw a nail sticking out of the front tyre. I was relieved that my dad was there to change the wheel and he drove with us into the nearest town to get the tyre fixed.

When the mechanic saw the wheel he was shocked and warned that it was in a very dangerous spot and if I had driven on the motorway with it in that condition, I would definitely have had a blowout. I was stunned by the news but extremely grateful that something or someone had warned me. Later when it was all fixed and as I was driving home along the motorway with the three children asleep in the back of the car, I felt the presence again and it sent shivers up my body. I asked who was there and a voice in my head said, 'Angel Michael.' We made it home safely and it was sometime later when I was pottering around a bookshop that I picked up a book about angels. I opened that book on a random page and nearly dropped it when I saw the image of the guardian angel Michael. I read on and was stunned to learn that he is the angel that protects motorists.

Carla, 41, mum of three, County Dublin

⁂

I ATTENDED A WORKSHOP in IET (Integrated Energy Therapy) recently – it was very nice and involved meditation and relaxation and writing down issues we had and trying to sort them out with the assistance of Spirit. I have found several people close to me following alternative ways of addressing Spirit since the decline of the Catholic Church. But the amazing thing is when you talk about angels, the response is fascinating. Some women will laugh out loud. Others will nod their heads in agreement that it is all nonsense but I have a theory that they are hiding behind their real beliefs. Every religion on earth regards, respects and acknowledges angels – they may not be called the same thing, but their energetic presence has always been used to express details and, like many spiritual practices such as Reiki and yoga, there is a requirement to focus on the forces that make us living and thinking human beings. This force may be called God, Spirit, energy, the universe, Allah, Buddha or whatever you choose and what I am finding is that this energy that we all seem to want help from is there for us.

Carol, 54, teacher, County Wicklow

෴

I ALWAYS ASK MY ANGELS to get me parking spaces and trolleys that don't need coins in the supermarket – it works almost every time! Don't forget to thank them – they love that!

Pauline, 66, counsellor and psychologist, County Dublin

I thank and respect my angel guides and the love and light that they send into my life.

What are we doing here?

None of us really know what we are doing here. We can guess and surmise and hope, but there is no guarantee that even after death we will be any wiser. However, one conclusion that most people reach at some stage in their lives is the fact that they are on a journey. We enjoy using the analogy of a train ride. If you ever find yourself stuck in a train at rush hour, maybe look around and watch the body language of your fellow passengers. Each and every person will have a different perception of the experience. Some may be anxious because they need to get home to relieve childcare, others because they have a date. Some might be happy not to be home at all after having a row with their partner before leaving that morning. Those sitting down are comfortable, those standing up might want a seat. Everyone perceives their journey through life in a different way.

As women we spend so much of our lives looking after others, in our jobs, in our homes and in our relationships – it is difficult to stop and spend time thinking about why you are here in the first place. But we like to think that there is a bigger plan that pulls us to the great light, energy, universe or whatever you want to call your god and that is love.

So why not hop aboard and enjoy the ride! 🐦

BEING A WOMAN is incredible. As women, we need sometimes to go against what nature makes of us – The Mother, The Wife, The Best Friend, The Neighbour, The Employee, to name but a few – and always take time to nurture our own Spirit and soul! We can keep giving but in life tragedy and 'shit' happens so we need to be ready and able to manage it. I have noted that if you are strong and stable as a person before the bad stuff occurs, you have a good chance of getting through it. Friends and honesty in friendship and relationships are crucial. I look around sometimes and wonder how many people are truly honest with themselves and their lives – I think very few! We need to stay as grounded and real as possible to be 'True Women' – while also having good friends and family that we can laugh and enjoy life with. You know life is only the now – we must aim to do the best in the now that we can, and you know sometimes we just get fed up – but that's allowed. We must always look for the rainbow and the happy times and aim for them for sure.

Linda, 39, accountant, County Dublin

꙳

As women, we spend a huge amount of time worrying about what other people think. As a doctor, I often see women suffering in bad marriages, afraid to leave because of what other people might think. I see people unable to pay debts, facing bankruptcy because they have borrowed beyond their means so that they can impress other people. I see people afraid to face the truth in their own lives, afraid to admit failures, afraid to ask for help all the time because of what other people might think.

One thing I know for sure: Other people's heads are far too miserable a place in which to leave your sense of happiness.

Juliet

I BELIEVE we were put on this earth to love.

Siobhan, homeopath, County Dublin

❧

BE AND DO THE BEST we can. Make and keep friends. Help each other. Have fun. Raise and/or be a positive family member. Learn and share. But yes – love.

Aisling, 41, Montessori teacher, County Cork

❧

WE ALL WERE PUT HERE to live a journey ... our life on this earth is a short journey, we face many tests from God, and if we are good people, we will pass to the other life which is longer and much better than the life we are having now. This is what I believe as a Muslim girl.

Wonderfulra Rasha, medical student, Libya

❧

I THINK WE ARE ON this wonderful earth to learn from each other and everything around us. To love and share. I believe in life there is something to learn from everyone and everything. Enjoy.

Venetta, 42, mum of four, County Dublin

Most of us ask ourselves at some point of life to discover the meaning of life and our true purpose. To be honest, it's difficult for me to find answers. Recently, I've been through a very spiritual experience. I don't know, it's like something lights me up and makes me feel so relieved and simplifies my answers 'to do what I love and what I have passion in'. I read about this before but I couldn't feel it at that time.

It was like linking pieces together and makes it clear to see. This increases my satisfaction and reflects on my perspective to see things.

Aya, 22, medical student, Benghazi, Libya

🕉

We are spiritual beings residing in physical bodies for this lifetime. Treat your body as your temple, nourish your mind with positive thoughts and meditate every day to align more closely with the inner self. Also, trust that the Universe or God (it doesn't matter what you call it) will look after you. Ask and it is given.

Anita, life coach, County Dublin

🕉

We aren't just a family – the whole world is a family – we just don't know each other yet!

Nicole, 6, schoolgirl, County Dublin

🕉

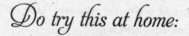

Do try this at home:

On a daily basis ask yourself, 'What do I want from life?' A lot of us go around miserable saying we aren't happy because we aren't getting or doing what we want. But in order find out what you want, you need to be very clear. Write it down. It is a great way to bring clarity and focus to your question.

You can subdivide the questions into sections:
• Emotional needs
• Material needs
• Spiritual needs

Be honest with yourself no matter how bizarre the request.

The amazing outcome of this is that you usually already have or have access to what you want.

It is also a good idea that while you write these points you also acknowledge the things that you already have that are important and fulfil your spiritual, emotional and material needs – this will help you give thanks and gratitude and help you feel content.

A BUDDHIST MONK told me that bringing up children is a spiritual practice.

Strong Angel, healer, County Dublin

I ALWAYS TELL my young nieces that the two things in life that are most destructive are envy and self-pity.

Susanne, In Her Prime, author, County Tipperary

❧

WE BRING OURSELVES with us wherever we go. You won't change your life by looking for a picture-postcard view of life. We all have to come home to ourselves. We can move house, change partner, lose weight, but ultimately, it's not the external things that are going to bring us inner peace. Certainly, aspects of our lives will help harmonise what is going on inside us – and provide the space for us to grow. But always remember, we have to take responsibility for our feelings. We can wake up and be happy or sad. It's within us. Don't blame anyone else. We allow others to affect us in different ways, but it's really us who are drawing up the rules.

Mary, journalist, County Dublin

❧

AS WOMEN, we are inclined to put everyone else's needs first and often feel guilty if we take time out for ourselves. We have so many roles – daughter, girlfriend, wife, mother – sometimes it's easy to lose our sense of self and what we really want or need. So next time you notice you'd like time to yourself or want to treat yourself when it's not even your birthday, consider this. Focus your attention on your heart, feel its rhythmic beat, the heart tirelessly beats, pumping blood around our entire body enabling our body to function. However, before the heart sends this blood to other organs and cells, it delivers some to itself first

– without doing so, it would not be able to succeed in its function to serve the rest of the body. It is not a selfish act but a necessary one and a beautiful example of self-love. Nourishing and loving ourselves opens us up to healthy and loving relationships with others, and when you've done this simple exercise, go guilt-free towards your heart's desires.

Siobhan, 43, spiritual advisor, County Dublin

Forgiveness –
I refuse to hang onto grudges or hurts.
I will fill my heart with
love and light.

Where are we going? The life after

In order to sustain life, a planet has to be a certain distance from a star, have water, have oxygen, lots of all the right minerals and carbon – it's a very, very long shot. To have sentient life on any planet in any universe, the conditions are very tight – yet here on Earth, we actually have it on our very own planet, and guess what? We're actually experiencing it!

Why on earth would you want to spend a single moment not loving every single thing about it?

We don't know if we are going anywhere when we leave our physical bodies, but there is enough evidence of people having out-of-body and clairvoyant experiences to suggest that there is some sort of existence after life. We have to remember that we are all made of energy and that energy has to go somewhere – it can't just disappear. It is up to each and every one of us to come to our own conclusion as to what the afterlife might be.

Michelle's granny told her a story once when she was about ten years old. She said that her mother – Michelle's great-grandmother – suffered from a terrible fever and was at death's door. She recovered from the illness and told her children about a beautiful place that she had been while she was unconscious. She said that it was beside a river and the trees were the nicest she had ever seen – she travelled through a bright, white light to get there and she didn't want to leave and come back to Earth. All the people that she loved who had died were there and at peace. She told all her children that this place was waiting for her when she died and she no longer had a fear of death. Michelle's grandmother took great comfort from her story and told it to her.

So many people who have near-death experiences go through the same white light to a similar place of their dreams – our energy carries on.

Juliet had a consultation with a patient one day who had suddenly become very depressed. She told Juliet that she actually wanted to kill herself. Juliet was quite frightened by this and took the phone off the hook to talk to her for an hour. They talked at great length about her wish for death. And so Juliet asked her, 'What do you think happens to us after we die?'

The patient confessed that she hadn't really thought about it. Her preoccupations were all with trying to end the life she had. Yet she was prepared to embark on a journey without actually knowing the destination. She hadn't considered what might happen after she died.

Juliet asked her to think about it for a moment, because she was taking a decision to go to a place she didn't know, and from which she had absolutely no chance of coming back. It might well be a better place. None of us know. None of us have been there yet. And we all will certainly be there one day. But for the moment, it is a mystery to all of us.

The patient said she hadn't actually thought about the fact that she was going to a place that she couldn't come back from, a place she knew nothing about, and that the more she thought about it, the more she didn't want to go. Even if the place turned out to be so

much better than this world – and she most certainly hoped it did
– she quickly decided that she didn't want to go there yet.

Shortly after this she became quite well again, and came back to
thank Juliet. She'd explored her universe – the dark side of it, and
what might be on the other side, and she'd come to realise that life is
very short, and that she definitely didn't want to let go of it yet! She's
still well today and very much in touch with her spiritual side. ✍♥

THE FINALITY OF DEATH is what really troubles us, the uncertainty
even in those who have strong belief in their resurrection,
reincarnation, eternal reward or cessation of suffering. And it is
certainly true that human life will cease come what may. Rather
than bury our heads in the sand, it might be worthwhile thinking a
bit more about leaving our families and friends, with regret but only
the happiest memories and the knowledge that we have shared with
them to the best of our abilities.

Nuns have it right – they have a party with lots of smiles, beautiful music and ceremony, and affectionate reminiscences of their sister who is going to her eternal reward.

Perhaps the people who succumb to a terminal illness feel that
their 'fight' has been worth the ultimate finality, though dejection
at the failure of their response to prolonged therapy and worry
about expenses can enormously disrupt family life. It's worrying, in
fact, that the positivity of thought and possibility of conquering a
terminal disease are linked in our minds; undoubtedly, the more
active one is in mind and body, the better the quality of one's daily
life, and quality of life is what it's about – eradicating the disease is
only a part of it.

The most important resolution is to stop procrastinating. Don't
wait until your life expectancy is in single figures – weeks, months

or years – but do the things you want to do, see the people you want to see, look with new eyes at the countryside, the gardens, the skyscape. Reminisce with old friends, dine out with new friends, go to art exhibitions, the movies, the concerts. Tell your children or grandchildren your favourite jokes, what you did when you were their age.

Let people know that you love and value them. Don't save up for a future which might not exist for you without making sure that you're investing in the present.

Jacqui, grandmother, Australia

❧

LIFE IS JUST LIKE THIS. Extremely happy moments today, tears and sadness tomorrow. But we women are so brave. Live your pain and get ready to be happy again! I am living a bad moment in my life too, but I won't give up being a happy woman again.

Dora, mum of triplets, Brazil

❧

IN MY 'BELIEF SYSTEM' all we learn, everyone we meet, everything we do (i.e. living) teaches us things and exposes us to others' spirits – and we kind of absorb that. It's sometimes called life lessons and that is what guides us. Nature/nurture – all that kind of stuff. We grow, we learn, we reproduce, we try to make it all better for them. That's the higher power – it's in us.

Marie, 41, secretary, County Dublin

Go FORWARD – keep a happy heart.

Marie Therese, granny, mum and godmother, Scotland

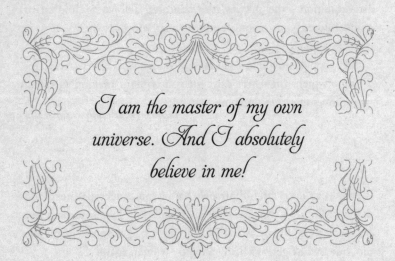

I am the master of my own universe. And I absolutely believe in me!